PEACE AND SECURITY IN KENYA

Peace and Security in Kenya

The USAID Approach

GALEEB KACHRA

The Kent State University Press   *Kent, Ohio*

© 2025 by The Kent State University Press, Kent, Ohio 44242
All rights reserved
ISBN 978-1-60635-497-1
Published in the United States of America

Cataloging information for this title is available at the Library of Congress.

29 28 27 26 25   5 4 3 2 1

To all who served USAID since President John F. Kennedy founded it in 1961—Americans and non-Americans alike, staff, contractors, grantees, sub-grantees, consultants, and vendors worldwide. You dedicated time and energy to promoting hope, improving global security, and enhancing quality of life.

You worked in remote parts of the globe, often at great personal risk. Many sacrifices—partners, children's education and stability, health, and death—were made in the line of duty.

Your legacy endures in the countries and institutions you helped build, the lives you touched, and the ideals you upheld. This holds equally true for American peace and security and for the American farmers, contractors, and suppliers whose quality of life was also improved.

CONTENTS

AUTHOR'S NOTE

This book was written before 2024. In February 2025, the Agency for International Development (USAID) was largely shut down. The physical sign, website, and social media accounts were removed. Readers may have to infer USAID in the past tense. However, the primary message of this book is that America's overseas peace and security programming is crucial to our own national security. This programming must be intentional and broad—it does not depend on the name of the agency or the office that manages overseas programs that serve America's domestic peace and security interests through international development.

This book was written by Galeeb Kachra in his personal capacity under the US Constitution First Amendment rights and Kenyan Constitution Article 33 rights. He has had no relationship with USAID since 2015 and no relationship with the government of Kenya post-childhood.

The opinions expressed in this book are the author's own and do not reflect the views of any current or former agencies, departments, or ministries of the US government or the government of Kenya. Nor does the author's opinions reflect the views of the State University of New York or any international or non-governmental organization.

ACRONYMS

BBC	British Broadcasting Cooperation
BLUF	Bottom Line Up Front
CDCS	Country Development Cooperation Strategy
CIC	Commission for the Implementation of the Constitution
CIPEV	Commission of Inquiry into the Post-Election Violence
CoE	Committee of Experts (Kenyan Constitution)
CRS	Congressional Research Service
CVE	Countering Violent Extremism
DC	District of Columbia
DFID	Development for Internal Development (UK)
DG	Democracy and Governance
DPGL	Development Partners Group on Land
DRC	Democratic Republic of Congo
EACC	Ethics and Anti-Corruption Commission
EEZ	Exclusive Economic Zone
FAF	Foreign Assistance Framework
FSO	Foreign Service Officer
GAO	Government Accountability Office
GJLOS	Governance, Justice, Law and Order Sector
ICC	International Criminal Court
IEBC	Independent Elections and Boundaries Commission
IT	Information Technology
KANU	Kenya African National Union
KLA	Kenya Land Alliance
KTI	Kenya Transition Initiative
MP	Member of Parliament
NATO	North Atlantic Treaty Organization
NGO	Non-Governmental Organization
NLC	National Land Commission
OTI	Office of Transition Initiatives (part of USAID)
PEPFAR	Presidential Emergency Program for AIDS Relief

PSC	Parliamentary Select Committee
TJRC	Truth, Justice and Reconciliation Commission
UK	United Kingdom
UN-Habitat	United Nations Human Settlements Programme
US	United States
USAID	US Agency for International Development
VOA	Voice of America

INTRODUCTION

"President Joe Biden and First Lady Jill Biden will host President William Ruto and First Lady Rachel Ruto of the Republic of Kenya for a State Visit to the United States on May 23, 2024. The upcoming visit will mark the 60th anniversary of U.S.-Kenya diplomatic relations and will celebrate a partnership that is delivering for the people of the United States and Kenya. The visit will strengthen our shared commitment to advance peace and security, expand our economic ties, and stand together in defense of democratic values."

—The White House, "Statement from White House Press Secretary," February 16, 2024

Bottom Line Up Front (BLUF)

What is the point of this book? My teenagers have taught me one important modern communications lesson: Get to the point. We are driven by social media, distracted by scrolling headlines, and informed by smart speakers. We need the message up front before deciding whether to swipe left or scroll down. This book centers on the phrase "peace and security," found across a broad spectrum of governing documents and strategies. Because the term is ill-defined, international development professionals are unable to effectively design or account for programs that promote our peace and security. In this book, I unpack the use of the term and define it. Using Kenya as an example, I demonstrate how the United States promoted American peace and security through traditional development programming instead of relying on arms and military training.

The United States promoted peace and security in Kenya after its flawed and disputed 2007 general election. Kenya was on the brink of civil war, at its most fragile period in its short 60-year history. Over a 24-hour period, Kenya plummeted from a tranquil tourist destination into disarray, deaths, displacement, and destruction. According to the Human Rights Watch, "The scale and speed of the violence that engulfed Kenya following the controversial presidential election of December 27, 2007, shocked both Kenyans and the world at large. Two months of bloodshed left over 1,000 dead and up to 500,000 internally displaced persons in a country viewed as a bastion of economic and political stability in a volatile region."[1]

In the runup to Kenya's general election and over the eight years that followed (2007–2015), the United States spent $28.8 billion in Kenya, including $20.5 billion on health and $3.8 billion on humanitarian assistance, as shown in the following chart.[2]

Yet the United States recorded spending 4 percent on peace and security, funds that are meant to contribute to America's safety. That 4 percent target achieved the first of three shared goals identified in the 2024 White

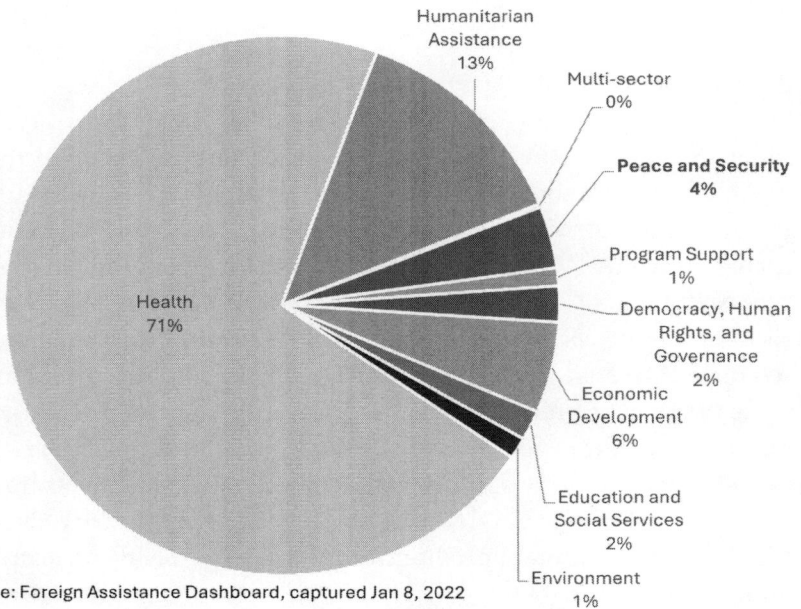

Source: Foreign Assistance Dashboard, captured Jan 8, 2022

House press statement that opened this chapter. In reality, the United States spent a lot more on peace and security in Kenya but, because the term is ill-defined, our real accounting of the sector is fragmented and incomplete.

The United States' national security strategies identify democracy, economic growth, and good governance as prerequisites to peace and security in any nation, including our own. However, these stated strategies do not align with our Foreign Assistance Framework (FAF), which distinctly separates peace and security from democracy, governance, and economic growth, as shown in the previous chart. If we want to advance America's peace and security, we must provide our development professionals with a clear definition of the term; change how we account for activities in the sector; reinforce its relationship with foreign development assistance programming; and consider having a bigger, more robust programming toolbox. Instead of shying away from it, we must embrace the fact that development interventions commonly used to attain other objectives, such as judicial and constitutional reform, can play a tremendous and powerful role in advancing US peace and security objectives. All this is demonstrated in this book.

The Mysteries Unraveled

This book, which presents my personal perspective on peace and security programming for the US Government, unravels a series of mysteries I discovered when engaging with colleagues during my decade with the US Agency for International Development (USAID). I was working for the Office of Transition Initiatives (OTI), whose mission statement, "[to] support U. S. foreign policy objectives by helping local partners advance peace and democracy," left no doubt of the nexus among US foreign policy, peace, and our programming.[3]

As I helped manage a multiyear, multimillion-dollar program collaborating with hundreds of local organizations to help Kenya recover from the postelection violence and to create a foundation for future stability, I tried to make sure each activity was carefully designed and contributed to our objective. But as I compiled data to submit to Washington, DC, reporting against the peace and security indicators in the FAF (see chapter

3), I wondered how this program was contributing to *American* peace and security. As the February 2024 White House press release stated, the partnership was delivering for both Kenyans and Americans. Was I, indeed, making my country safer by assisting Kenyans to adopt a new constitution, address land reform, build their judiciary, or counter violent extremism? To answer this question, I first had to unravel the definition of "peace and security" and look at the intent of foreign assistance (chapter 2). Then I needed to investigate whether our program was advancing both Kenyan and American peace and security. Therefore, the other chapters detail four examples of peace and security programming based on my firsthand experience in Kenya between 2008 and 2014.

The Author

I was not an observer of the US government's approach to peace and security in Kenya. Nor was I sitting ringside. I was one of the ring*leaders.* Working for USAID, I moved into my new taxpayer-funded residence in Nairobi a few months after Kenyans signed the 2008 peace agreement, and I remained there through the 2010 Constitutional Referendum and the 2013 General Election. I was a senior USAID official in Kenya, overseeing one program, the $60 million Kenya Transition Initiative (KTI). I advised on its activities—527 activities over six years—which comprised primarily grants given to local government, civil society organizations, and informal groups.[4]

That ringleader was both Kenyan and American: I am a third-generation Kenyan, born and raised in Nairobi. Yet I am an American immigrant success story; I migrated as a high school senior, was educated and lived in the United States, passed my citizenship test, and became an American citizen 10 years before joining USAID. Then, in 2008, I was posted to Kenya in a foreign service capacity.[5] Culture never leaves an individual; my Kenyan counterparts spoke to me in Swahili while we dug into *nyama choma,* Kenyan-style, dry, and extremely chewy, barbequed goat. Together, we all shared our personal perspectives, only as Kenyans would with each other.

My kids felt neither Kenyan nor American; they were typical third culture kids for our seven-year posting in Kenya. While all embassy families have this third-culture dichotomy, ours was exacerbated by my being back home. When I moved back to Nairobi, recollections of people, family, friends, roads, and hidden gems quickly reappeared. I was able to share my childhood memories with my children over that seven-year period, not during a four-week summer trip from America to the homeland as many of my peers do and have done with their children. With this unique perspective as a Kenyan, American, parent, diplomat, and development specialist, I untangle our peace and security programming in seven different chapters, none of which addresses arms, defense force training, bilateral negotiations, or intelligence services. Rather, I focus on aspects that development specialists, policymakers, and foreign assistance accounting systems unsuccessfully compartmentalize into different sectors.

Chapter Outline

This chapter sets the stage for my narrative. After presenting the chapter outline, I explain why I chose Kenya as my case study, and then introduce USAID, its funding structure, and one of its offices, the OTI, which is affectionately referred to as the "Marines of USAID." I end the chapter disclosing my inherent bias and prejudice.

Chapter 1 addresses the first example: America's successful contribution to peace and security, which focused not on arms, diplomacy, or negotiations but on a robust and renewed judiciary in Kenya. Americans learned during the 2000 Supreme Court decision in *Bush v. Gore* that security and stability depend on a credible judiciary.[6] The tale begins in the Kenyan city of Eldoret with a stolen 40-foot shipping container and an unhappy chief magistrate. It ends at the World Bank, one block from the White House in Washington, DC. I describe how we contributed to peace and security by offering Kenya assistance in developing a new confidence in their judiciary.

Based on this judiciary example, I realign the reader's understanding of peace and security in chapter 2. I explain why international "peace and security" is important for US national security—why, for instance, would the 2024 White House press release about a state visit by the president of Kenya to the United States include the phrase "peace and security"? I explore how governing documents, laws, and foreign policy professionals define and use the term, describe essential underpinnings that drive my interpretation of the phrase, and boldly redefine it. I draw on examples of traditional and nontraditional tools the United States has used and continues to use to promote peace and security overseas.

Having established a focused definition of the phrase, the remaining chapters focus again on Kenyan–US examples. Chapter 3 places attention on the most pivotal moment in Kenya's postcolonial period, marked by their embrace of a new constitution, which finally freed Kenyans from the constraining and culturally inappropriate British constitution they inherited from Lancaster House in London—without any public consultation. In Kenya's 2010 referendum, two out of every three Kenyans cast their vote in favor of a radical, modern, supreme law of the land that offers a solid foundation for peace and security. The 18-month constitutional process was the glue that held Kenyans together as they recovered from the horrific violence following the December 2007 general election, a period in which thousands of Kenyans were slaughtered by their own countrymen and hundreds of thousands were displaced. The chapter also explores America's role in Kenya's constitutional evolution, the 14-year history of Kenya's current constitution, its implementation successes and challenges, and even Kenya's foray into the global peace and security theater with respect to the 2024 crisis in Haiti.

Chapter 4 is less uplifting. It describes the ghost that will forever haunt Kenya, much like the memories of the slave trade present today in the caves of Wasini Island or Kenya's rocky south coast. Since the British stole Kenya's prime Highlands in the early 1900s, multifaceted concerns about land—ownership, administration, injustices, and fraud—remain Kenya's primary topic of conversation in traditional media, social media, public transport, dinner parties, country clubs, and roadside cafes. Land in Kenya is a trigger point, much like abortion and gun control are in America. Discussions about reparations for land injustices continue in both Kenya and the United States. In this chapter, I describe America's failures (and successes) as we tried to help Kenya address its intractable land issues.

Chapter 5 addresses the newest and least understood topic within a traditional peace and security portfolio, one with scarring and visible roots in Kenya's 1998 bombing of the US Embassy but deeper roots in the 1980 Norfolk hotel bombing in Nairobi. I describe what a nascent countering violent extremism (CVE) policy and programming looked like, what it should be, and how I—as a Kenyan-born, Muslim, American, development specialist, and diplomat—tried to change its trajectory.

The last chapter concludes with advice for foreign policy and international development professionals regarding peace and security programming, especially among our African allies. We must add new tools to America's peace and security toolbox and innovate, but, mostly, we have to move tools from other sectors' toolboxes. We must also remove the constraints that force us to report in predetermined categories of programs, constraints preventing us from thinking of countries and communities as systems.

Why Kenya?

If this book is about *American* peace and security, why do I focus on Kenya? Barely two months before Kenya's parliament approved the draft constitution in April 2010, sending the constitution to a national referendum, Michael Ranneberger, a former US ambassador to Kenya, told the American Chamber of Commerce in Nairobi that "Achieving implementation of the reform agenda is the central objective of U. S. policy in Kenya. Success in implementing key reforms will help ensure future democratic stability and prosperity."[7]

Throughout the speech, the ambassador rattled off details of specific US investments in Kenya. We are "contributing approximately $3 billion annually to Kenya's economy and development . . . a $560 million program to fight HIV/AIDS is the largest we have with any country in the world. . . . The United States is supporting activities valued at more than $3 million annually aimed at promoting reconciliation and mitigating future conflict."[8] He noted, "over 10,000 Americans call Kenya their home. More than 300,000 Kenyans live in the United States."[9]

Yet, none of these facts tell me why the United States chooses to invest so much in Kenya; we only know that "the United States is by far Kenya's largest and most important partner."[10] More telling is the message that the numbers give. Only 0.1 percent of the ambassador's list of total contributions was for peace and security programming because of the flaws in the accounting of peace and security activities. After all, the entire $60 million KTI program was geared at promoting peace and security.

According to the late Joel Barkan, a former State Department political officer, political scientist, and professor of political studies at the University of Iowa, Kenya is an "anchor state" and a focal point of America's Africa policy. In *Foreign Affairs,* he defined anchor states as, "countries that are key to the stability of the region because of location and resources."[11] He explained:

> Kenya has become the platform for U. S. operations in East Africa and the Horn. It houses the largest U. S. embassy on the continent and regional headquarters for a host of U. S. activities and agencies, including the security and military assistance, the Agency for International Development, the Library of Congress, and the Centers for Disease Control . . . [and] the U. S. Navy and Air Force may use the port of Mombasa and Kenya's international airports at Nairobi and Mombasa.[12]

Barkan later wrote, "During the past decade, however, the focus of U. S. Africa policy has shifted again to one that balances support for democratization in those countries where the prospects for democracy are promising with support for regimes that take a strong stand against terrorism and share US security concerns."[13] In its simplest terms, the United States believes that if Kenya falls, America will lose an important regional anchor that has served it since the onset of the Cold War. Because of Kenya's strategic, geopolitical importance to the United States, USAID's OTI designed and launched the KTI four months after Kenyans laid down their machetes; reeled in their mutual, ethnic, and class-derived distrust; and signed a peace agreement. Because of this importance, in May 2024, former President Biden hosted President Ruto on the first state visit of an African head of state to the United States in more than two decades.

What was the Program?

USAID staff designed the KTI to promote reconciliation and tolerance, jumpstart local economies, and foster peace and democratic political reform. From the beginning, KTI partnered with both grassroots and national-level civil society organizations, political leaders, and key local and national government institutions to achieve its guiding objectives: (1) to enable public institutions to undertake fundamental reforms and to manage instability and uncertainty, and (2) to mobilize the public, especially the youth and key change agents, to demand accountability and reform.

What is USAID?

Even after a decade working for USAID, I find it challenging to explain what the agency is and what it is about. I have had lots of practice explaining it to my parents, friends, other aid workers, and government officials in the countries where I have worked. My simplest response has been: It is a US government agency that leads America's official international development and disaster assistance activities around the world, and it is funded by taxpayers via Congress. During an official visit to the Langata Women's Prison in Nairobi, the prison warden did not blink when my Department of State colleague introduced himself. However, when it was my turn, she asked, innocently, "USAID . . . is that a Non-Governmental Organization?" My State Department colleague grinned. I was flabbergasted, as it is the antithesis of a nongovernmental organization (NGO).[14] I explained that USAID was part of the US government's efforts to support humanitarian and development projects around the world. I offered, as an example, the building next door to her office, which was a USAID-funded clinic. Despite seeing the USAID logo on the signpost right outside the building, she had not realized we were part of the US government.

I could not blame her. The clinic was likely funded and established by an NGO, either a private contractor or nonprofit organization (NPO) working on behalf of USAID. Many of the USAID employees I interacted with during my decade at USAID privately thought of themselves primarily as NGO development experts as opposed to agents of the US government.

In formal settings, USAID employees describe the agency as an independent federal agency created in 1961 by former President John F. Kennedy after Congress passed the Foreign Assistance Act. During new employees' orientation into the agency, regardless of the type of position they will hold or the office they will work in, they quickly learn it is separate from the Department of State. Common comments include, "We don't report to them or work for them," "We are separate from them," and "They cannot tell us what to do." My personal favorite quotations are from USAID mission directors. USAID's larger overseas field offices are known as "missions" and are headed by a mission director, who is a senior US government foreign service officer (FSO). More than one mission director has told me an ambassador cannot tell us what to do, dictate how we spend our money, or approve or disapprove our programs. Yet, an ambassador is a plenipotentiary, a diplomat who represents the president. The mission director and all of us who work at the embassy should be subservient to the ambassador.

An American relative of mine, keen on trying to understand what I did, what role I played for the US government, and how I spent US citizens' tax dollars, once made the mistake of explaining to an acquaintance in my presence that USAID is under the State Department, and I was under the secretary of state. But I had had much USAID-indoctrination, so I fired off a quick rebuttal: We are *not* part of the State Department. Every few years, triggered by a new administration, Congress, secretary of state, or USAID administrator, the Washington scuttlebutt circles back to the State Department's inevitable "takeover" of USAID. However, staff brush it aside, saying a takeover is always discussed but will never happen. Yet, the USAID and Department of State budgets are combined. Moreover, doesn't the USAID administrator report to the secretary of state? Or is USAID considered an independent federal agency? Note that in February 2025, the executive branch dismantled USAID as an independent entity and subsumed some of its functions into the State Department. However, the rest of this chapter describes USAID as it was up to January 20, 2025.

The USAID website is silent on this ambiguity. What I do know, from documented laws and executive orders, is that Congress passed the Foreign Assistance Act on September 4, 1961, to consolidate all US foreign assistance. Thereafter, former President Kennedy issued Executive Order 10973 on November 3, 1961, establishing USAID: "SEC. 102(a) The Secretary shall establish an agency in the Department of State to be known as the Agency for International Development."[15] When I joined USAID, this executive order was not mentioned in the agency's new employee orientation material, nor can it be found on USAID's website.

Staff are simply told that former President Kennedy created USAID in 1961 in response to the Foreign Assistance Act, which is the framework for the agency. As an employee, not once did I ever hear about an executive order requiring the secretary of state to establish USAID *within* the Department of State. I first read the executive order after I had already left USAID and was conducting research for this book. It was a surprise. Perhaps my relative was right in that I did work for the secretary of state. However, as long as I was with USAID, like all my other colleagues, I vehemently denied we were part of the State Department. Was it the truth? Was it a cultural myth perpetuated over the years? Or was it only wishful thinking? After I left the agency, I decided I had to dig deeper.

Congress passed the "Foreign Affairs Reform and Restructuring Act of 1998," which among other things defined USAID as *an independent establishment.*[16] The 1998 act also required that "The Administrator of the Agency for International Development... report to and be under the direct authority and foreign policy guidance of the Secretary of State."[17] Additionally, the act states that "Under the direction of the President, the Secretary of State shall coordinate all United States assistance."[18] USAID's budget is part of the US government's foreign operations budget, commonly known as the "150 Account." The budget includes all civilian international affairs programs, including USAID, which accounts for approximately only 35 percent of the account.

On paper, I conclude USAID is therefore part of the Department of State because (1) the administrator of USAID reports to and is under the Secretary of State; (2) USAID's budget is combined with the Department of State and other US government civilian programs; (3) foreign policy guidance comes from the secretary of state; and (4) all US assistance must be coordinated by the secretary of state. If our national security warrants international peace and security and our Department of State plays a critical role in American foreign policy, then USAID must be an implementing agent of that foreign policy and must engage in a wide variety of peace and security programming.

The agency is headed by an administrator, who is appointed by the president. During my 10 years with USAID, I worked under *four* different administrators and several acting administrators. One administrator was great, he was long-serving and dedicated. One resigned in embarrassment after the details of a Washington, DC, sex scandal broke out in 2007. Ironically, this same administrator had encouraged abstinence, discounted the use of condoms, and started to deny funds to organizations helping commercial sex workers. The last administrator I worked under resigned after serving a mere five years. One blog on a USAID alumni association forum labeled him as, "the Second Worst USAID Administrator in 30 years."[19] I don't have a benchmark from which to evaluate this claim because I was not engaged with USAID for the entirety of those 30 years. As I was overseas in Kenya for his entire tenure (2009–2015), I was insulated from the Washington, DC, gossip. I do recall, however, being appalled by the tone of his agencywide emails and his firm belief that all development problems could be solved with simple technological solutions.

Structurally, USAID is divided into bureaus, each headed by an assistant administrator. In USAID's headquarters, in Washington, DC, there are functional bureaus (e.g., Global Health, Food Security) offering technical assistance to the field programs; regional bureaus (e.g., Africa, Middle East) providing headquarter administration, coordination, and oversight of programs in the field; and other support bureaus (e.g., Management, Legislative and Public Affairs, and Policy, Planning and Learning). During my tenure with USAID, my office was in a functional bureau, Democracy, Conflict and Humanitarian Assistance (DCHA). After I left USAID, the bureau was split into the Bureau for Humanitarian Assistance and the Bureau for Conflict Prevention and Stabilization.

Who Funds USAID?

USAID was created in the early 1960s, at the height of the Cold War, when Congress authorized and funded the consolidation of disparate foreign assistance programs. With a budget request of approximately $30 billion in 2023, it is not a small agency within the US government portfolio (I use 2008–2013 data in this book to coincide with my term in Kenya).[20] Its budget resembles the core budget of the Federal Emergency Management Agency (FEMA), which is responsible for assisting communities in both preparing for and responding to disasters in the United States and its territories. USAID's budget is slightly greater than America's National Aeronautics and Space Administration (NASA) ($26 billion) and Federal Aviation Administration (FAA) ($24 billion), and it is substantially greater than the National Oceanic and Atmospheric Association (NOAA) ($9 billion), which covers oceans, fisheries, marine endangered species, and weather tracking.[21] Comparing US state budgets, USAID's annual budget exceeds the annual budgets of approximately one-half of the 50 US states.

There are several nuances to these USAID budget numbers, which are important to understand within the context of the scale of USAID's peace and security sector. These nuances also explain why the ambassador can tell the Chamber of Commerce that the United States is spending $3 billion in Kenya, presumably in 2010, but the ForeignAssistance.gov dashboard shows $570–$901 million annually between 2009 and 2011. If the total number we contribute is under- or overreported, the accounting of individual sectors cannot reflect our government's true level of support.

The first nuance stems from the difference between what Congress appropriates and what each and every agency actually spends. While Congress consolidated much of America's international development in the 1961 Foreign Assistance Act, the executive branch has considerable leeway on where funding goes. Congress also provides funding for international development under other accounts. For example, the FAA can assist countries with international air travel structures and procedures as it impacts the United States, while the Department of Interior can assist with international endangered species habitat and planning.

When I first arrived in Kenya, I took a new employee tour of the US embassy. I was stunned to find several doors with logos I did not expect—Library of Congress and the Departments of Interior and Transportation. In 2012, the State Department's Office of Inspections identified 19 different US government agencies based at the embassy in Nairobi, and even cautioned that the "Ambassador needs to broaden his understanding of why various agencies are part of his mission."[22] I envision a kindergarten sandbox with a host of US government agencies playing together or by themselves, collaboratively sharing or reluctantly giving or taking, arguing, and ignoring one another.

Agencies do, with difficulty, transfer funds among each other, and funds even flow among other international agencies. Therefore, USAID can end up spending more than its base budget because of these transfers. For example, USAID manages some of the contracts under the

Presidential Emergency Program for AIDS Relief (PEPFAR); in Kenya in 2013, USAID's obligations totaled $480 million while the Department of Health and Human Services (DHHS) obligated $208 million. One of my first tasks at USAID Washington, when I started in 2005, was to arrange for a transfer of funds from the World Bank, through the government of the Democratic Republic of Congo (DRC), to USAID for a program to re-integrate ex-combatants. The six-year program in Kenya received funds from several different accounts, including multiple accounts within the Department of State and one from the United Kingdom. On more than one occasion, I felt like a panhandler on Nairobi's streets, walking around the embassy with a collection box for the program. There had to be an element of truth with this analogy because the money I received from our head office in Washington, DC, accounted for less than half of the program's total budget.

The implication of this first nuance is that USAID's budget is one-third to one-half of the US government's budget for foreign assistance. The dashboard page on the ForeignAssistance.gov website shows that USAID's obligations in 2013 comprised 37 percent ($17 billion) of all US foreign assistance ($46 billion). In Kenya specifically, USAID accounted for $480 million (53 percent) of the total $910 million of US foreign assistance obligations.

The second nuance is about what USAID reports spending in a particular country such as Kenya. This spending is not *in* that country but *for* that country. Less than half of USAID's budget is spent overseas. USAID used to have a library and public information center in the Ronald Reagan Building in downtown Washington, DC. One prominent display is forever emblazoned on my brain: "Contrary to popular belief, more than half of USAID's spending occurs in the United States."[23] USAID has an office in Washington, DC, with staff who get paid, receive benefits, and use information technology equipment all bought and paid for in the United States. When USAID issues a contract or a grant to an implementing partner, that partner is most likely a US-based organization. For example, I oversaw contracts with large USAID contractors, including Chemonics, Development Alternatives, Inc. (DAI), TetraTech, and Associates in Rural Development (ARD).[24] Each organization is a US-based for-profit commercial company. Each maintains an office and staff in the United States. When USAID issues a contract with funding for consultants, equipment, or supplies, much of those funds are spent in the United States. USAID procurement rules try to maximize US-based purchases, including equipment, bulk food, vehicles, and airline tickets.

The third nuance relates to the US government's accounting terminology. Agencies submit budget requests to Congress, which then appropriates money for a particular account. Congress may even issue a recission, reducing the appropriation amount after it has been signed into law. Once an agency has its obligation, it has to sub-obligate funds for a particular purpose. The numbers above and the foreign assistance dashboard report on obligations. The $910 million obligated for Kenya in 2013 represents the total in grants, contracts, or other agreements the United States *signed* in 2013. A US government agency cannot send a check to a contractor or vendor unless the government has set aside funding for that particular purpose. But there is a delay, sometimes years, between an obligation being issued, using those funds, invoicing, and receiving payment. For example, in 2013, our program issued a contract to Chemonics, which may have placed an order for thousands of copies of the new constitution in mid-2014 and invoiced USAID at the end of 2014, after ensuring the items were delivered to rural parts of Kenya and all the paperwork was in order. USAID may not have paid that invoice—that is, released funds—until 2015.

These three nuances—the number of agencies in the international sandbox, the total amount of spending in the United States, and the delay between an obligation and the flow of cash—depict the complexity of the entire system and confuse the public. No one can accurately describe exactly how much each government agency spent, from all annual budgets, on Kenya *in* Kenya in a given year. Thus, the amount spent on peace and security in a particular country in a given year remains amorphous.

The Marines of USAID

The previous two sections described what USAID is and what it does, and its funding. I also briefly explained USAID's broad structure of bureaus, which I knew nothing about when I applied for a job with the agency in 2005. I was exploring positions in international development and saw an announcement for a USAID program manager for the Iraq program at the USAID's OTI and decided to apply because it was based in Washington, DC. I didn't get that specific role, but only a few months later, I onboarded with OTI as a program manager for the DRC.

I quickly discovered OTI was very different from USAID's other, more well-known, offices. USAID's main offices occupied the second to ninth floors of the Ronald Reagan Building in Washington, DC. I was told to report to OTI, housed in the third basement level, below the car park. Its location deep underground symbolized the office's uniqueness and separation from the rest of the agency, a difference responsible for OTI's nickname, "the cowboys in the basement." OTI earned both this honorific and another, "the marines of USAID," because it inherently operated differently and staff adopted a singular attitude compared to others at USAID. This attitude focused on getting things done quickly and working around bureaucratic hurdles. As one non-OTI USAID official retorted in response to yet another failed attempt to secure a bureaucratic approval, "You never take 'no' for an answer."

I was part of OTI, which is the political arm of USAID, within the DCHA Bureau. The office is more like a fingernail than an arm, given that its small budget represents less than 0.5 percent of the agency's budget. OTI uses the term "political" with confidence, even though most others within USAID and outside of USAID would shirk from connecting development and political objectives. Indeed, OTI is not shy about its mandate. Its website states, "Although our interventions may appear similar to development activities, they are political in nature."[25] Moreover, its mission is, "in support of US foreign policy, OTI seizes emerging windows of opportunity in the political landscape to promote stability, peace, and democracy by catalyzing local initiatives through adaptive and agile programming."[26]

What does all this mean, and how does it differ from the rest of the agency? In 2014, the agency's mission was to "partner [with other countries] to end extreme poverty and to promote resilient, democratic societies while advancing our security and prosperity."[27] OTI's mission was clearly a subset of the agency's overall mission, as the office was a small part of USAID. On the one hand, both missions touch on democracy, a core US value. As for OTI, it is seen as the entry point, one *beginning* the road to peace and democracy, with an emphasis on short-term targeted assistance. On the other hand, the agency as a whole is focused on the long-term goals of ending poverty (2014) and promoting democracy (2014, 2018). OTI's ten-year report (2004) explains this distinction: "USAID's Office of Transition Initiatives (OTI) was created in 1994 to bridge the gap between relief and development and provide short-term political assistance to countries in crisis.... OTI was charged with responding rapidly to dynamic situations and unfolding emergencies, in effect acting as the first responder to political upheaval."[28]

OTI's mission statement included assisting with both political transitions and stabilization programs. Its efforts supported political change such as the United States-led invasion of Iraq (the Second Gulf War), the Kenyan reform agenda after the 2007/2008 postelection violence, the Orange Revolution in Ukraine in 2012, and the 2010–2011 Arab Spring revolutions in Libya and Tunisia. When I joined USAID in 2005, OTI was managing programs in the DRC, Burundi, Iraq, and Afghanistan, all of which involved stabilization. "Stabilization" was a buzzword within the international arena, one that US politicians and bureaucrats used liberally. It implied the settling down of hostilities after a conflict or war. For OTI, "stabilization" meant it became engaged after a battle or civil war when the country was trying to come to some semblance of peace before development agencies could engage in longer-term programming.

OTI's core funding comes from a special account established by Congress. The transition initiatives account within the foreign assistance budget is an annual earmark for "programs targeting key transitions to democracy for countries in crisis and quick-impact activities for conflict prevention or stabilization."[29] The budget is extremely small, averaging $50 million before I left in 2015 and $80 million in 2023. That accounts for only 0.3 percent of USAID's annual budget. This budget is extremely flexible; OTI can use it in any country after giving Congress a five-day advanced notice. The funds also come with a special notwithstanding authority, which basically allows OTI to override, with justification, any other statutory restriction when using these funds. I used this authority once in my tenure with USAID. Congress has restricted USAID's ability to assist law enforcement, but we used notwithstanding authority to fund improvements in police stations in support of Kenya's reform agenda.[30] Unfortunately, authorities are tied to specific funds; this authority did not extend to all other funds we received for our Kenya program.

With this unique approach to programming, within a US government bureaucracy known to take years to initiate a new program, OTI was able to send an assessment team to Kenya in March 2008, one month after the peace agreement was signed, award a multimillion-dollar contract in May, launch the program in June, and field USAID staff to Nairobi in September (after renovating office space within the embassy in Nairobi). Because of the speed, flexibility, and attitude, I loved working for OTI and considered it a privilege. I was proud of being called a "cowboy in the basement" or a "Marine of USAID." One of our beneficiaries, British author Michela Wrong, eloquently explained this attitude:

> Then, miraculously, a *deus ex machina* emerged in the form of Galeeb Kachra, a dynamic young American working for the Office of Transition Initiatives. OTI, he explained in a call from Nairobi, was a branch of the USAID development agency specialising in rapid initiatives promoting change in countries moving from authoritarianism to democracy. Getting copies of my book to ordinary Kenyans was exactly the kind of project OTI relished. He was already hard at work, pulling together a multipronged distribution operation to bypass a gagged retail industry.[31]

Throughout this book, I will provide practical programming examples to further justify these honorifics.

Inherent Bias and Prejudice

Everyone has bias and inherent prejudice. All good nonfiction authors articulate their perspectives in their writing and then let readers judge for themselves. What are the inherent biases underlying my definition? I am a former African citizen, an American Muslim, a former 10-year American diplomatic aid worker, and the spouse of an American Pakistani. I have lived and worked in three countries—the United States, Kenya, and Pakistan—on three different continents.

I am neither an academic nor a social scientist, but I do have a bachelor's degree in systems engineering (systems thinking, not information technology systems) and in Islamic Studies and Arabic. I consider myself a grounded, practical pragmatic; a doer; a manager; and a reformer.

I understand one small segment of USAID, having worked for one of its offices, the Office of Transition Initiatives, for a decade. During this period, I conducted in-country transition program performance reviews in Zimbabwe, Pakistan, and Sudan; remotely managed final evaluations for political transition programs in Bolivia and Sri Lanka; provided technical assistance on peace and security program design in Colombia and Jordan; and assisted with field-based startups of an ex-combatant reintegration program in eastern Democratic Republic of Congo and a political development program in western Pakistan. While in Kenya, I collaborated with other bureaus of USAID and proactively tried to understand their strengths, weaknesses, and systems. But I also reached across the aisle, to the Department of State and other agencies. My USAID colleagues in Kenya would joke that I spent more time with the embassy's political officers than USAID's development specialists. That was true because my work in Kenya aligned more closely with the former than the latter.

This book is based primarily on my period in Kenya, managing KTI. I lived and breathed KTI for six years; I worked for OTI for a decade. I strongly believe in OTI's mission, the role of the KTI program in Kenya, and the applicability of my experiences to other contexts. Therefore, while I do point out flaws or failures, these may be fewer than the reader expects.

Conclusion

This book, which defines a Kenyan application of American peace and security programming, reflects my unique qualifications and way of thinking. It will be short, to-the-point, and punctuated with real-world examples and personal anecdotes. The topic is becoming more important as our twenty-first-century world evolves. The devastating impacts of climate change, Russia's invasion of Ukraine, domestic and international radicalization (Muslim, Jewish, and Christian fundamentalists, white supremacists, and antigovernment anarchists), and global political uncertainty will continue to challenge US foreign policy experts. Meanwhile, universities multiply and morph their peace and security academic programs. Americans are becoming savvier and more connected with what Congress appropriates and how the executive spends taxpayers' funds. Yet our attention spans are decreasing; we want instant answers.

US peace and security experts, academic and professional, must be able to articulate, in a simple tweet or webpage, what we want for global peace and security, why the United States cares, and how we can achieve it. The bureaucrats must understand and acknowledge each agency's strengths and weaknesses in providing peace and security programming before intentionally deciding which agency is best positioned for a particular type of effort as authorized by Congress and within the confines of the US Constitution and its interpretation.

CHAPTER ONE

Judicial Reform

"We found an institution so frail in its structures; so thin on resources; so low on its confidence; so deficient in integrity; so weak in its public support that to have expected it to deliver justice was to be wildly optimistic. We found a judiciary that was designed to fail."
  —Chief Justice Willy Mutunga, "Progress Report on the Transformation of the Judiciary: The First 120 Days," speech, Nairobi, Kenya, October 19, 2011

Bottom Line Up Front (BLUF)

The 2007/2008 postelection violence in Kenya was triggered by the "massively flawed" December 27, 2007, general election because the opposition party led by Raila Odinga did not see the judiciary as a "credible mechanism for resolving electoral disputes . . . [his party] refused to take the matter to the courts, pointing out that they were controlled by Kibaki."[1] The country was thrown into weeks of violence, resulting in the murder of thousands of Kenyans, the displacement of hundreds of thousands of people, and charges of crimes against humanity against six Kenyans at the International Criminal Court (ICC). December 2007 to February 2008 was Kenya's worst three months. Yet, when Raila Odinga lost the August 2022 election 15 years later, he voluntarily turned to the courts, pleaded his case, and accepted their final decision, stating, "In this regard, we respect the opinion of the court although we vehemently disagree with their decision today."[2]

The judiciary has brought peace and security to Kenya through concurrent changes in laws, personalities, infrastructure, and perception.

In less than two decades, it went from being a mistrusted and mocked institution to a modern, trusted institution. The old judiciary was stuck in the past, inheriting not only corruption and bureaucracy from Kenya's colonialists but also the white wigs worn by judges and attorneys alike. Only a new constitution heralding in a new supreme court and a new chief justice could give the judiciary a new life. It also symbolically rid Kenyan judges and attorneys of the comical headgear and references to "My Lord" and "My Lady."[3] This transformation was sparked by the violence, made possible by the new constitution and facilitated by several foreign powers, including the United States. Although the judiciary had failed Kenyans in 2008, now, with support from the international community, Kenya has been transformed; all of this and helped bring peace and security to Kenya in the wake of the 2013 and 2022 presidential elections.

The Problems and Solutions

The 2008 peace agreement, brokered by Kofi Annan to end the postelection violence, included an agenda of longstanding issues that needed resolution.[4] Eight influential Kenyans, including Martha Karua, the former minister of justice, signed the agreement. Affectionately known in the media as Kenya's "Iron Lady," Karua served as minister of justice through 2009, ran for president in 2013, and ran as Odinga's deputy president in 2022.[5] One of the 2008 agreement's longstanding issues was judicial reform, partly because in 2007, Raila Odinga's supporters took to the streets and violence because their leader had no faith in the judiciary.

However, in 2022, Odinga's supporters begrudgingly but peacefully accepted their leader's acknowledgment of the court's verdict. Odinga is not the first politician to sway his followers' confidence in or disdain for the judiciary. His 2022 announcement echoed statements made after Florida's supreme court decision in 2000. Al Gore, in a televised address to the nation on December 13, 2000, after losing the US presidential election over issues with vote counting in Florida, said, "While I strongly disagree with the Court's decision, I accept it."[6] America moved on peacefully.

When then-President Trump lost the 2020 election to Joe Biden, he sent mixed signals about his trust in the judiciary. He turned to the courts, filing "62 lawsuits in state and federal courts"; two different lawsuits he filed were refused by the US Supreme Court.[7] But, unlike Gore in 2000 and Odinga in 2022, Trump, in 2020, did not accept the results and has been accused of instigating an attempted coup by encouraging the storming of the US Capitol on January 6, 2021.[8] With this strategy, Trump's anti-judiciary persona aligns more closely with Odinga's 2007 decision.

Then-President Trump both trusted and mistrusted the judiciary simultaneously, while Odinga's perspective changed over time. In merely 15 years, Odinga and Kenyans alike had pivoted from having no trust in the judiciary to having complete faith in it. As former Vice President Joe Biden lectured Kenyan students in 2010, "too many of your institutions have lost the people's confidence."[9] What makes a losing politician trust the judiciary and how can governments and development partners help advance judicial reform to further improve peace and security? This chapter concludes that judicial reform is better connected to US peace and security interests. It offers a tangible, practicable, and bite-sized intervention that makes sense. However, I also reemphasize the need for development and security professionals to select carefully from the menu of development challenges when identifying peace and security interventions that can help nations achieve positive, measurable, and meaningful results.

USAID's experiences in Kenya between 2008 and 2014 show that improving confidence in the judiciary requires momentum in three parallel forces: processes, perceptions, and people. Each differs in its contribution to the problem and the opportunities it affords for US interventions to advance peace and security.

Processes

The first force that significantly impacted Kenyans' perceptions of the judiciary was based on their interaction with the processes of justice. Studies, reports, personal conversations with court users and attorneys, and my own observations all came to the same conclusions about pro-cesses.[10] For one, trial files were often lost, either by mistake or because one party had "paid" for the file to disappear. Files were also stolen; the court had insufficient, insecure, and inadequate storage space. Moreover, there were no electronic files. Upcoming hearing dates and changes to those dates were not communicated to the parties and their attorneys. Citizens would travel, at a considerable expense, from their rural villages to the city only to find that the hearing had been delayed. When one entered a court building, one was intimidated and lost: There was no information desk, signage, or posting of the day's docket. Justice was delayed because magistrates took longhand notes; there were no stenographers or recording equipment. Instead, secretaries had to type up a backlog of notes before a magistrate could consider all the evidence, review the notes, and reach a decision.

Kenya's post-2010 court system mirrors Britain's and America's, replete with a hierarchy of lower and superior courts. Kenya's lower courts include magistrate courts, presided by a chief magistrate, while the superior courts include the high court, court of appeals, and the Supreme Court, each having both appellate and original jurisdiction. For example, Kenya's Supreme Court has exclusive original jurisdiction for presidential election disputes.

Unfortunately, while the reform effort, supported by the international community, was focused on the higher courts, most of the public only interacted with the justice system in the magistrates' courts. If the structure of that interaction could be changed, the momentum could trickle up, and the public could see that the peace agreement and international effort have brought judicial reforms to Kenya. That was our goal as we initiated a partnership with a visionary magistrate in Eldoret, Kenya. Unlike many other Kenyan officials whom I have met, Chief Magistrate Mbogo, who had only recently moved to Eldoret when I met him, had identified discrete, workable solutions for many of the problems in the court building. Together, we designed a grant package, which he agreed to sign given his responsibility for the court's operations. To avoid any perceptions of corruption, we offered only an in-kind grant; our KTI contractor would procure each item, directly contract each supplier or expert, and directly pay for expenses such as travel, hotels, and flights. This is the way KTI operated; that is the way most OTI programs worked worldwide. It was extremely labor-intensive for OTI's contractor, but it was extremely effective when trying to support the grassroots or local government entities that could not qualify for US government cash grants.

We also agreed to host a formal event with the chief justice and US ambassador *only* if the project was successful. These two elements, an in-kind agreement with no exchange of cash and a soft launch that delayed a formal event until after results could be demonstrated, were two ways KTI differed from other donor initiatives.

The Eldoret project comprised simultaneous but separate components (a physical filing infrastructure, case management software, court-user forums, directional signage, text messaging updates, and customer service desks), allowing any individual one to fail without jeopardizing the entire project. Most worked well. Unfortunately, however, the court transcription using voice recognition did not work. We could not overcome the cumulative problems of bad acoustics in old, open courtrooms; the lack of microphones for the magistrate, lawyers, and witnesses; and the inability of the American software to decipher Kenyan accents. We abandoned it after a few unsuccessful adjustments and reboots.

The court became a regular site visit for development partners, reformers, and even industry representatives. I would regularly receive calls or emails asking about visiting the court. My standard answer was, "You can contact the chief magistrate in Eldoret. The project is a government of Kenya judiciary project, not a USAID project." I would always encourage visitors to go to Eldoret only after having first visited another court because one cannot appreciate change without a good benchmark. The most convenient location was Kitale, less than two hours north of Eldoret.

The Eldoret judiciary contributed staff and personnel to the reform project; they saw it as their project operating with USAID assistance and reached out to their headquarters in Nairobi for additional support. As part of their contribution to the grant, the ministry assigned a fulltime computer expert to Eldoret, the first judiciary information technology (IT) expert to be posted outside Nairobi. The Eldoret chief magistrate oversaw a smaller station in the town of Kapsabet, an hour away from Eldoret. He wanted to replicate the project there and learn from their initial mistakes. He took complete ownership of the replication and ensured that the Kapsabet staff were fully vested in the project. He even transferred some Eldoret staff to provide consistency in the implementation and to learn from the Eldoret example. Version two was better than the first; an internal USAID review found that staff morale in Kapsabet offered a better work environment and much quicker progress.

On April 19, 2013, the judiciary sent a letter to KTI, stating, "The Judiciary is grateful for the support that USAID has provided over the years. This support provided insight as to what the Judiciary can be able to achieve if it harnessed concerted efforts."[11] A representative in the justice solutions practice area of Cisco, an American-based, multinational digital communications technology firm, offered a comparison to global justice reform:

> The main thing that sets Eldoret apart from all other courts I have seen is PRIDE. These people are proud of their court, and proud to have taken responsibility for solving judicial issues faced throughout Kenya (the world for that matter), and with USAID support, have created a model court that will most likely become a template for a nationwide solution.
>
> I was very impressed in that it seems that a thorough needs assessment was done for each one of the issues faced by Eldoret, and a proper solution was created for each one, with a great "bang for the buck." Even more impressive is that all the separate solutions synergize very well together to increase productivity and transparency, while at the same time greatly reducing areas of possible corruption. Believe it or not—what you have been doing in Eldoret is pretty cutting edge in court technology worldwide.
>
> Kudos to you and your staff. It makes me proud to be an American when I see things like this.[12]

The court project became one of KTI's flagships. KTI replicated (and customized) the project in both Kericho and Mombasa. A new chief magistrate in Mombasa had previously been posted to Eldoret and said to me, "Give me everything you did in Eldoret."[13] We added customer surveys and a robust media component (social and traditional) to capture and disseminate the impact.

But the replication of a handful of projects, funded by KTI in partnership with the Kenyan Judiciary, was not enough to change perception nationally. As Maya Gainer writes: "'The [Eldoret] system was intended as "a testing ground,"' said Long'et Terer [a lawyer and former Chief

Executive Officer of The National Council for Law Reporting]. 'It's a fairly simple system, but it showed all of us that it's possible to have a system in place.' ... However, scaling up an electronic case management system to cover the entire country was no easy matter."[14]

Kenya needed national change: better court buildings, files, electronic case management, customer care centers, and text messaging communication with court users. One of the Eldoret court staff met a World Bank staff member and showcased the court project. The bank was interested; I met with their representatives in Nairobi and conceptualized a new idea. This time the Eldoret court, together with USAID, would submit a concept for replicating the effort in 10 magistrate courts within easy access to Eldoret. I had based the partnership on a previous USAID and World Bank partnership, one that I had been engaged in while working in Washington, DC.

During my first month at USAID in 2005, I was asked to figure out how to receive World Bank funds that were available to the DRC. At first, the finance, accounting, and legal staff with whom I had talked within USAID said that it was not possible, that USAID could only use funding that had originated from Congress. This was not true; USAID had other means, including the authority to receive *gifts*. For example, in Fall 2005, OTI received $4.6 million from the World Bank and used it to reintegrate an additional 9,000 ex-combatants and 4,000 community members in eastern DRC after demonstrating a multiyear pilot project funded by USAID. I don't know how much money USAID received from nonfederal sources when I first started, but I do know that in my last year at USAID, when I arranged for a transfer of $2.4 million from the UK government to USAID for my program in Kenya, the agency was receiving significant funds from other sources and had even developed a new policy chapter on "Gift and Donations and Dollar Trust Fund Management."[15]

With support from the KTI staff, the Kenyan judiciary finalized and submitted the proposal, but the World Bank staff balked. They decided to wait until the new senior judicial leadership, required by the new 2010 Kenyan Constitution, was in place and had demonstrated its intent to reform the judiciary. This happened quickly and, by 2011, the new chief justice and new chief registrar began working with the World Bank on a project appraisal document for a new $120 million judicial performance improvement project, which included components of our demonstration projects. Over a few months, I met with various World Bank teams in Kenya to help explain the successes and challenges of our pilot projects.

After the proposal was submitted to the bank's headquarters and before the board's vote in November 2012, I met with bank staff and other US government officials from the Treasury and the State Department at the bank's head office in Washington, DC, to further explain the pilot programs and their relationship to the new proposal. A few days later, the United States supported the project by voting for it at the board meeting, and the board approved the $120 million project.

The project was modified in 2016 and completed in 2021. The World Bank's final indicators included an increase in court users who were satisfied with the delivery of court services in project courts from 35 percent in November 2012 to 65 percent in July 2021 and an increase from 50 to 70 percent over the same period in users reporting timely court services.[16] The final outputs included over 25 new courts, each with two to 12 courtrooms, nine mobile courts, upgrades to registries, storage containers, files, case tracking systems, equipment, web portals, training, and furniture.[17]

Perceptions

Consultants, change management experts, and strategic planners use the term "SMART" when establishing target objectives, outcomes, or results. It refers to *S*pecific, *M*easurable, *A*chievable, *R*elevant, and *T*imebound. The SMART approach distinguishes judicial reform from land reform in Kenya. Evaluating judicial reform boils down to two basic indicators: Are cases moving through the court system promptly and, second, are the judgments relatively fair, reasonable, and grounded in law, as opposed to being political or bought? A judiciary reformer can identify opportunities to enhance one or more improvements that influence these indicators, design interventions for them, and measure and report on their progress using SMART indicators.

Kenyans I met during my term as the deputy country representative for a USAID program in Kenya were intimately familiar with Kenya's judiciary woes. Discussions with advocates, magistrates, judges, and judiciary staff led to unanimous and unambiguous findings that can be summed up in two simple quotations: "Why Hire a Lawyer when you can pay the judge?" and "I have to pay to ensure files do not get lost or for lost files to reappear."[18]

Kenyans were not the first to buy, or pay off, a judge. The British can be credited with bringing that practice to Kenya during the creation of the country. The colonial administration was under significant pressure from the white settlers to address the 1950s brutal Mau Mau effort to free Kenya. They arrested Jomo Kenyatta in 1952, accusing him of being the mastermind of the Mau Mau independence movement. The British needed a conclusive and firm verdict for their trial, which was a political farce. They flew in a "potbellied and bespectacled" retired judge who had served 12 years on Kenya's Supreme Court and as Fiji's attorney general.[19] Judge Ransley Samuel Thacker "apparently had no qualms about selling his verdict long before the trial began. He insisted upon twenty thousand pounds to ensure a conviction, and in what must be described as one of his most self-incriminating moves as governor, Baring complied."[20]

This simple example of the British's desperation and blatant disregard for justice is a footnote in history. Yet, it exemplifies two significantly important facets of an historical narrative. The first relates to the term "rebels." America, like every nation, is quick to amend labels depending on the political whims of those who write history. When we assisted the Afghans in their war against the Soviet invasion in 1979, America called the *mujahidin* "freedom fighters." Then, when the *mujahidin* fought against the US invasion of 2002, we labeled them "terrorists." The British labeled Kenyatta the "terrorist leader" of the Mau Mau uprising against the white settlers and arrested him in 1952. In 1961 the British released him and a year later he became Kenya's first president.

The second facet has deeper implications for Kenya's growth potential, one that Kenyans personally struggle with. Corruption permeates all levels of society, from an individual traffic policeman receiving mobile money bribes to multimillion-dollar government procurement corruption schemes. It manifests itself in different ways, driven by political and tribal patronage, human greed, and a multigenerational way of life. This culture of corruption, which existed in different forms before colonialism, was molded by colonial institutions and has developed and become more complex since independence with population growth, development, and information technology.

In some ways, this culture of corruption mirrors that of other countries. For example, both Pakistan and Kenya are high on the corruption indices. In the words of *The Telegraph,* a British Newspaper, "The president of Pakistan will always be known as 'Mr. 10 Per Cent' even to many of those who hail his wife, Benazir Bhutto, as a martyr and national hero."[21] Both Kenya and Pakistan consistently rank among the top one-third of corrupt countries in Transparency International's annual Corruption Perceptions Index, which is based on perceived levels of public sector corruption. The 2023 index is bookmarked by Denmark (rank 1, score 90) and Somalia (rank 180, score 11). Seventy percent of countries ranked higher than Kenya (rank 126, score 31) and Pakistan (rank 133, score 29). By comparison, in the same year, 13 percent ranked higher than the United States (rank 24, score 69).[22]

Yet, based on my experience in both countries, I found blatant corruption at every level of public service in Kenya but not in Pakistan. In Kenya, not only does any transaction require a bribe but also the public servant is blatantly obvious about his or her intent. Just as Judge Thacker demanded money for a definitive verdict, police, desk clerks, land registrars, procurement officers, and building inspectors ask for *kitu kidogo* or "something small" to grease the wheels of government service.

Britain's export of professional corruption was not limited to the judiciary. It transcends the private sector. Procurement in any country offers one of the biggest opportunities for individuals to receive financial windfalls from potential bidders, and Kenya's history is punctuated by innovative and largescale corruption scandals, each registering in the tens of millions of dollars. While the international community frequently mumbles about Kenyan greed, it forgets that procurement corruption is global and began in Nairobi before Kenyan independence. In the 1950s, the British, through an understaffed and corrupt city council, issued tenders for multiple housing estates around Nairobi at a scale that "surprised even Kenya's most cynical observers."[23]

Kenyans are unfortunately too familiar with corruption in land transactions, which also started when the British introduced land tenure systems to Kenya. In 1955, the British government established the Rose

Commission to investigate corruption and fraud within the Nairobi City Council. According to Sir Alan Rose, the chairman, "even in the City Fire Brigade, a group of senior European officers were involved in a longstanding scam to 'sell' city property, and then have it brought back at a margin."[24] The commission "reached the unequivocal conclusion that bribery and corruption were 'by no means uncommon' among city office holders at 'all levels and in all departments'; that the scale of cash inducements involved to secure services or preference from the Council was often significant; and that such behavior was accepted as the norm and widely tolerated."[25]

Unfortunately, corruption is so widespread and deep in Kenya that the courts are helpless against it. Even a significantly stronger, independent, and organized judiciary cannot singlehandedly destroy corruption. The public prosecutor, anticorruption commission, police and investigators, and lawyers all need to transform. But most importantly, and perhaps impossibly, the ethic of Kenya's elite needs to change. None of these transformations are within America's manageable interest under a peace and security agenda.

The elite, which I discuss more in-depth in chapter 4, are the same ones who took advantage of a dysfunctional judiciary. They knew they could get away with all sorts of corruption, fraud, and even murder because of an ineffective judiciary and a weak director of public prosecution. Yes, murder: Kenya's history is rife with incidents of political and politically related murder. Pinto de Gama, a journalist and activist; Tom Mboya, an educator and activist; and Robert Ouko, a politician; are just a few of Kenya's assassinated political and cultural figures. Even during KTI's short lifespan, I heard about the disappearance or accidental deaths of civil society activists and potential International Criminal Court (ICC) witnesses. Foreign journalists were not exempt. In 2022, Pakistan investigators claimed "the Kenyan police were apparently 'used as instruments' in . . . a planned, targeted assassination" of an outspoken Pakistani journalist in October 2022.[26]

In 2014, only a year after confirming charges against six Kenyans, including former President Uhuru Kenyatta and current President William Ruto (before they became presidents), the ICC dropped all charges against the former president. According to Reuters, "Prosecutors blamed their failure to put Kenyatta on trial on political interference and massive interference with witnesses, especially after Kenyatta was elected president in 2013."[27] Charges against current President Ruto were dropped in 2016. I compare the confirmation of charges against these elite Kenyans with the US House of Representatives' impeachment or bringing of charges against former President Donald Trump for crimes associated with the January 6, 2021, insurrection of the US Capitol. In both cases, the elite walked free, but the difference is that, for Kenya and the ICC, there was no trial and the flow of justice was interrupted. In contrast, the US Senate did find Trump not guilty, thereby completing the congressional judicial process.[28]

The development partners had to operate against this depressing backdrop of the reality of corruption in Kenya's judiciary before the 2010 Constitutional referendum. USAID's global judiciary reform programs have focused on judiciary independence without an explicit connection to peace and security. For example, USAID's 2002 "Guidance for Promoting Judicial Independence and Impartiality," part of its technical publication series, notes that "Judicial independence lies at the heart of a well-functioning judiciary and is the cornerstone of a democratic, market-based society based on the rule of law."[29] In Kenya, USAID's support of the justice sector has focused primarily on strengthening civil society or contributing to a multi-donor, sector-wide fund for various government of Kenya initiatives. The first large allocation was initiated in 2004 for the Governance, Justice, Law and Order Sector (GJLOS) reform program across 34 ministries, departments, and agencies including the judiciary. One independent evaluation of this program criticized donors for cherry-picking, arguing, influencing the program's direction, and advancing their own interests.[30]

While the 2010 Constitution brought immediate hope to Kenyans, the international community was filled with trepidation. After we initiated support for the Eldoret Magistrates Court, one of Eldoret's court staff showcased the project to a World Bank representative who was impressed but cautious. We heard that the bank was holding off on providing any new support to the judiciary. While the new constitution radically altered the structure of Kenya's judiciary, the bank and other donors wanted to see who was going to take the helm and in what direction they were going to steer.

A postelection-violence change in Kenyans' perception of the judiciary required more than a radical approach. Kenya had tried *radical* change in 2003, and it had failed. That effort, led by former Justice Aaron Ringera, identified multiple courts of appeals judges, high court judges, and magistrates believed to be corrupt; Ringera officially named them and demanded their resignation without due process.[31] The 2010 effort was, by contrast, a systematic transformation. The new constitution introduced a bill of rights; a new supreme court with term limits; minimum qualifications for all judges; and requirements that a Judicial Services Commission (a judiciary body independent from the executive branch) make appointment recommendations to the president, and that these appointees are approved by the National Assembly. The 2010 Constitution also required that the attorney general, auditor-general, and chief justice be fired.[32]

As we funded various civic education programs to teach Kenyans about the draft constitution and help them make informed decisions at the polling booth, we found that this systematic judicial transformation appealed to them. USAID and other donors provided technical assistance while drafting the constitution; it also aided parliament and its subcommittees after adopting the new constitution to assist with the myriad new laws, which the constitution required to be passed within a short timeframe. Some of these USAID efforts, and the obstacles we faced, are discussed in chapter 3.

KTI explored ways to maintain positive public perception. Specific to judicial reform, but focusing on the thorny land issues, we funded a local human rights civil society group that promoted access to justice by identifying, documenting, and disseminating examples of successful land cases under the new constitution. As with many KTI grants (and those of USAID's Office of Transition Initiatives programs worldwide), the most important beneficiaries are not those reached through the grant's activities. Recipients of the disseminated findings, delivered either in the form of booklets, outreach efforts, or media dissemination, were actually secondary. Organizational staff were the primary beneficiaries because their mission revolved around access to justice for human rights issues. Land evictions and ownership rights were among the matters they dealt with daily. Some individuals involved in legal justice focus on the trees and not the forest because they work on individual cases with real people. By showing them how Kenya's Constitution was tangibly changing the corpus of land case law for the public's benefit, we could renew their confidence in both the new constitution and the transforming judiciary. They subsequently passed that confidence on to their hundreds of potential and actual clients.

USAID and other donors tended to focus on top-down judicial reform. Changing laws or appropriating funds does not always translate into tangible changes in practice or improvements for the public. In discussing the county context, the 2014–2020 Country Development Cooperation Strategy (CDCS) highlighted this problem, stating, "After years of ignominy due to poor performance and suspicions of corruption, the justice sector is being transformed, with an increasingly positive public perception of the Judiciary. However, problems remain. Equality before the law has not been achieved; ordinary citizens do not receive the same treatment as the elite. The culture of impunity persists, with few corruption cases ever prosecuted."[33]

Against this bleak picture, the United States steered away from judicial reform, noting in the 2020–2025 CDCS that "USAID/Kenya will not be undertaking a robust program on judicial reform."[34] Yet, 31 pages later, there is an acknowledgment that "Judicial reform is progressing well," citing that "USAID/Kenya worked with the judiciary to help build capacity for electoral dispute resolution prior to the 2013 election and this was a vital component of the elections preparations."[35]

Kenya's Supreme Court dismissed a challenge to the 2013 election following the process required by the 2010 Constitution. The same court passed a landmark ruling that clarified one aspect of the constitution: The constitution requires that, in order for a presidential candidate to win, the candidate must receive "more than half of all the votes cast in the election."[36] Every election in every country rejects ballots that are blank, spoiled, or stray. Spoiled ballots include those that are damaged beyond readability or those with more than one mark, rendering the voter's intent indecipherable. Stray ballots are those inserted into the wrong box. Kenyans vote for six distinct positions during a general election and must deposit six separate, color-coded ballots into six separate, color-coded boxes. While election officials guide voters as much as possible without interfering with their right to vote as they please, a few ballots always end up in wrong boxes. Consequently, they cannot be counted because vote counting must be completed, signed, and certified for each box before the next box is opened.

This requirement, as well as all the other strict counting protocols, is not purely theoretical. Although I was not in Kenya during the 2022 election process, I found myself explaining to several Kenyans that the initial rumors of election rigging, which they were hearing about and retweeting, were farfetched. The irony amused me. Despite the proliferation of rumors, none of them believed that the US 2020 election had been stolen. Furthermore, even though they were not American and had never voted in or seen a US presidential election process, they knew that elections in the United States are extremely complex and decentralized. For example, in Virginia, where I last voted in person, ballots are collected at each polling center, tabulated at the local general registrar's office (usually at the county level), and uploaded to the state's central system. Each state's electoral college votes are then tabulated to determine the winner. In both the United States and Kenya, fraud at one polling center or county, in the form of ballot stuffing or replacement, is unlikely to noticeably change the vote count. If it is blatantly obvious that the number of votes exceeds that of registered voters or those who checked in on a particular day, then fraudulent activity can easily be identified.

In Kenya, widespread fraud is difficult to organize and ascertain. I describe my involvement as an observer in Kenya's 2013 presidential election, the first under the country's new constitution, in chapter 3. Each person (polling official, political party observer, media representative, or international observer) in the Kenyan polling station vote-counting room had the opportunity to scrutinize each blank, spoiled, or stray ballot and reach a unanimous decision about whether to set the ballot aside. This effort, running late into the night, occurred at every single one of the 50,000 polling stations countrywide.

The challengers to the 2013 Kenyan election results wanted blank, spoiled, and stray ballots to be included in the denominator of the calculation of "more than half of all the votes cast."[37] Kenya's Supreme Court established its newfound authority by concluding such ballots are invalid and not to be counted in either the numerator or denominator. That precedent played a significant factor in the decision on the 2022 Kenyan election petition.

In contrast to 2013 and 2022, Kenya's Supreme Court threw its own citizens and the world a curve ball in 2017. As one opinion piece in the *Al Jazeera* said: "It put Chief Justice David Maraga in history books as the first African chief justice to oversee the annulment of election results."[38] The court's decision hinged not on fraud but on processes and rule of law, reprimanding the elections commission for not following its own requirements: "The discontent and criticism of the election were never about Raila Odinga losing it as some have alleged—it was about having a winner who was worthy of the title 'democratically elected.' And the Supreme Court found that the Independent Elections and Boundaries Commission (IEBC) simply did not deliver on basic democratic principles of transparency and rule of law that should guide any election."[39]

In throwing out the entire election result and calling for a fresh election, the court firmly exerted its newfound authority over election disputes and significantly improved the perception of a systematically transformed judiciary. This decision cost Kenyans millions of dollars, as another election had to be held. Despite the trauma of it, luckily, the constitution allowed for such a ruling; indeed, the constitution had established the broad framework for the court's decision and had articulated the requirements for holding another election.

While US election processes may be strong, both its domestic case law and foreign policy can easily be perceived as contradictory and whimsical. For instance, the US Supreme Court's 1896 decision in *Plessy v. Ferguson* established the separate but equal doctrine, which facilitated further segregation by race. Yet the United States would later criticize South Africa for its own form of apartheid. In another example, while the United States was fighting World War II and the mistreatment and murder of Jews, the US Supreme Court upheld the practice of interning Japanese Americans on the US West Coast. Following the 2018 alleged assassination of *The Washington Post* journalist Jamal Khashoggi, the US Justice Department determined that Saudi Arabia's Crown Prince, Mohammed bin Salman Al Saud, was "recently made the Saudi prime minister and as a result, qualifies for immunity as a foreign head of government."[40] (According to *The New York Times,* the Biden administration found the prince responsible but withheld issuing penalties in light of US–Saudi relations.[41]) Yet, in December 1989, four months after I emigrated to the United States, America initiated "an invasion of Panama . . . to depose and capture Manuel Noriega, the country's military dictator, who had been indicted in the United States on drug trafficking charges."[42]

For the most part, the American public does not discuss these hypocrisies outside of social media and backroom conversations. But they are not rare occurrences when considering America's long history. The Congressional Research Service (CRS) itself identified a disconnect in the US position on Kenya's flawed 2007 elections: "On December 30, the United States government reportedly congratulated President Kibaki. . . . The U.S. position shifted somewhat by January, as the Assistant Secretary declared that 'serious flaws in the vote tallying process damaged the credibility of the process.'"[43]

While critics or political and jurisprudence analysts may identify flaws with the above examples of contradictions, the Kenyan public discusses these inconsistencies in roadside cafes and at private dinners. Perception, not fact, leads to breakdowns in peace and security, including the 2007/2008 postelection violence in Kenya and the January 6, 2021, insurrection and attack on the US Capitol.

Peoples

The second force that requires improvement is that of the people within the judiciary system. When Kenyans overwhelmingly voted for the 2010 Constitution, they fired their attorney general, auditor-general, and chief justice. They also introduced a new director of public prosecutions and a permanent Ethics and Anticorruption Commission. The selection process for the first people to apply for these positions was transparent and bold; Kenyans were enthralled by live television interviews of candidates for the Supreme Court chief justice and the interview panel did not hold back its punches. For example, it questioned Aaron Ringera on his 2003 radical surgery on live television. (In 2003 Justice Ringera investigated, publicly named, and purged over 20 judges and over 70 magistrates in a radical effort aimed at restoring public confidence in the judiciary.[44])

Americans would detest foreign influence in the nomination and selection of our judges. The same holds for Kenyans or any other sovereign people. Development specialists and diplomats have to let Kenyans and their new democratic processes take shape of their own accord. KTI's Kenyan staff are well-connected, respected, and influential among non-traditional civil society groups in Kenya. These include small women's groups, youth groups, and other informal groups and startups that lack the financial and institutional structures to manage donor funding. On many occasions, our staff, including myself, were approached by a Kenyan who wanted to implement a great idea but lacked the means to do so. Sometimes these ideas targeted potential nominees, either directly or indirectly, for office. In 2011, one such young man approached our staff. His youth group members were concerned about the blatant, uninformed support the Maasai elders and wider community had thrown behind a nominee for the new position of director of public prosecution simply because he was from their tribe. But the Maasai youth were not convinced. Social media and the internet outside of their community had cast doubt on the nominee's credibility, owing to his association with several high-profile corruption scandals and his lukewarm support for the constitutional review process. They looked to the new constitution's elaborate vetting process for senior officials and hoped that the constitution would pivot Kenyans to participating in meritocracy instead of tribalism when considering nominees for public office.

Their grant proposal was creative: It spoke to the heart of democracy. We funded multiple meetings with Maasai community leaders across four counties, focusing on the new constitution's "Leadership and Integrity" section. Local representatives were selected to meet the nominee, and expectations were presented to him. The grant also included a media briefing on the outcome. Our grant was conditional; we did not allow the youth group, with US funding, to try to influence the selection process. While many donors would have been more interested in the outcome, we were more invested in the community engagement process and the leadership. The fact that the youth took the initiative, stood up, had a plan, secured funding, and performed, said many positive things about Kenya's future.

Eleven years later, while remotely monitoring the 2022 general election, I was pleasantly surprised to see votes cast contrary to tribal affiliations. Following lessons learned from the 2017 general election and the landmark decision made by Kenya's Supreme Court to throw out the 2017 election in totality, the elections commission posted every polling center result on its web portal. I had previously witnessed the 2013 election firsthand in Nairobi, as I described in chapter 3. That year, I had been asked to sign a 34A form, the primary document used to record the results at each polling station, because I was in the vote counting room as an observer. Although I declined as a foreign diplomat out of respect for a sovereign process, I was able to study the form. It contained the name of the center; the total number of ballots cast for each candidate; the total number of voters, ballot papers, disputed votes, and names; ID and telephone numbers; and the signatures of all witnessing political party representatives or observers.

In 2022, although I was thousands of miles away, I could point critics of Kenya's election process to these approximately 50,000 34A forms, duly witnessed and uploaded to the election commission's portal, to allay fears of tampering and vote rigging. It was easy for those who lacked firsthand, insider experience with the system to doubt the results; they would not have had trust in the process given the unexpected shift in tribal affiliations. The outgoing president, Kenyatta, a member of the influential Kikuyu tribe, was time-barred, meaning his term limit was up, by the 2010 Constitution. With no other Kikuyu frontrunner in the 2022 race, many were surprised when Kenyatta threw his weight behind the opposition candidate, Raila Odinga, instead of Kenyatta's own deputy president, William Ruto. Odinga is a member of the Luo tribe and had challenged Kenyatta in 2017. Ruto is a member of the Kalejin tribe. Kenyatta had convinced the Kikuyu elders to back Odinga and was banking on the majority of Kikuyu to follow his vision. The results were far from close. Unfortunately for Kenyatta and Odinga, many Kikuyu backed Ruto in numbers sufficient enough for him to win the close election. For example, even in Kiambu County, home of the Kenyatta family and a Kikuyu stronghold, Odinga secured only 25 percent of all votes cast in Kiambu County in 2022. These surprising results were echoed across the adjacent Kikuyu-dominated counties: Odinga secured only 20 percent in Nyandarua, 16 percent in Nyeri, 14 percent in Kirinyaga, and 17 percent in Muranga. Even the Kikuyu Council of Elders "admitted that it had failed to read the political mood"[54] before publicly backing Odinga at Kenyatta's behest.

As I watched the results and the subsequent Supreme Court case (televised live) and decision, I thought back to all the amazing, creative, and forward-thinking youth I had met in Kenya between 2008 and 2014, including those involved with the Maasai leadership grant. These youths are Kenya's pivoting force, using the constitution as their armory. They have the most to gain and the most to lose—be it cost of living, climate change, unemployment, or frustration with the challenges of life and the political process.

The US government and other development partners can do little, except back reformers. We found creative opportunities to support key people within the judiciary when we believed that their interests matched ours. For example, we supported the Eldoret court's chief magistrate, as discussed earlier; he later went on to become a judge in the land and environment court. We also supported other chief magistrates in their efforts to improve processes within their respective courts, and the chief registrar in her efforts to secure World Bank funding. On many occasions, I was asked why the United States would not come out against a particular individual for their alleged corruption history, or why we would not publicly back a particular reform-minded candidate. I would always answer that a foreign government should neither support nor oppose individuals nominated for public positions, such as candidates for chief justice or the director of public prosecution. That responsibility, rightly so, is solely in Kenyan hands. Nor would Americans accept foreign interference in their elections and appointment processes.

Conclusion

In our program's final evaluation, Barkan noted that "KTI's grants to computerize the case record system at the magistrate courts in Eldoret and Kapsabet have had a profound demonstration effect of what is possible in the area of judicial reform. They have not, however, transformed the judiciary."[45] No single project or action, Kenyan-led or foreign-funded, can transform any country's judiciary. However, our pilot project in Kenya did serve its three intended purposes to (1) contribute to the public's perception of a systematically transformed judiciary, one that can be trusted; (2) demonstrate bottom-up transformation; and (3) incubate an idea that others, with deeper pockets, could build upon. KTI spent approximately $250,000 and leveraged $120 million for Kenya's judiciary. But even the World Bank-funded project is insufficient, on its own, to improve confidence in a judiciary. Improvements require parallel changes in the processes in the courthouses, people within the judiciary, and perceptions of judicial reform.

Judicial reform is an essential element of peace and security; a stronger, more trusted judiciary offers a suitable alternative to conflict and violence. As such, US peace and security professionals can and should focus on judiciary reform and include it in the menu of opportunities for peace and security programming. Furthermore, US peace and security programming should not attempt to influence Kenyan appointments or elections, either within the judiciary or any aspect of the government. Instead, within the remit of judicial reform, the United States should focus on processes, perceptions, and the Kenyan people's capacity to advance their own objectives.

CHAPTER TWO

Defining Peace and Security

"It is with great humility and pride that I accept this inaugural Women for Peace and Security Award. I do so with deep appreciation of the contribution of NATO to advancing gender equality in the arena of peace and security."

—Speaker of the House Nancy Pelosi, speech given in at NATO parliamentary assembly, Lisbon, Portugal, 2021

Bottom Line Up Front (BLUF)

The United Nations Charter, now over 75 years old, calls upon nations "to unite our strength to maintain international peace and security."[1] Over 30 national constitutions, spanning the Marshall Islands to Morocco, use the phrase "peace and security." At home, four recent US national security strategies use the phrase, as does the US Foreign Assistance Framework (FAF). Between 2001 and 2020, the US government spent $836 billion in foreign assistance.[2] Peace and security constituted the single largest program area, representing 35 percent ($293 billion) of the total.

Although the United States spends a lot of money on peace and security and uses this phrase in critical documents, it is inadequately defined. I believe our foreign assistance framework, as presented, does not best support our national security strategies, nor does it encompass all efforts to promote peace and security worldwide. If we consider a holistic definition of the phrase and account for other development and diplomacy efforts that do promote peace and security, we could design more intentional and effective programs, while better justifying our efforts to American taxpayers.

This chapter begins by exploring the phrase "peace and security" from multiple angles in the hope of articulating the best definition. After defining the words in the phrase, I then explore diverse uses of the phrase, such as those used by Nancy Pelosi (in the quotation at the beginning of the chapter) and in international and US laws and strategies. Next, I turn to the US FAF, explaining both the framework itself and its first category, peace and security. Before presenting my own definition, I first set up two critical underpinnings for our international peace and security efforts—paternalism and domestic affairs. My definition sets the stage for exploring the US involvement in Kenya's search for peace and security following "a time of extreme danger in Kenya a few years ago—the beginnings of a civil war."[3]

Is it a Phrase or Two Words?

Is "peace and security" a single phrase or a combination of two different terms? If a high school English teacher asked this question on a test, their students would break it up into two parts and correct a grammar mistake. The revised question might then be, "What are peace and security?" But in the context of a United Nations objective, the US government, or a university program, the words form a singular undefined phrase. Since a grammatical approach fails to shed light on the meaning, let us distill the phrase into its components: the words themselves.

The word "peace" means tranquility or calmness. It is more often described by what it is not. For instance, it is the absence of conflict, war, or turmoil. By denoting a state of bliss or calmness, peace is not relegated to a building, street, neighborhood, or country. We do not restrict our daily use of this word to the physical environment. The Arabic greeting, "*As-salamu alaykum*," translated as "May peace be upon you," is used by all Arabic speakers, Muslims and non-Muslims alike. Peace, in this case, could be spiritual, emotional, or metaphorical. The greeting, "Peace," symbolized by the popular emoji, ✌, can be applied to many different connotations and contexts, while the phrase "Peace-out" is a popular alternative to "Goodbye." "Peace," therefore, is a complex word like many in the English language; it has multiple meanings and connotations. Its specific meaning depends on the user's intent and the context in which it is used.

The writings of famous philosophers on peace have influenced our understanding of it, as will be articulated in-depth later in this chapter. For example, in 1651, Thomas Hobbes focused on social contracts and a strong central authority to maintain peace, while John Locke (1689) prioritized individual rights and freedoms as a foundation for peace and security. Later, in 1795, Immanuel Kant suggested that nations with a representative form of government are more accountable to their citizens and less likely to engage in war. Centuries earlier, the Muslim philosopher Ibn Khaldun (1377) wrote about peace being more than an absence of conflict but a marker of a strong, civilized society. Today, we see the word "peace" in two other US government-established and government-funded entities. The US Peace Corps, whose mission is to promote friendship, understanding, and peace, and the US Institute of Peace (USIP), established by law to promote "international peace and the resolution of conflicts among the nations and peoples of the world without recourse to violence."[4]

"Security" is an even more complex word than "peace," and it has multiple meanings. A banker or loan officer would automatically think of an asset used to guarantee a loan. Yet a high school senior's admission into an Ivy League university can offer security for their own life, while someone with job security is guaranteed to have the job as long as they want. Both a US Supreme Court justice and a tenured professor have job security. But there are other angles to the term. An office building or museum may have a security office staffed by private security guards. Over 50,000 agents provide security for the Department of Homeland Security's Transportation Security Administration (TSA).[5] Their job is to protect travelers, employees, or visitors and to maintain an environment free from turmoil, theft, or violence. In this case, security is closely related to one interpretation of peace; it is the absence of something undesired, free from threat or danger. Like peace, security can also refer to an emotional state, when one is free from doubt or anxiety. A common application in this case is the emotional security a vulnerable infant or elderly parent has when they are loved and cared for. Like peace, one can only understand the word "security" if the user's intent and context are known.

A book, an academic program, or a government objective categorized as peace and security must therefore begin with the applied context. The phrase is not about an individual's emotional health or the protection of a masterpiece at an art museum; it is an academic and career discipline within the context of foreign policy and international relations. The latter encompasses international development, international trade, military relations, and diplomatic activities.

Who Uses the Phrase "Peace and Security"?

Having explored the grammar and definition of the words in the phrase, we can now turn to its usage in documents forming the bedrock of international relations, US foreign affairs, and academia.

United Nations

The preamble of the United Nations' founding charter was signed in 1945. Since this book focuses on one African country, Kenya, I would not normally use a document that preexisted independent African nations. Africa comprises over 50 nations; by 1945, only three had gained independence. But this document is one of the earliest sources of the phrase "peace and security." The preamble to the UN Charter calls upon all of us "to unite our strength to maintain international peace and security."[6] Article 1 of the Charter elaborates upon the duty of member nations to take effective, collective measures to prevent and remove threats to peace, to suppress acts of aggression, and to settle international disputes. The 8,900-word, 111-article document uses the phrase "peace and security" 32 times but never defines it. Given the role of the UN Charter, a document binding together countries in their relationships with each other, and in the absence of any definition, the phrase likely applies only to international and not to domestic peace.

The United Nations has a variety of departments, commissions, and agencies including UN Women, which is dedicated to gender equality and women's empowerment. Their peace and security web page states that "UN Women works to promote peace by supporting women of all backgrounds and ages to participate in processes to prevent conflict and build and sustain peace."[7] Because the page's title is "Peace and Security," the word "security" could be inferred as a process preventing conflict while building and sustaining peace. The United Nations' main page on peace and security aims to "restore peace after the outbreak of armed conflict" and "promoting lasting peace."[8] It describes the roles of the security council, general assembly, and peacekeepers in maintaining international peace but offers no definition of this phrase, which is also used as the web page's title.

National Constitutions

Setting aside the unhelpful UN Charter and a few UN web pages, we can now turn to national constitutions. According to the Constitute Project, the specific phrase "peace and security" appears in 31 constitutions, most recently Burundi and the Union of the Comoros in 2018.[9] Most constitutions use the phrase within the context of international peace and security. Two countries, however, expand the concept of national security to domestic affairs.

The 2010 Constitution of Angola states, "the objective of national security shall be to guarantee and safeguard national independence and sovereignty, territorial integrity, the democratic state based on the rule of law, liberty and the defence of the territory against any threats or attacks, as well as achieving cooperation for national development and contributing towards international peace and security."[10] This is an objective of national security, not a definition. But the phrase "guarantee and safeguard . . . the democratic state based on the rule of law, [and] liberty" implies that national security must be concerned with domestic democracy and governance.

More elaborately, chapter 14 of Kenya's 2010 Constitution is dedicated to national security. Moreover, it actually starts with a definition: "National security is the protection against internal and external threats to Kenya's territorial integrity and sovereignty, its people, their rights, freedoms, property, peace, stability and prosperity, and other national interests."[11] This definition is incredibly broad, placing peace and prosperity under the rubric of national security, thereby expanding the scope of national security agencies (e.g., Kenyan Defense Forces, National Intelligence Service, and National Police Service) to areas of economic and social development, governance, human rights, and rule of law. In other words, their functions and responsibilities are to protect against threats to the public's rights and prosperity.

➤ In summary, of the 31 countries using the phrase "peace and security" in their constitutions, none define it, while two use the term "national security" to refer to domestic concerns such as rule of law or human rights. Perhaps the US legislative or executive branches can shed some light on the definition.

US Congress

The US Congress passed the International Peace and Security Act of 1961 (22 U.S.C. 2301) alongside the Foreign Assistance Act, which I introduced us to in the introduction. In a single sentence in the Peace and Security Act, Congress seeks to "promote the peace of the world and the foreign policy, security, and general welfare of the United States."[12] But instead of linking our security with the peace of the world, it presents both as targets of communism. Most of the rest of the act focuses on military assistance and on combatting communism. The act also establishes a nexus between our allies' security, stability, and "rapid social, economic, and political progress."[13]

In 2017, Congress passed the Women, Peace, and Security Act, whose formal text reads, "to ensure that the United States promotes the meaningful participation of women in mediation and negotiation processes seeking to prevent, mitigate, or resolve violent conflict."[14] Unfortunately, Section 4 of the act, the statement of policy, abandons domestic conflict and our own peace and security by focusing solely on "overseas conflict."[15]

Therefore, Congress does not give us a solid definition of peace and security, nor a clear link between our domestic peace and security and that of other nations. It does, however, echo the Kenyan and Angolan Constitutions by linking social, economic, and political progress with security and stability.

US National Security Strategies

Our national security strategies, first released in 1987 as required by law, take a similar stance.[16] The 2010 strategy underscores the need for the United States to help, worldwide, strengthen and integrate human rights, promote democracy, develop institutions, facilitate the freedom to access information, promote economic opportunities, support global health, and promote food security. However, that same strategy acknowledges that only if we maintain our values at home first can America help other countries around the world do this and, in turn, promote US national security. As the 2010 document states, "in keeping with the focus on the foundation of our strength and influence, we are promoting universal values abroad by living them at home and will not seek to impose these values through force."[17]

During my decade with USAID, I never engaged with US national security strategy when designing programs. It was not required reading for new USAID employees; nor was it the subject of discussions around the water cooler or in leadership forums. However, it should have been because it forms the foundation of our international development programs and justifies why the US government is spending American tax dollars overseas.

The phrase "will not seek to impose these values through force," may elicit an eye roll or an exacerbated sigh. There are many instances in America's long history where our actions contradict this statement. We have blatantly conducted political assassinations and launched invasions to oust or kill a sitting government leader. These are serious acts of force. We justify these acts with the rhetoric of a credible national security or need for justice, such as our invasions of Afghanistan and Panama. We veil some acts under a mantle of a multinational force, such as that used in Iraq and Libya. Regardless of our published intent, the United States likely has an underlying, unwritten objective to impose values that differ from what the targeted country holds at the time.

America's 2015 national security strategy emphasizes the need to lead by example. It ensures that military action, diplomacy efforts, development assistance, matters of economy, and sanctions are all part of our strategic toolbox. This strategy goes further than the 2010 document by identifying rule of law, service delivery, and economic opportunity as root causes of conflict that can overtake state structures, thus further threatening our interests. The strategy articulates a nexus between these root causes, extremism, weak state structures, and violence against these structures. The insurrection in Washington, DC, on January 6, 2021, is a classic example of this nexus. While it appears that America proved to be strong in response to this event, the command structures, intelligence sharing, and weakness in our security and justice systems, echoing some of our 9/11 failures, simultaneously indicate components of a weak state.[18]

The strategy wraps a critical element of the notion of peace and security around the rubric of prosperity: "To prevent conflict and promote human dignity, we will also pursue policies that eradicate extreme poverty and reduce inequality."[19] I had to read that again. "To prevent conflict," we will "eradicate extreme poverty and reduce inequality." This gives a very difficult mandate—promoting prosperity, economic growth, civil rights, and equality—to our national security agencies, just as Kenya's Constitution does. The US strategy, therefore, suggests that the mandate of the National Security Agency, and that of the Central Intelligence Agency, Federal Bureau of Investigation, Department of Defense, and Department of Homeland Security and other security agencies, must include addressing homelessness, health care for all, and a woman's right to choose.

As for the 2017 national security strategy, it acknowledges the vital role that targeted development assistance, aimed at enhancing conditions abroad, plays in bolstering US national security. In doing so, it defines the role of foreign assistance in this way: "By modernizing U.S. instruments of diplomacy and development, we will catalyze conditions to help them achieve that goal."[20] Without necessarily spelling out how, the strategy creates an undeniable link between economics and stability: "Stable, prosperous, and friendly states enhance American security and boost U.S. economic opportunities."[21]

Four years later, the United States went even further. In the 2021 Interim National Security Strategic Guidance, former President Biden unequivocally states, "I firmly believe that democracy holds the key to freedom, prosperity, peace, and dignity. We must now demonstrate— with a clarity that dispels any doubt—that democracy can still deliver for our people and for people around the world."[22] This prodemocracy guidance is perhaps even more brazen than the rhetoric employed during the anticommunist movement of the 1960s. By comparison, the Foreign Assistance Act of 1961, the act that conceived USAID, begins with the following phrase: "to promote the foreign policy, security, and general welfare of the United States by assisting peoples of the world in their efforts toward economic development and internal and external security, and for other purposes."[23]

In essence, each American may or may not personally believe that democracy is the only key to peace. However, US national security strategies unequivocally maintain that domestic security, stability, and economic growth require security overseas and, moreover, that secure nations require democracy, human rights, and improved living conditions. This is the very premise, discussed hundreds of years ago by philosophers such as Ibn Khaldun and John Locke and, more recently, in Kenya's Constitution. The US Congress acknowledged this premise as critical for the stability of foreign nations and it, therefore, forms the structure of my own definition of peace and security presented later in this chapter.

Academia

Universities also use the phrase "peace and security." Ethiopia's Addis Ababa University has an Institute for Peace and Security Studies that offers master's degrees and PhDs in Peace and Security Studies. The institute "also conducts academic and applied research in the area of peace and security that takes into account the interaction between governance, human security, socioeconomic development and sustainable peace."[24] This close link between social development and peace echoes the Kenyan and Angolan Constitutions, documents produced by the US Congress, and US national security strategies.

Georgetown University and Columbia University in the United States also have peace and security programs. Columbia's is called "Youth, Peace, and Security," and it focuses on "the linkages between youth, social conflicts, violence, peace, and security."[25] Georgetown's program echoes the Women, Peace, and Security Act by focusing on the role of women in preventing conflict and building peace. Both universities link peace and security with other aspects of a nation's development; Columbia links it with youth and social conflicts while Georgetown links it with "growing economies, and addressing global threats like climate change and violent extremism."[26] The Center for Peace and Security Studies at University of California San Diego remains more neutral by focusing on research for "new and emerging modes of interstate conflict."[27]

The application of the phrase "peace and security" to global academic programs resembles the diverse use of the term across international and domestic users. These applications begin to show that the internal governance and development conditions of a particular country are tied to global peace and security, which, in turn, impact our own national security. Having addressed the phrase in UN documents, national constitutions, domestic and international law and agencies, and academia, we can now turn to our FAF.

USAID's Evolving Mission Statement

USAID is an important toolbox in the US government's ability to advance American peace and security by influencing and assisting foreign nations. But does USAID's leadership and the professionals that work for the organization recognize and embrace this toolbox? No USAID official should be able to deny that USAID is a tool of America's foreign policy and a contributor to US national security. Yet, USAID's constantly evolving mission statement is vague.

USAID's website notes that, "since 9/11, America's foreign assistance programs have been more fully integrated into the United States' National Security Strategy."[28] The term "security" morphs with each iteration of USAID's mission. In 2024, the term "national security" was not in the statement: "On behalf of the American people, we promote and demonstrate democratic values abroad, and advance a free, peaceful, and prosperous world."[29] Yet, at the end of 2022, it was: "USAID's work advances U.S. **national security** and economic prosperity, demonstrates American generosity, and promotes a path to recipient self-reliance and resilience."[30] In 2019, the mission emphasized USAID's role with the clause, "in support of America's **foreign policy**," but did not use the term "security."[31] In the February 2018 Department of State and USAID Joint Strategic Plan for 2018–2022, the USAID administrator, Mark Green, focused on USAID's "critical role in furthering America's interests around the globe," stating, "while America faces an unprecedented array of national security threats, USAID's international development efforts support the U.S. Government's response to counter and prevent them."[32] In 2014, the USAID's mission statement was to "partner to end extreme poverty and to promote resilient, democratic societies while advancing our **security** and prosperity."[33] On February 3, 2025, echoing this vague and evolving mission, the Department of State issued a media note stating that "the United States Agency for International Development (USAID) has long strayed from its original mission of responsibly advancing American interests abroad, and it is now abundantly clear that significant portions of USAID funding are not aligned with the core national interests of the United States."[34]

The US Foreign Assistance Framework (FAF)

The lexicology of the phrase "peace and security" and its diverse applications failed to offer a meaningful definition. Perhaps the accounting system the United States uses to track American foreign assistance, the FAF, can offer foreign policy and development specialists a solid definition.

In 2006, a year after I started working at USAID, the US government introduced significant changes to its foreign assistance program. First, Randall Tobias was appointed as the first US director of foreign assistance. Internally, USAID staff referred to his office as "F" for "foreign assistance." Tobias, in this new position, reported to then–Secretary of State Condoleezza Rice and assumed both the ranks of ambassador and deputy secretary of state. Second, in this same position, Tobias concurrently served as the new administrator of USAID. Third, as the head of F, he was tasked with transforming, once again, the government's approach to foreign assistance. I say "once again" because calls for USAID's reform are as old as the agency itself. With this charge, he was to provide strategic direction and guidance to all foreign assistance, not just USAID's. Many different agencies have foreign assistance programs. As an example, according to the ForeignAssistance.gov dashboard web page, between 2000 and 2020, 17 different departments or agencies spent more than $1 million on or in Kenya, while another four reported some expenses less than $1 million. All were playing in the international development sandbox, spending US tax dollars on or in Kenya.[35]

In Nairobi, I interacted regularly with representatives of the Department of Defense, Department of State, Centers for Disease Control, Department of Homeland Security, and the Department of Justice. All were either based in Nairobi or frequented East Africa while providing technical assistance or funding to the government of Kenya and its people. We shared housing compounds, schools, office cafeterias, and recreational facilities.

There was, and probably still is, an overwhelming desire to improve coordination or further consolidate foreign assistance to reduce or remove redundancies, leverage resources, and synergize efforts. Unfortunately, agencies do not consistently coordinate on program objectives, activities, and, most importantly, with local partners. The people who work in these agencies want to coordinate, but they often cannot because the agencies have different mandates, structures, and objectives. The biggest obstacle, in my opinion, is statutory. Over many years, the US Congress has introduced and amended statutes that are contradictory. They also require two different agencies to do the same thing in the same place. Five US government entities fund HIV/AIDS projects in Kenya, while four support antipoaching and wildlife efforts.[36] This is inefficient. It promotes unnecessary competition; requires multiple offices and staff in the country; duplicates management and oversight efforts; and relies on redundant accounting, technology, and contracting personnel. On the ground, Kenyan entities working on HIV/AIDS or wildlife management must learn to work with different US agencies, use different funding and reporting rules, and often compete for funding that flows from the American taxpayer, albeit through different channels.

The F office introduced a new framework for coordinating, thinking, and reporting. Each agency, regardless of enabling legislation or funding stream, had to use the same set of objectives and indicators. Would this remove all the overlap on the ground? No, but a common framework would allow the US government to articulate, comprehensively, what it was doing overseas. Before the framework, neither the government nor the American public could get a clear and immediate governmentwide picture of US foreign assistance in a particular country. There were too many funding streams and agencies. With the framework, ideally, one could ask, "How much assistance has the United States given Kenya in wildlife protection, and what are the most recent impact indicators?"

This framework catalyzed a powerful foreign assistance dashboard, which has surpassed the vision presented in 2006.[37] For example, a user selecting "Kenya" from the ForeignAssistance.gov dashboard page would see that the United States obligated $1 billion in 2012.[38] The website shows the breakdown by program area and a further delineation into each activity (contract or grant) that contributed to the program area.

The F structure provides a menu of seven main program areas, the first being peace and security. The others are democracy, human rights and governance, health, education and social services, economic growth, humanitarian assistance, and program development.

Peace and Security Objective within the Framework

Despite a new framework and a powerful dashboard page on the ForeignAssistance.gov website, the American taxpayer cannot find a definition of peace and security. I served in multiple roles during my decade with USAID. Two required I enter program data to inform the new F framework, or "feed the beast," the phrase we Washington-based bureaucrats frequently used when faced with another bureaucratic information-gathering or data-entry task. I thought I knew the F framework well, having had to enter this data. But I could not find an adequate definition of peace and security in the manuals or instructions. Nor have I stumbled across anything during the years I spent researching for and writing this book. This lack of definition reminds me of a typical Kenyan four-way intersection in a Nairobi suburb; there are no lane lines, no traffic lights, and no stop signs. Everyone has an objective and knows where and how to go, yet accidents are rare. However, Kenyan intersections are not defined as they are in America, that is as either a four-way stop, two-way stop, rotary, or one that uses a traffic light to direct traffic. Similarly, the F framework has no definition but has an objective for peace and security that gives the following indication of where and how to turn: "To help nations effectively establish the conditions and capacity for achieving peace, security, and stability; and for responding effectively against arising threats to national or international security and stability."[39]

An objective is not a definition. Practitioners think of it as a definition but, under scrutiny, such a definition would be considered circular; this objective, for instance, uses the words "peace" and "security"—the very concepts it is trying to define. Breaking down this objective into its two clauses and analyzing the contributing vocabulary and sentence structure may, then, inform how one articulates a definition.

This objective is saying we, the United States, want to help nations achieve peace, security, and stability. There are prerequisites to this outcome, namely, conditions and an internal capacity. The words "peace" and "security" were defined earlier in this chapter, but what about "stability"? This new word, "stability," comes from stable, meaning unmoving or unwavering. Think of an earthquake-resilient building or a suspension bridge. Both are designed to sway a little under extreme forces. Both are stable if they manage to absorb those forces and remain true to their intent. Within the context of peace and security, then, stability, like security, is perhaps another prerequisite to peace. It is a condition every country must have, one allowing it to withstand both internal and external shocks.

USAID documents also define the specific conditions and capacities it believes American allies need to establish. What are these? The rest of the framework defines these well. Each foreign assistance objective has various program areas. Those under the peace and security objective include violent extremism, trafficking in persons, narcotics, and weapons of mass destruction. Therefore, the word "capacity" denotes the foreign government's abilities, personnel, tools, systems, and structures it can deploy to address each topic the United States deems important.

Drilling down further in the framework, one sees that each program area has multiple elements. For example, the program area "Transnational Threats and Crime" includes element 4.2, "Deter Cybercrime, Intellectual Property Theft, and Corporate Espionage." The explanation states its objective as "build[ing] their capacity to identify, investigate, prosecute, judge, and prevent crimes committed through the criminal misuse of information technology."[40] This element defines one kind of capacity that the United States believes a country needs to address cybercrime, intellectual property rights, and corporate espionage.

The term "conditions" is much more amorphous than "capacity." Each country has unique underlying conditions that may make it more susceptible to things the United States deems undesirable, such as trafficking, violent extremism, or narcotics. Some program elements are designed to address these conditions. For example, the Trafficking in Persons (TIP) program area, also under the remit of peace and security, includes an element for prevention, described as increasing "public awareness of human trafficking and its dangers by supporting public information and education campaigns and programs that promote behavior change and positively inform cultural and social norms."[41]

Under this objective, the United States appears to want to help reduce human trafficking overseas, for instance, child trafficking, forced labor, or confined conditions on fishing factory ships. American assistance could educate the private sector about all forms of human trafficking, offer outreach to communities vulnerable to trafficking, provide vulnerable populations with educational or employment opportunities, or support local organizations in eradicating all forms of human trafficking. In other words, the United States is saying that it wants to change the conditions that encourage and facilitate trafficking in persons. If we do change these conditions, we think we are helping the other nation advance its peace, security, and stability and, therefore, America's own.

Defense Spending

Although I have dissected the peace and security objective's first clause, "to help nations effectively establish the conditions and capacity for achieving peace, security, and stability," there are some fundamental questions I never heard discussed around the water cooler at USAID, the Department of State, or any of the half dozen embassies I spent time in.[42] If America wants to *help* a nation establish these conditions and capacity, does the United States have a competitive advantage in the marketplace? All business professionals know they must be best placed to provide a product or service, must have something others cannot provide at the same price or cheaper, and must know how to provide it. This, of course, was the impetus for the Cold War, especially in Africa. The former Soviet Union and the United States pitted themselves against each other by offering money or goods to new and struggling African countries. Today, the key ingredient to supporting peace and security is still money, much of it in the form of defense equipment and training.

For example, total US foreign assistance between 2001 and 2020 was $836 billion. Peace and security was the largest program area, accounting for $293 billion, or 35 percent of total foreign aid.[43] American defense spending is substantial—$243 billion, or 83 percent of total peace and security spending. Over the same period in Kenya, the Department of Defense accounted for $774 million, or 6 percent of all US obligations in Kenya. Of this, $520 million was under the peace and security objective.[44] Furthermore, according to ForeignAssistance.gov, most of this ($303 million) was for training and equipment. In other words, 62 percent of US peace and security assistance in Kenya was provided by the Department of Defense.

Underpinning the dollars is a competitive advantage in technical assistance and technology, a competitive advantage the ForeignAssistance.gov website cannot depict or define is American military might. For example, in the words of one National Public Radio reporter, in September 2021, "Australia bailed on a submarine contract with France worth $66 billion last week, choosing instead to work with the United States and the United Kingdom."[45] The new deal was for nuclear submarines instead of France's diesel-electric ones. By selling submarines to Australia, the United States was able to market its technical superiority and promote the specific companies that produced them. American arms deals reflect the same attitude. We give billions of dollars' worth of military aid to both Egypt and Israel.[46] Who pays for this aid? The US taxpayer does, through Congress and then via the Defense Department, and finally to the US companies making those arms and the firms transporting and maintaining them in Israel and Egypt.

But the conditions necessary for achieving peace extend beyond arms, improved defense infrastructure, and military forces. It includes underlying, structural, historic, and cultural conditions. Defense contractors, tanks, or submarines cannot create such conditions. In 2021, despite decades of American investment in Afghanistan's security sector, the American public was stunned when the Taliban recaptured their country in almost the blink of an eye. This demonstrates how vital it is that the United States offer something more than military equipment and training, as I will argue in the next section when presenting my own definition of "peace and security." But first, I must untangle the rest of the peace and security objective.

Whose Peace and Security?

I now return to the F framework objective for peace and security: "to help nations effectively establish the conditions and capacity for achieving peace, security, and stability; *and for responding effectively against arising threats to national or international security and stability.*"[47] This clause is the most important for US foreign policy and for the American taxpayer because it attempts to explain *why* the United States invests overseas in peace and security. Moreover, the framework should justify why the United States has spent $11 billion over the past two decades in Sub-Saharan Africa on this single foreign assistance objective, that is, to help nations "respon[d] effectively against arising threats."[48] What threats? Clearly, threats "to national or international security and stability."[49] But does the term "national" refer to the United States or to the country being helped per the first clause of the objective ("To help nations")? There is a significant difference between these two perspectives.

The polarization between these two perspectives creates a disconnect among US foreign policy, development, and defense professionals. Some understand the clause as referring to the national security of the country being helped, while others interpret it as America's security. In reality, the American taxpayer, the one footing the bill, knows that the United States is a "government of the people, by the people, for the people."[50] As such, they expect any foreign assistance programs, including those with a peace and security objective, to have a direct, describable, and tangible nexus to American security and stability.

This perspective is not amorphous; the entire impetus for the Foreign Assistance Act of 1961 was to counter the threat communism posed to America. Section 101 of the act states that "Congress declares that the individual liberties, economic prosperity, and security of the people of the United States are best sustained and enhanced in a community of nations which *respect individual civil and economic rights and freedoms* and which work together to use wisely the world's limited resources in an *open and equitable international economic system.*"[51]

The premise for the US invading Afghanistan and spending billions between 2002 and 2021 was to find Osama bin Laden and prevent Al-Qaeda from using Afghanistan as a base for attacking the United States, as it did on September 11, 2001. Today, the threat may not be Al-Qaeda, but other strands of violent extremism, both domestic and international. Other global threats, including climate change and viruses, persist across the globe and continue to threaten the United States. American peace and security programs should be addressing all of these dangers.

But what if the word "national" in the F framework objective refers to the recipient country? Then the United States would be helping the other country mitigate threats to that nation's own internal security and stability. For example, the United States has been helping both the Democratic Republic of Congo and Uganda tackle internal threats from the Lord's Republican Army, a Christian religious extremist group that has killed over 10,000 people on both sides of the border and abducted twice that number of children.[52] The United States has also invested in training and equipping Kenya's security forces to help them allay internal and external threats from Al-Shabaab, an extremist militant organization based in Somalia. How is this interference in a nation's domestic issues beneficial to US peace and security? How would Americans feel if other countries tried to interfere with, under the rubric of assistance, domestic US issues such as gun control, domestic nationalist terrorism, or school shootings? American states do not want the federal government interfering in some of these issues and those matters do not have much potential to threaten the peace of our Canadian and Mexican neighbors.

The US foreign assistance framework was a noble and important endeavor, aiming to collate all US assistance and thereby inform the American taxpayer. Unfortunately, the framework has failed to adequately define the terms it uses. Furthermore, the objective of peace and security uses vague terms such as "conditions" and "capacity"; nor does it distinguish between America's and the foreign nation's national security. As a consequence, the development specialist cannot successfully implement US foreign policy and contribute to America's national security without a noncircular, all-encompassing definition of "peace and security." Before beginning the process of defining the phrase, however, we must first look at two underpinning concepts: paternalism and global versus local peace.

Underpinning Concepts

America's systems of government, social structures, and economy are relatively robust. They generally withstand local, national, or international shocks such as the 2000 Florida election, acts of domestic terrorism, market crashes, cyberattacks, and the COVID-19 pandemic and global shutdowns. Many Americans have adopted a paternalistic mindset, believing that the United States has something to give or for others to mimic; there is the belief that other countries should embrace America's national ways to flourish, and many perceive that these robust systems are grounded in democracy and capitalism, as is noted in the

2021 Interim National Strategic Guidance. The 2017 National Security Strategy echoed the same mentality: "Around the world, nations and individuals admire what America stands for. We treat people equally and value and uphold the rule of law. We have a democratic system that allows the best ideas to flourish. We know how to grow economies so that individuals can achieve prosperity."[53]

My definition of "peace and security" is underpinned by two concepts, which in this message are critical to US international peace and security efforts—paternalism and domestic affairs.

Paternalism

A fundamental principle of international assistance is self-help. Congress echoes this principle in the statement of policy in Section 502 of the International Peace and Security Act of 1961: "The Congress hereby finds that the efforts of the United States and other friendly countries to promote peace and security continue to require measures of support based upon the principle of effective self-help and mutual aid."[54] This section is also part of the Foreign Assistance Act of 1961, which also unequivocally states in section 102(b)(1), that development is primarily the responsibility of the people of the developing countries themselves: "Assistance from the United States . . . shall be concentrated in those countries that take positive steps to help themselves."

The statuary message has trickled down to the foreign assistance framework. The first part of the peace and security objective begins with the clause, "to help nations" Yet this simple phrase has a hidden connotation. It implies other nations want US help. A manufacturing firm may hire a consultant to identify bottlenecks in its processing and to improve delivery times. But before doing this, the firm must have recognized there is an inherent problem and have the will to address it. Furthermore, the problem must be substantial enough for the company to set aside funds for a consultant, develop a scope of work, select a firm or individual, commit management and employee time to meeting with the consultant and then give them access to the entire plant and employees, brainstorm potential problems and solutions, review a draft report, pay the consultant, and then actually implement the findings. This effort requires serious commitment. When someone *wants* help, they should really *want* it. They must demonstrate its importance. They must commit time and resources to the process.

Not all countries the United States engages with around peace and security concerns acknowledge they have a problem and commit to addressing it. Unless thousands of troops are amassed on their border, no sovereign nation, including the United States, would turn to others and admit they have a security problem. More likely, these countries simply want US assistance to advance their own interests. US policymakers have blindly believed the countries want America's help and, therefore, justify this need as an overriding principle in the foreign assistance framework objective with the phrase "to help nations." If a policy maker unambiguously states the country wants and needs US help, then the practitioners who implement the policy will simply follow suit. Many US government development experts do not allow themselves to honestly question *whether* the other country *wants* the assistance. They are programmed to believe, in line with a paternalistic undercurrent pervasive among Americans, that they know best. This flaw is not reserved for Americans working in international development; it is inherent in human nature. Parents and older siblings maintain they know what is best for the younger generation. Western powers think the same way. Winston Churchill, England's prime minister during World War II, once described his belief about equal rights to an Indian Kenyan delegate: "Certainly, if the individual becomes civilized and lives in a civilized way, in a civilized house, and observes civilized behaviour in his goings on, and in his family life, and he is also educated sufficiently . . . it is absurd to go and give the naked savages of the Kikuyu and the Kavirondo equal electoral rights, although they are human beings—you cannot do that."[55]

In pursuing this type of assistance, the United States is also implying that the recipient country is bereft of said conditions and capacity for peace. The 2017 National Security Strategy phrase does not employ the words "strengthen" or "improve" but "establish." To establish something inherently implies that it was completely missing beforehand. This is what many Americans believe; after all, this is *our* foreign assistance program and *our* overarching objective and it is in *our* best interest to convince, cajole, or even force the other country into accepting our assistance.

The first clause of the framework's objective is "to help nations establish conditions and capacity for achieving peace, security, and stability." The rest of the clause then qualifies the first three words, as discussed above. It implies that the United States wants to establish the conditions and capacity in those target nations. I had to read that again to absorb its meaning; the United States wants to help nations establish certain conditions for stability. Given this, does the US federal government help its own states to establish these conditions for domestic stability? No, not unless it is invited. Even if an earthquake or wildfire decimates part of an American state, the governor must request federal assistance before the president, through the executive branch, can act. Many countries for whom America provides peace and security assistance have not asked for it. Instead, the United States has taken it upon itself to provide it, in service of its own national security interests.

Some Americans may object, saying Churchill was a British colonialist who believed in white, Christian, and European supremacy over Africans, thereby implying that America's attitude toward Africa is different. But this is not the case. Following Kenya's 2017 general election, the United States delivered its own modern, toned-down rhetoric that, unfortunately, still portrays an attitude of Americans knowing what is best for an African nation. In March 2018, Kenya's top diplomat, Macharia Kamau, the equivalent of the US secretary of state, published an opinion entitled, "US intervention in Kenya? No thanks" in response to an opinion published by former US diplomats to Kenya.[56] Macharia was diplomatic. He first politely acknowledged the Americans' credibility, writing "that Mark Bellamy and Johnnie Carson are accomplished US diplomats [and this] is not in doubt. It may also be assumed that their relationship with Kenya as former ambassadors in Nairobi gives them a more than average understanding of Kenya's politics, economy and even social aspects."[57]

Johnny Carson was the US assistant secretary of state for African affairs under Hillary Clinton. He served as the US ambassador to Kenya (1999–2003), Zimbabwe (1995–1997), and Uganda (1991–1994). William Mark Bellamy was the principal deputy assistant secretary of state for Africa and had been the US ambassador to Kenya after Carson from 2003–2006 under former President George W. Bush. He also served as a political officer in Zimbabwe in the 1980s. Therefore, both are senior career American diplomats with African experience. Having set the stage for a sharp rebuke, Macharia then noted that "their article, published here at *African Arguments* on 27 February, in which they call for US intervention in Kenya is a clear demonstration of how preconceived notions and stereotypes about Africa by Western technocrats override any practical experience and knowledge they may have acquired on the continent."[58]

What was this about? In their publication, entitled "How and why the US should intervene in Kenya," former Ambassadors Bellamy and Carson presented their paternalist opinions about Kenya and their belief that the United States is in a unique position as the only viable savior for Kenya:[59]

> As was the case during the horrendous postelection violence of 2007, Kenya today *needs outside assistance* to help it alter course. Such help is unlikely to materialise *unless the US* uses its unique relationship with Kenya to catalyse an international response . . .
>
> However, the US must make it crystal clear privately that *there are limits to what the US can tolerate* if it is to maintain its close relationship and that continuing to amass executive power unconstitutionally and flaunt the rule of law seriously tests those limits . . .
>
> While the two countries may be valuable security partners, *Kenya needs the relationship more than the US*. The partnership is not a "get out of jail free" card for the Kenyatta government. Nor is it an excuse for the US to overlook Nairobi's refusal to respect fundamental democratic norms.[60]

These former senior US diplomats used extremely interesting phrases such as "Kenya today needs outside assistance." I teach my children the difference between "needs" and "wants." A sovereign country can want assistance, however, no other country, except an imperial or colonial power, would say outside assistance is "needed." Even the United States has a policy for humanitarian assistance. Following even the most catastrophic earthquake or other natural disaster, the country or the state governor must officially request assistance before the federal government can respond through USAID or the Federal Emergency Management Agency (FEMA). Bellamy or Carson would have received dozens of such requests during their long careers.

The excerpt's second phrase is an empty threat: "There are limits to what the US can tolerate." No country knows or can articulate those limits. We know from recent political history that US presidents drawing such red lines have had to back down. The two authors themselves recognize that sanctions and public shaming efforts, two tools in America's diplomatic toolbox, are ineffective. The United States cannot effectively use the rhetorical leverage it postures. As KTI was wrapping up following the 2013 general election, I took a job with a US-based NGO to serve as the deputy for a new USAID program in Kenya. It was an ambitious, $50 million devolution support program aimed at helping Kenya's 47 new counties that the new constitution had created. The KTI assets (vehicles, computer equipment, furniture, etc.) were to transfer over to the new program. Yet, four months into the new program, the only two expatriates on the organization chart, the program lead and I, resigned because the US embassy could not secure long-term work permits for us. Nor could the embassy arrange for the transfer of six relatively new Toyota Land Cruisers from the KTI program. These vehicles were parked in an embassy parking lot for more than six months, mired down in struggles between the United States and Kenya, over power, taxes, registrations, and import duties. Like our work permits, the cars were effectively stuck in a diplomatic and bureaucratic quagmire, over which the United States had no leverage despite our $60 million KTI program and new $50 million devolution program support to Kenya.

This quagmire does not reflect Bellamy's and Carson's belief that "Kenya needs the relationship more than the US." It is also contrary to what I frequently heard during my seven years in Kenya. I was often told the United States needs Kenya more than Kenya needs the United States because of the war on terrorism and because Kenya offers America a stable base in the Horn of Africa. Nairobi hosts the largest Embassy in sub-Saharan Africa, over 400 official US government personnel (in 2012), and Manda Bay near Lamu in Kenya "is an important operational base for U.S. Africa Command forces in the region."[61] As discussed in the introduction, Kenya is an anchor state for the United States while Kenya easily turns to other states, including China, for financial assistance. It does not *need* the United States in the same way that Bellamy and Carsen believe.

Then–Vice President Biden, in his 2010 address to University of Nairobi students, correctly avoided this paternalistic attitude that Bellamy, Carsen, and other US diplomats and development specialists hang on to. Biden noted that "The United States strongly supports the process of constitutional reform, including providing assistance for voter registration and civic education, so that Kenyans are able to familiarize themselves with the draft constitution your parliament passed and allow you to make informed decisions. But, let me repeat, this is your decision, your decision alone. And the people of Kenya must make this choice—a choice for Kenya by Kenyans."[62]

Paternalism, like colonialism toward Africa, must end before America can successfully foster secure peace in the world. There is also a second prerequisite: America must address its own internal peace and security problems.

Acting Locally

Consider these proverbs and bumper stickers: "charity begins at home"; "think globally, act locally"; "fix your own house before meddling in someone else's affairs"; or "put on your own oxygen mask before helping those seated next to you." The latter is drilled into every air passenger today. But how many understand why we put our own masks on first? I had to think about it when flying with two young children. I could get my mask on in a couple of seconds; getting one on my six-month-old infant would be a little more challenging but they would not rip it off. My two-year-old was a completely different case. I may have to console and even perhaps restrain them once the mask is on to prevent her from ripping it off. When I walked through the scenario, half-listening to the flight attendant drone on, I understood why I had to get my own mask on first, get oxygen into my system, and then assist my kids. The take-home message echoes first-responder training: Take care of yourself first; if you are a mess, you can't help anyone else.

Let's think about peace and security at home first. If "peace" is defined as the tranquil, undisturbed state of affairs within a nation allowing its citizens to constantly flourish, as echoed by Ibn Khaldun, Hobbes, Locke, and Kant, then the United States has never experienced constant and lasting peace. In fact, throughout the millennium of European presence in North America, beginning with Leif Erickson's arrival in Newfoundland in approximately 1,000 CE and ending with the January 6, 2021, insurrection at the Capitol building, America's history has constantly indulged in the opposite of peace.

From the first European settlers through the War of Independence, slavery, the genocide of Native Americans, the Civil War, and the Texas War of Independence, the United States is no different from other nations whose history is also punctuated with episodes of turmoil manifested as *us* versus *them*. Yet our history manifests bouts of violence we bring upon ourselves. Sometimes, this violence is triggered by government action. For example, from the internment of American citizens of Japanese origin during World War II, the 1970 Kent State Massacre of students by the Ohio National Guard, and the race-related riots from the 1960s to those triggered by police brutality against Rodney King in 1992 and George Floyd in 2020. Yet, in other cases, we perpetuate this violence without direct government provocation. Attacks on Muslims, Hindus, and Sikhs after 9/11, as well as regular mass shootings, punctuate our daily news. Schools, synagogues, nightclubs, malls, and offices are not immune to violence.

I was living in Nairobi in 2013 when terrorists attacked the popular Westgate Mall in Westlands and gunned down over 60 innocent civilians, including children, in cold blood. The US embassy's private security guards contacted me as I was on my way home as the attack unfolded. The event catalyzed into a multiday siege; helicopters and smoke were visible from my garden. Our side of the city shut down for a few days, and we were on an embassy-imposed lockdown. It was scary. Social media exploded; our friends and family across the globe wanted to know if we were okay. Eventually, it was over. Rumors of US and Israeli security assistance and a botched Kenyan military response permeated social media. I do not know what actually happened; each report and analysis contradicted the previous one. All we saw, once the dust settled, was the physical destruction of a significant portion of the building and multiple funerals scheduled for the following week.

Over the following months, a few foreigners chose to pack up and leave. Some had been in the mall at the time and had witnessed, firsthand, the senseless killings. One person I knew had spent hours inside a bank vault with her young child. Another had to answer the question, "What was Prophet Muhammad's mother's name?" to avoid being gunned down. We had to teach our young kids how succinctly and confidently to respond when instructed: "Prove you are a Muslim." Family members back in the United States asked me if I was also thinking of coming home. Wasn't it unsafe to live in Kenya, they asked, because an attack like this could happen again? My quick retort could not be challenged. I noted that five days prior to the Westgate Mall attack, a single gunman killed 13 people at the Navy Yard in Washington, DC, while less than two months earlier, three people were gunned down at a local government meeting in Pennsylvania. At the time, both the Sandy Hook school shooting and the Aurora, Colorado, movie theater shooting had happened within the past year. Violent acts perpetrated by terrorists, whether international or domestic, can happen anywhere at any time. The United States is not immune. Americans were not moving out of Washington, DC, or Pennsylvania. No. They stayed there and we stayed in Nairobi.

Things are far from perfect at home. Don't we need to improve our own house first? As OTI's deputy country representative and a former Kenyan, I participated in the selection process for the program officers. Many applicants came from the peace and reconciliation sector and noted in their interviews that they were educated Kenyans who had accumulated experience in Kenya and then taken those skills to East and Central Africa. In response to the interview panel's question—"Why are you applying for this job?"—some noted they were engaged in peace and reconciliation activities elsewhere. They added that, when Kenyans started killing each other and almost collapsed into civil war after the December 2007 elections, their counterparts suggested they go home and fix their own country first.

America's national security strategies reflect this need. The 2021 document stated, "one thing is certain: we will only succeed in advancing American interests and upholding our universal values by working in common cause with our closest allies and partners, and by renewing our own enduring sources of national strength."[63] Threats to our own national security know no borders; they can come from extremists, biological or computer viruses, and climate change. Therefore, America must think locally before it can act globally.

Acting Globally

As embodied in the definition offered earlier, "security" contributes to achieving peace. The United States, from its very beginning and through to today, believes it can promote security at home if it promotes security overseas. This belief manifests in two primary ways: the protection of commercial interests and of the nation's geopolitical or ideological interests.

Overseas commercial interests comprise two main categories: transportation and fixed assets. In the first few years of a century, a US Navy frigate was ordered to escort merchant vessels off the coast of Africa.

These vessels, laden with goods for or from US ports, were vital to the supply chain fueling the American economy. The navy's orders were to protect the vessels from African Muslim pirates. These pirates, working in small clusters using small, fast, and easily maneuverable boats, could sneak up unseen on large ships, board them, and disable the crew. Crews generally do not carry small arms and can easily be disabled during their long, monotonous days at sea. Pirates were capturing vessels, steering them to African ports, selling or using the goods, and ransoming the crew.

These were the Somali pirates operating in the early 2000s. The US Navy was part of a multinational force patrolling the north Indian Ocean and Red Sea, but this description is equally applicable to a different African coast, in a different century, with a different type of frigate. In the late eighteenth century, the United States. disbanded its small navy after the end of the Revolutionary War. However, after Barbary pirates from the North African provinces (Algiers, Tunis, Tripoli, and Morocco) began attacking European and American merchant vessels, capturing crew and passengers and enslaving them, the US Congress appropriated funds for a new permanent navy under the Naval Act of 1794. The famous USS *Constitution,* or *Old Ironsides,* currently docked in Boston, is one of the first of three ships built for this purpose.

Every country has the right to protect its international shipping but needs the willingness, means, and infrastructure to provide adequate protection. This type of protection could be extended into the skies; American fighter jets could be called on to protect US-flagged commercial aircraft. In 2019, the United States also established its newest branch of the armed forces, the Space Force, partly to protect US space assets from attack and debris.

Protecting offshore fixed assets, under the umbrella of peace and security is the second type of commercial interest protection. American military deployments to Saudi Arabia after Iraqi invaded Kuwait in 1990, protected US commercial oil assets but also had unintended consequences. As described in the 9/11 Memorial & Museum in New York City, the presence of US troops on Arabian soil near the holy cities of Mecca and Medina, the birthplace of Islam, contributed to Osama bin Laden's hatred of America. But Americans can understand the need for its government to protect the lifeblood of the American economy—oil. We can understand the importance of sending troops to the Panama Canal

Zone the year after Panama claimed independence from Colombia and the United States was extended the right to build the canal to link our eastern and western seaboards. Security for geopolitical or ideological interests has probably earned the most headlines accusing the United States of paternalism. Indeed, American forces are currently sprinkled across the globe. Manda Bay in Kenya or Camp Lemonnier in Djibouti may be less known than US troops who are permanently stationed on the demilitarized zone (DMZ) on the Korean peninsula, in Japan, or in Germany.[64] These facilities form an integral part of the US peace and security infrastructure assets.

Beyond physical bases, the United States has extended its security footprint overseas by attacking anti-American, antidemocratic, or anti-capitalist ideology. We have used a vast spectrum of tools in our peace and security toolbox; some have been locked away in the archives of history and others should be locked away forever. At the top of this list are political assassinations. One senate committee report stated, "We have found concrete evidence of at least eight plots involving the CIA to assassinate Fidel Castro from 1960 to 1965," and the "Committee has received solid evidence of a plot to assassinate Patrice Lumumba."[65] Lumumba was the first prime minister of the Congo following its independence from Belgium in 1960. Castro was the leader of Cuba from 1959 to 2008. The United States perceived a threat from both leaders with their pandering to the former Soviet Union. In both cases, the United States was worried about the spread of communism. More recently, the killing of Osama bin Laden in Pakistan in 2011 is a form of revenge assassination for American security.

The fear of communism also drove the creation of the Foreign Assistance Act, which led to the creation of USAID. President Kennedy emphasized the need to put both economic and military support in our foreign assistance toolbox when he signed the act into law: "It provides military assistance to countries which are on the rim of the Communist world and under direct attack. It provides economic assistance to those governments which are under attack from widespread misery and social discontent which are exploited by our adversaries, and this permits us to speak with a much stronger and more effective voice."[66]

The United States also pressures governments and world leaders through diplomacy (e.g., pushing Kenya to adopt a multiparty system under President Moi) or sanctions (e.g., those leveraged against Libya, Iran, and North Korea). These tools are also part of America's peace and security toolbox. Another related instrument is arresting, deposing, or killing a world leader. America's military action in 1989, namely, arresting Panama's president, is a classic example of this strategy. Other examples of countries in which this tool has been used include the Philippines, Grenada, Dominican Republic, and of course, Iraq with the US invasion in 2003.

These disparate examples of American actions overseas under the peace and security umbrella demonstrate how extensive the United States' toolbox is and how difficult it is for all Americans to agree on the fundamental question: Do these tools help strengthen our national security? Each American could define scenarios in which using a particular tool (e.g., assassination, sanctions) was both appropriate and inappropriate. The exercise becomes extremely argumentative. In the end, foreign policy and international development specialists must use the right tool at the right time, within the right context. They must believe the United States is best placed to use that specific instrument and that we have something important and unusual to offer. But, first, they need a good definition of "peace and security."

Definition

In an attempt to clearly define the phrase "peace and security," I started with the dilemma of whether the term is grammatically singular (e.g., a kind of compound noun) or two separate words. Then, as I considered various uses of the phrase across the globe and in America's own laws, national security strategies, and its foreign assistance framework, I failed to find an appropriate, noncircular, comprehensive definition that professionals can use in designing US peace and security programs. My definition, however, is underpinned by two overarching concepts—paternalism and domestic affairs. Both are extremely important to the United States' presentation of its peace and security programming to its allies across the globe. I now present my own definition and rationale.

The "What"

As I define it, peace and security is a singular phrase representing an ideal end-state for every nation or community. For nations, it is the state of affairs allowing each citizen to maximize their potential by working, studying, innovating, producing, and being a steward of their neighbor, community, and the environment. This state of affairs is only possible under a continued state of both *peace,* that is, the absence of physical, verbal, or emotional turmoil, and *security,* the long-term presence or guarantee of the desired outcome. Otherwise, peace may be short-term or fragile. The peace Kenya enjoyed after the signing of its 2008 peace agreement was extremely fragile; it required the implementation of Agenda 4, which addressed longer-term issues, to turn it into a secure peace.

The essential ingredients of peace and security, or what I call secure peace, are depicted by the mnemonic, PARADISE, described and illustrated below:

- *P*eace, or the absence of war, conflict, crime, and turmoil
- *A*cceptance of our diversity, equality, and pluralism
- *R*ule of law and human rights
- *A*dministration of government services and responsibilities
- *D*emocracy or a government comprising the people's representation and voice
- *I*nnovation allowing each new generation to be better placed than the previous one
- *S*tewardship of neighbors, communities, humanity, and the earth
- *E*conomic growth

The previous chapter described Kenya's efforts, with US support, to secure peace through a more robust judiciary. USAID's effort to improve the judiciary contributed to three parts of my mnemonic: Faster and more efficient decisions contributed to an improvement in the *r*ule of law and human rights such that the losers of the 2013, 2017, and 2022 general elections trusted the renewed judiciary. The *a*dministration of government services and responsibilities were enhanced by USAID's pilot efforts and the longer-term World Bank funded program. There was also a level of *i*nnovation, which allowed the newer generation of court users to be better placed than the previous generations.

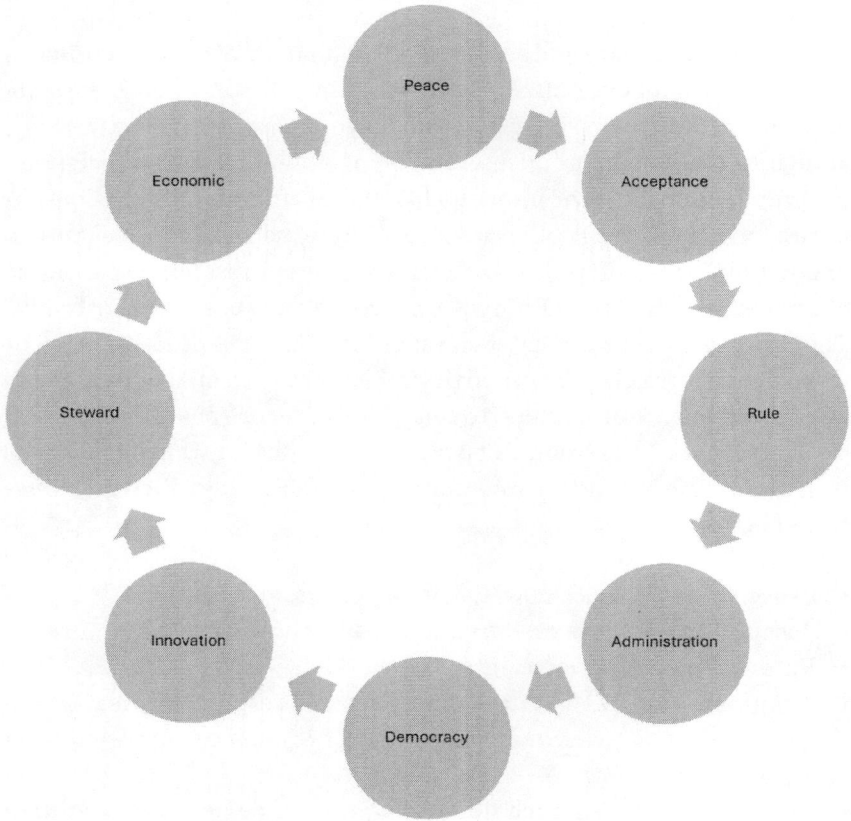

The "Why"

Explaining *why* is often more important than explaining *what*. I get better results if I articulate *why* when presenting, proposing, or, especially in the case of children, asking that something (e.g., a chore) be done. Due to psychology, the explanation that "dirt attracts mold and bugs, please vacuum your bedroom" yields much better results than the imperative, "please vacuum your bedroom floor." Human nature keeps us on the defensive. When I hear a request or suggestion from someone else, I automatically adopt to a defensive mode. I am likelier to get a positive response if I include an explanation alongside a request: "Ambassador, in order to ensure the corrupt leader does not sue the bookshop owners, I would like to have individual newspaper vendors, who have little to lose and are not worth suing, sell the book on the streets."[67]

The USAID's Office of Transition Initiatives (OTI) drilled this concept into anyone working with or for them. When proposing a new country program, a shift in programming, or a new activity, managers asked *why* before asking *what*. Notably, the first required data field in OTI's global program database was *why*. In my work with the National Environmental Policy Act (1970), on environmental impact statements, I found a similar regulatory requirement. Before embarking on an environmental analysis for a proposed project, we have to explain the "purpose and need"—a fancy term for *why*. Likewise, declarations of independence, international resolutions, and constitutions all start with clauses articulating the need for the document. Anyone who has participated in a model United Nations conference has had to write a preamble to their resolutions, first describing the reasons or justification for the proposed action or decision. Why not apply this logic to all international development programs and definitions?

For my own definition, I combine the sources introduced above— English grammar and lexicology, United Nations documentation and processes, national constitutions, US national security strategies, and the US foreign assistance framework. I add to these sources my own decade of experience with USAID—three years in Washington, DC, seven years in Nairobi, and numerous short-term assignments in Asia, the Middle East, Africa, and South America. The result is my own explanation of why the United States invests in peace and security programming overseas, outside of its territorial jurisdiction, and under the rubric of international development:

1. Recognizing that American security, stability, and economic growth at home is dependent on secure international peace.
2. Appreciating that secure international peace is the sum of each nation's secure peace.
3. Acknowledging secure peace requires self-worth, human rights, and improved living conditions.
4. Noting that democracy, which is any form of government by the people, holds the key to freedom, peace, and dignity.

Therefore, to ensure secure peace for all Americans, the United States will defend its global interests; improve its domestic quality of life, human rights, and good governance; and assist its allies in their efforts to secure or maintain their own peace and security.

The US 2021 Interim National Security Strategic Guidance explains the first point, justifying America's involvement in another nation's domestic affairs to advance US peace and security: "Leading the world isn't an investment we make to feel good about ourselves. . . . it's in our undeniable self-interest."[68] The strategic guidance document presents four powerful examples to explain how America's overseas investments improve the country's own national security:

- When we strengthen our alliances, we amplify our power and our ability to disrupt threats before they can reach our shores.
- When we invest in the economic development of countries, we create new markets for our products and reduce the likelihood of instability, violence, and mass migrations.
- When we strengthen health systems around the world, we reduce the risk of future pandemics that could threaten our people and our economy.
- When we defend equal rights of all people—of women and girls, LG-BTQI individuals, indigenous communities, people with disabilities, and people of every ethnic background and religion—we help ensure those rights are protected for our own children here in America.[69]

My explanation reflects US national security strategy by articulating America's belief in its right to both defend itself and be proactive where needed. In fact, the department responsible for America's armed forces since 1789, shortly after independence, to 1947, after World War II, was the War Department. It was not named the Defense Department. In 1947 it was rebranded as such to be politically correct. The British government reflected the same thinking; its War Office existed from 1857–1964. Then, it was renamed the Ministry of Defense. Military engagement, whether under the umbrella of war or defense, constitutes only part of this right to act in self-defense. For the United States, being proactive also justifies our involvement in another nation's domestic problems and governance. As the 2010 national security strategy documentation states, "The United

States supports the expansion of democracy and human rights abroad because governments that respect these values are more just, peaceful, and legitimate. We also do so because their success abroad fosters an environment that supports America's national interests."[70]

My definition of "peace and security" replaces the word "help" with "assist." "Help" has a paternalistic connotation: "If you help someone, you make it easier for them to do something. . . . [It means you are] doing part of the work for them."[71] "Assist," however, is a more formal offer of supplementary support or aid, making it easier for the recipient to do the task.[72] The term "assist" also avoids another pitfall foreign policymakers and development specialists often succumbed to. Every country, including America, has internal struggles or domestic issues that have little bearing on its national security, stability, and economic growth, nor on international peace. Each country should determine what assistance, if any, it wants from the international community. For example, the United States invited an election observation mission from the Organization for Security and Cooperation in Europe to observe our midterm and presidential elections.[73] We also invited the world to assist us recover from Hurricane Katrina in September 2005, with countries from Bangladesh ($1 million in humanitarian aid) to Britain (500,000 military ration packs) pledging assistance.[74]

Conclusion

America believes its system of governance and markets is the best and, perhaps, the only way to achieve prosperity. Moreover, the United States seeks to advance global peace and security because the American people believe this outcome will enhance US security and economic opportunities. Security ensures long lasting peace, and peace provides for a higher ideal end state. Therefore, I think of peace and security as a long-lasting or secure peace, and define the higher ideal end state in terms of the mnemonic, PARADISE. This end state also requires other intermediate outcomes: peace, acceptance, rule of law, administration, democracy, innovation, environmental stewardship, and economic growth, which are all reflected in the works of our historic philosophers, Ibn Khaldun (1377) and his seventeenth-century European counterparts. Former Vice

President Biden presented his own version of PARADISE to University of Nairobi students in June 2010:

> Your coalition government has agreed to a reform agenda that would bring about the fundamental change that Kenyans are seeking. If implemented fully, corrupt officials will be finally held accountable. The judiciary and the police force will place the pursuit of justice above the pursuit of personal gain. Land rights and ownership will be governed by the rule of law, not by the whims of the powerful. Kenyan women and girls—the most untapped resource of this nation and almost every nation in the world—will be ever better positioned to contribute to their communities and their country at every level. And a new constitution will put in place a framework to accelerate those reforms, including reducing executive power by building up the checks and balances of your parliament and your judiciary.[75]

If we, as Americans, use any number of tools in our peace and security toolbox to help countries achieve any of these intermediate outcomes, we are helping to advance a secure peace.

Having offered a new definition of "peace and security" and a mnemonic to appreciate the *what* and understand the *why,* I can now turn to the *how.* The following chapters, like the previous one, explore many applications of US peace and security programming in Kenya that contributed to this broader definition of the term and advanced America's own interests.

CHAPTER THREE

A New Dawn

"I want to emphasize the unwavering determination of the United States to push for and support implementation of the reform agenda. President Obama and Secretary Clinton believe strongly that Kenya must seize this historic opportunity to bring about fundamental change....

The constitution is, in many respects, the *sine qua non* of the reform process. Without a new constitution, implementation of other reforms will not prove sufficient to steer the country in the right direction. If a new constitution is put in place, then implementation of other reforms, along with the new constitution, will help ensure future democratic stability and prosperity."

—Ambassador Michael Ranneberger, "Reform, Partnership, and the Future of Kenya," speech, American Chamber of Commerce, Nairobi, January 26, 2010

Bottom Line Up Front (BLUF)

A constitution is a nation's supreme law; it establishes governance structures and defines the relationship between the state and the people. Constitutions vary. They may be empowering, progressive, and visionary, or they may be restrictive, out of touch with the times, and closedminded. This chapter demonstrates how the United States meaningfully contributed to long-term peace and security in Kenya by strategically and tactically using diplomacy and development to advance Kenya's constitution building process during three distinct periods: (1) 1960, before independence; (2) 1990–1991; and (3) 20 years later in 2009–2010. The United States invests in such efforts because, as discussed in chapter 2, it seeks to promote peace and security across the globe and, as demonstrated in the quotation above, believes constitutions are inextricably linked with stability, peace, and governance.

I played a lead role in US efforts in Kenya as the deputy country representative for USAID's Kenya Transition Initiative, a program set up specifically to help Kenya rebuild after the 2007/2008 postelection violence. Between February 2008 when the peace agreement was signed and August 2010 when Kenyans overwhelmingly voted for a new constitution, the nation successfully completed the first task listed in the agreement's fourth agenda. This agenda identified long-term issues and solutions for prosperity, none of which could commence before the first task of completing a comprehensive constitutional review process. Like many Kenyan roads, the process was riddled with potholes, diversions, and corrupt policemen. Members of the Kenyan elite who did not want a new constitution attempted to stall, delay, or derail the process.

Since 1963, Kenyan politicians have used, abused, or modified their constitution to advance their nefarious ways—holding on to power, crushing the opposition, fixing legislative and administrative structures, and facilitating rampant corruption to feed Swiss bank accounts. They did not want Kenyans to have a document focusing on the common person, one that could be a new, powerful, protective document with the potential of ushering in a new dawn.[1] Using both blatant and subtle tactics, they obstructed those charged with developing the new document; hampered public access to the pre-referendum draft; used misinformation to pit communities against each other to facilitate a rejection at the polls; introduced 150 self-serving legislative amendments to the final draft; illegally changed the text *after* the public and parliament had approved the document; attacked US support with help from elected US officials; and attempted, in the spirit of the old Kenya, to amend the document during the COVID-19 pandemic.

Kenyans prevailed; they thwarted these tactics. They gave birth to a robust, forward-thinking, progressive, long-term master plan for Kenya. This document has survived a decade of attacks, established an intimidating legislative agenda, and begun to change the lives of ordinary Kenyans. It has even played a role in international peace and security, for example, the 2024 Haiti police crisis. With significant US support, it also helped establish and maintain peace and security for over 50 million people and a key US ally.

Peace and Security in Constitutions

The Kenyan example of a constitution providing peace and security echoes the role of the American constitution in bringing together 13 disparate American colonies in 1787. But this fundamental role of a constitution-type document spans almost 1,400 years when the Prophet Muhammad migrated from Mecca to Medina. The year 621 CE was momentous, marking the beginning of the Muslim calendar. The prophet and his followers were escaping persecution from Meccans opposed to the message of Islam. The prophet had also just lost his wife and uncle, two of his closest protectors. The people of Medina invited him to their city, known as Yathrib, to become the statesman and arbitrator between the various Muslim and Jewish tribes. Soon after emigrating, he led the development of the world's first written constitution, the Constitution of Medina. At the heart of this document was peace and security in the form of relations among communities, Muslim and non-Muslim; finances; the status of refugees; justice; and the protection of life and property. Researchers argue whether the document is a constitution, treaty, or compilation of various treaties.[2] Whatever type of document it is, in today's parlance, the Constitution of Medina reflects the mnemonic PARADISE by encompassing both internal and external peace and security elements, including conflict among communities and underlying elements such as justice.

Likewise, the preamble to the US Constitution encompasses elements of PARADISE—defense, justice, general welfare, and posterity: "We the People of the United States, in Order to form a more perfect Union, establish Justice, insure domestic Tranquility, provide for the common defence, promote the general Welfare, and secure the Blessings of Liberty to ourselves and our Posterity, do ordain and establish this Constitution for the United States of America."[3] The articulation, here, of elections, governance, war, and justice, as well as the Bill of Rights, provides a comprehensive framework for the nation's peace and security.

Both the Constitution of Medina and the US Constitution package peace and security—represented by defense and relations among different groups—with prosperity. Kenya's Constitution follows suit but goes one step further. First, it defines "national security" as "the protection against internal and external threats to Kenya's territorial integrity and sovereignty, its people, their rights, freedoms, property, peace, stability and prosperity, and other national interests."[4] Then, it assigns the mandate of national security to the country's national security entities, namely, the intelligence service, police services, and defense forces.

Kenya's Constitution distinguishes between two types of threats, internal and external. A threat to property from a cross-border land raid leading to death and the destruction of property would be considered an external national security threat, for example, the 2015 attack on Garissa College in northeastern Kenya in which at least 147 people were killed. An external threat to Kenya's resources may also manifest offshore in the form of illegal fishing within Kenya's Exclusive Economic Zone (EEZ), a threat the Coast Guard is mandated to address.

A domestic cattle stock raid would be an internal national security threat. One function of the Administrative Police Service is the provision of specialized stock theft prevention services (National Police Service Act, 2014, chapter 84, clause 27) because historically, stock theft increases tensions among communities and is accompanied by death and the destruction of property. Domestic terrorism, widespread postelection violence, and other manifestations of security threats would also fall under this umbrella.

In this broad definition and mandate, Kenya's Constitution unambiguously, yet perhaps inadvertently, expands the traditional scope of security services. The intelligence services, police services, and defense forces would be, according to the definition given in Article 238, responsible for addressing deforestation, flooding, or transportation inefficiencies because all three adversely impact property, prosperity, and "other national interests."[5] But the scope of the security services does not end there. They must encompass economic development, governance, leadership, and education because these, too, impact prosperity.

While the text of Kenya's Constitution itself is extremely important to internal and external security, as well as to prosperity, so is the process by which Kenyans adopted the constitution. According to Kenya's former Chief Justice Mutunga, "The making of the Kenyan 2010 Constitution is a story of ordinary citizens striving and succeeding to reject or as some may say, overthrow the existing social order and to define a new social, economic, cultural, and political order for themselves. Some have spoken of the new Constitution as representing a second independence."[6]

What better way to advance peace and security than by allowing Kenyans to reject the old, inherited colonial constitution developed in London—without public participation—and instead enable Kenyans to develop, approve, and protect their own guiding document? No longer can Kenyans blame the colonial powers and the power-hungry Kenyan politicians who amended, misused, or misinterpreted their nation's constitution to serve their own nefarious desires.

The US national security strategies and the Kenyan Constitution's definition of "peace and prosperity" are consistent in one overarching theme: National security is driven by domestic prosperity. Therefore, if the United States wants to advance peace and security in selected countries such as Kenya it must have a variety of available tools in its international development toolbox. The United States must focus on arms and agriculture, defense and democracy, intelligence and infrastructure. Placing attention on only traditional international relations, security infrastructure, and peacebuilding is not sufficient to advance peace and security. This holds true for dividing up responsibilities to keep USAID, the Departments of State, Health and Human Services, and the Departments of Justice, Defense, and the Interior squarely in their respective lanes. The policymakers and specialists in these agencies have three overlapping tasks, namely to stock and use a robust toolbox, share the tools wisely, and ensure internal obstacles do not obstruct program delivery.

This chapter explores the variety of roles US policymakers and development specialists have played in Kenya's constitutional history since 1960, the obstructions and counteroffensive moves the United States made, and what makes Kenya's Constitution a visionary document for promoting peace and security.

The Early Years: 1960–2007

Kenyans have been seeking to establish their own constitution since 1963, the year they secured independence from British colonial rule. Britain's Colonial Office and Kenyan political leaders gave the Independence Constitution to Kenyans following negotiations in 1960 and 1963 at the Lancaster House Constitutional Conferences. The final document was a relic of the postcolonial era; many countries have since sought out new postcolonial constitutions because such colonial documents "do not correspond to the democratic structures or to the political structures of these countries."[7]

Kenya's Independence Constitution

Kenya's Independence Constitution provided "a Bill of Rights, a multiparty system and a Westminster-style [bicameral] parliamentary government, led by a Prime Minister whilst the Queen remained formally the Head of State."[8] It provided for a system of regionalization to overcome potential conflicts among different ethnic groups. The regions were represented in the legislature's second chamber, the Senate. As Cornelia Glinz notes, "it produced a system of separation of powers on the vertical and on the horizontal level."[9]

In 1960, the United States was informally involved in drafting Kenya's first constitution. Former US Supreme Court Justice Marshall, operating in a private capacity before President Johnson appointed him to the court of appeals in 1961 and the Supreme Court in 1967, played an important role in framing Kenya's first Independence Constitution at Lancaster House in London in 1960.[10] *New York Post* columnist Murray Kempton "thought that Marshall's presence at the Lancaster House conference was "one of the most extraordinary events in colonial history. . . . There seems to be no record in diplomatic history of a private citizen of the United States sitting at a British government conference whose subject is Crown colonial policy."[11] Marshall spent time in Kenya beforehand drafting many provisions of the early drafts, including an important bill of rights that respected all Kenyans, black, white, and brown. Unfortunately, some of his contributions did not survive the British and Kenyan negotiations and edits.[12]

Kenyans blamed their woes on this Independence Constitution. However, what is rarely discussed is the quick and brutal alteration of the first constitution by Kenya's elite, including the first president, Jomo Kenyatta. The constitution fell victim to ideological differences, power struggles, and ethnic differences, the same issues responsible for almost plunging the country into civil war in 2007. Within a year of independence, in 1963, "Kenya began the perilous path that corroded the very principles the independence constitution stood for. The path that tore the concept of democracy to pieces through 38 hasty, self-propagating amendments aimed almost solely at centralising and consolidating power in the executive. So drastic and numerous were these amendments that the independence constitution completely lost its identity and became known, for over 40 years, as the 1964 constitution."[13] The queen, prime minister, bicameral parliamentary form, multiparty system, as well as regionalism, were quickly eradicated from both the text and Kenya's political structures.

The world saw Kenya becoming a *de facto* one-party state, with the president holding power over the parliament and judiciary. In his scathing book, *Rogue Ambassador: An African Memoir*, Smith Hempstone, former US Ambassador to Kenya (1989–1993), spoke to this quite differently:

It is inaccurate to speak of Kenya as a one-party-state. KANU [Kenya African National Union], the party that has ruled Kenya since independence in 1963, is firmly under the presidential thumb. Kenya is a one-man state, and that man is the president. Lacking any sort of vision of Kenya as a modern state, [President] Moi is seen by many—and probably sees himself—as a tribal paramount chief writ large. As such, he can kill who he likes and divert as much public money he pleases to his private purse. Since sexual potency is important in a leader, any woman he wants is for the asking and his bastards are said to people every district in the nation (how his correlates with his alleged Christian celibacy I do not know). Moi lives not in the real universe but in a fantasy world of his own creation, and this is heady stuff.[14]

Hempstone's published attacks on Moi echoed his four-year term as ambassador. Responding to a global change in US policy, the ambassador fueled the 1991 clamor for constitutional reform. This policy change followed the fall of the Berlin Wall and the fragmentation of the former Soviet Union. While the Cold War had previously "compelled the U.S. to support some extremely unsavory characters in Africa and elsewhere," the United States could now afford to be more selective and strategic.[15] It did not need to support anyone pandering to democracy.

Hempstone provided the external pressure while government-sanctioned political assassinations and human rights abuses drove the domestic movement. Fed up and frustrated, the Kenyan population turned to protests and demonstrations, many turning violent. The government responded with a heavier hand and a vicious cycle ensued. Ambassador Hempstone, recognizing this window of opportunity, pushed hard and ignored calls to resign. He steered the course and predicted the future. On November 26, 1991, he sent a cable to Washington, DC, stating, "I would predict that the Kenya that will emerge in mid-1992 will be a very different nation than that of today. . . . parliament will rescind Article 2(a) of the constitution allowing for multiparty elections in the future. Kenyans will be allowed more freedom of speech, assembly and travel."[16] Barely a week later, to everyone's surprise, former President Moi told the delegates at his political party convention to rescind section 2(a) of the constitution. Moi himself had introduced this section, a decade earlier, to memorialize a single-party system following the failed coup that threatened his young rule. With the rescission of section 2(a) came another surprise: presidential term limits.

Mass protests, diplomacy, rhetoric, and the might of the US government were not enough to tip the scales. Washington had threatened economic sanctions to bring about democracy to Kenya and ensure human rights. Moi's unexpected decision came on the heels of a donor conference in Paris. In a letter to former President George H. W. Bush, bipartisan members of Congress had "urged the president to freeze 'all military and economic aid until there is effective change' in Kenya's government policy, and to build in Paris 'an international donor consensus to condition future aid on actual evidence of long-term measures toward democratic reform.'"[17] Today, donors only threaten. They do not actually cut aid for fear of hurting the populace. In 1991, however, the donors pulled the rug out from under Moi, cutting aid to Kenya from $1 billion to $600 million and threatening additional cuts.

A year later, Kenya held its first multiparty elections. While Kenyans were hopeful for change, the ruling party managed to hold on to power, as it would again in 1997. In both elections, the party split the opposition to prevent any other party from garnering enough votes to topple the Kenya African National Union (KANU). The heavily amended Independence Constitution continued to govern Kenyan lives.

Modification Attempts: 1997–2005

In 1997, following renewed pressure for constitutional change, parliament passed the Constitution of Kenya Review Commission Act. This people's focused effort was, again, short-lived. According to the Kenya Human Rights Commission, the act "provided for people's representation in the constitutional review process, with Parliament only intended to technically approve the final draft."[18] Following a long tradition of amending the good out of the constitution, parliament bypassed the people's representation and reinstated itself as the key decisionmaker through a series of amendments in 1998, 2000, 2001, and 2004.

Despite the power struggles at the top over who would control the final version of the constitution, the groundwork had begun. In an extensive outreach effort stretching to all parts of the country between 2000 and 2002, the Constitution of Kenya Review Commission succeeded in collecting Kenyans' views. The act of traveling, collecting, and compiling perspectives gave Kenyans a sense of hope. Almost 40 years after they inherited the document from the British, they thought they could create their own national blueprint.

Why are people easily swayed in their recollection of historical facts, conveniently made to forget key details, or find scapegoats among those who may be peripherally guilty? Kenyans continued to blame the British for their constitutional woes, conveniently being led to forget that the Kenyan elite gutted the Independence Constitution a year after the British left. In the absence of Facebook, Twitter, and Google, and with only one television and two radio stations—one in English and one in Swahili, and both government-owned—the politicians controlled all messaging. They also oversaw the textbooks and versions of history learned in schools. The number one education goal in Kenya is national unity: "Education in Kenya must foster a sense of nationhood and promote national unity. Much as Kenyans belong to different ethnic groups, races, and religions, their differences should not divide them. They must live and interact in peace and harmony. Education is an avenue through which conflicts can be removed."[19]

In removing differences and conflicts, Kenyans are led to forget the details, differences, and dilemmas the nation has faced since colonialization. An analogy of this conscious effort to dilute and forget is taking a Sunday drive in Nairobi National Park. In the 1980s, my parents took me there specifically to see elephants, lions, or rhinos in a pristine environment. Decades later, the environment had changed drastically. When I took my own children there to see any animal we could find, we had to ignore the noise and encroachment of the city's new skyscrapers, railway, and highways.

I saw a similar kind of "forgetfulness"—namely, that one tends to forget the history and lessons of the past—while posted to Kenya. By the 2013 election, Kenyans had already forgotten the violence and polarization associated with the 2007 election. They had already forgotten about one corruption scandal when the next one hit the front pages. Sadly, this shortsightedness has and will continue to plague Kenyans, just as it does other communities around the world.

In 2002, before the Constitution of Kenya Review Commission could produce a new draft, Kenyans again went to vote. With the new term limits, former President Moi was barred from running again and his party lost. The succeeding president, Mwai Kibaki, promised to give Kenyans a new constitution and reconvened the National Constitution Conference. This conference adopted the "Bomas" draft (named for the venue hosting the conference) in March 2004. The document was on its way to parliament for review. But this time, a different force halted the process. The high court intervened, agreeing with a plaintiff that the constitution allowed parliament to *amend* it, but did not give any authority to parliament to *replace* it. The court decided that "the process denied the people of Kenya their sovereign right to approve a new constitution."[20]

The government took a detour. They dumped the Bomas draft, prepared a new "Wako" draft (named after Kenya's then–attorney general), and organized a referendum. Kenyans were not fooled. After complaining for 40 years about a document the British had given them, they were not going to approve one handed to them by another power.

In total, 57 percent of the votes were cast against the government's draft in November 2005.

Fifteen years later, the next commission to tackle the challenging task of giving Kenyans their own document would write this in their final report: "The [2005] referendum became the perfect forum for the political elite to air long standing grievances. Each group resorted to distortion and incitement based on ethnicity and tribal affiliation and raised hostility and animosity to levels that exacerbated the divides in Kenya. It was apparent a process of reconciliation was needed but no efforts were made to institute a process of national healing."[21] The commission concluded that the polarization Kenyans had witnessed in the 2005 referendum had "laid the ground for the catastrophic consequences of the 2007 elections."[22]

Ambassador Hempstone has documented the type and outcome of US assistance leading up to the 1992 election. But what, exactly, was the level of US development assistance to the constitution process between 2000 and 2005? USAID likely provided some technical assistance to the constitution commission and to civil society for education and outreach. The dashboard on the ForeignAssistance.gov website reports $13.3 million in USAID democracy and governance grants or contracts between 2002 and 2004. Unfortunately, the dashboard does not offer any details about this assistance.

During this period, the US flag was carried by ambassadors Johnnie Carson (1999–2003) and William Bellamy (2003–2006). In 2003, Ambassador Carson offered private remarks at the Wilson Center, soon after his return from Kenya, commenting on the constitutional reform process, stalemate, and the looming political crisis. As one report of the event states, "Carson said his private opinion was that the Kenya constitution, largely drafted by respected US constitutional scholar and jurist Thurgood Marshall, did not need to be replaced, only amended on several points and rationalized in terms of its flexibility on presidential power."[23]

In making these private comments at an event at the well-respected Wilson Center in Washington, DC, located in the same building as USAID itself, the former ambassador forgot that then-President Kenyatta had significantly altered Kenya's Constitution in 1964. Carson did not seem to recognize that the constitution Justice Marshall had worked on in London was not even close to what was governing Kenyans when Carson was the ambassador. Perhaps Carson was also inflicted with Kenyan's knack for forgetting details, differences, and dilemmas of history. The constitution needed a complete overhaul, not, as Carson opined, "only amendments on several points."[24]

Luckily, Carson had time to reflect on his shortcomings; six years later, he completely reversed his perspective on Kenya's Constitution. On National Public Radio's *Tell Me More,* he stated, "Kenya needs a new constitution, which allows for the sharing of power between the president and the prime minister. It needs to have power devolve from the center to the provinces, and there needs to be a land reform bill which addresses the issues of conflict over land."[25] We do not know what or who led Carson to this new realization but at least he had decided that the constitution needed to be replaced; it no longer needed, "only amendments on several points."[26]

Carson, like many other Kenyans and Americans, understood why Kenya needed its own constitution. While the period between 1997 and 2005 did not produce a new constitution for Kenya, it did create the perfect storm for chaos and upheaval. Many blame the 2007/2008 postelection violence on the centralization of power, weak administrative structures, and lack of checks and balances, all of which stemmed from the amended Independence Constitution. Despite the devastating outcome of the violence—thousands killed, even more displaced, and significant property damage—the violence rocking Kenya became the impetus for a commitment to new reforms, including a new constitution.

A Rocky Path: 2008–2021

Constitutional reform was therefore the number one long-term issue identified in the February 2008 peace agreement. This deal was mediated by former UN Secretary General, Kofi Annan, as chair of the African Union's Panel of Eminent African Personalities, and it brought an end to the violence and destruction that rocked Kenya after the December 2007 general election. On December 11, 2008, almost a year after the election, the president signed into law the Constitution of Kenya Review Act (2008), creating a Committee of Experts (CoE) and giving them 12 months to harmonize previous drafts, gather public comments, and propose a final draft to parliament. The act provided mechanisms for resolving disputes and required the elections commission to hold a public referendum on the final document.

The members of the CoE, comprising both Kenyan and international constitutional experts, were sworn in on March 2, 2009, more than one year after the peace agreement had been signed. Under then–US Ambassador Ranneberger, USAID's constitution-related assistance to the government of Kenya was both deep and wide. It included the Consortium for Elections and Political Process Strengthening (CEPPS); Parliamentary Support Program, implemented by the State University of New York (SUNY); drafting support for the CoE and parliament, implemented by the International Law Development Organization (IDLO); support for the Interim Independent Elections Commission (IIEC), provided through the United Nations Development Program (UNDP) and International Foundation for Electoral Systems (IFES); and the Kenya Transition Initiatives, implemented by Development Alternatives Incorporated (DAI) (2008–2011) and Chemonics International, Inc. (2011–2014).[27]

In using a wide bench for its constitutional reform support toolbox, the United States was able to use appropriate tools during the 18-month gestation period of the new constitution. This time began with the swearing-in of the CoE and ended with the August 2010 referendum. Each phase was punctuated by a unique and creative obstruction that kept reformers, including USAID staff, contractors, and grant recipients, constantly observing, forecasting, and strategizing. I felt like I was a Kenyan marathon runner who had entered the wrong race, dodging external obstacles in a steeplechase. At the same time, I was dealing with overarching internal obstacles—internal team conflict, leadership mistakes, rules, and policies. Below, I discuss these external and internal obstacles and how we approached each one while trying to support the Kenyan Constitution process.

Obstruction: Funding

On May 11, 2009, the CoE turned to USAID to help them get started; they had yet to receive any financial support from the government of Kenya. They had no office, equipment, or support staff. At the US embassy, we recognized the situation was not only symptomatic of a glaring lack of political will to support the CoE but was also demoralizing members and significantly undermining the pursuit and delivery of a new constitution for Kenya. Failure to start on the right track meant not delivering a new constitution and a high likelihood of renewed violence and bloodshed. It was imperative that the process would not be stalled by political brinkmanship or an unwillingness on the part of antireform elements in Kenya.[28]

The chairperson of the CoE publicly revealed this funding obstacle. He wrote in the forward to the CoE's final report, dated October 11, 2010, that "I can now confirm as true the rumour that owing to delays in the release of funds by the Government, the Committee Members initially actually contributed money from their own pockets to purchase stationery and other materials to at least commence the process."[29] Section 3.5 of the report stated, "a lot of time was lost in establishing offices and securing resources for the review process. In fact, the CoE commenced its work without financial resources and appropriate accommodation for its work."[30]

USAID mobilized quickly when approached. During our internal review process, my program team bluntly claimed that the CoE cannot work if they don't have desks and paper. We awarded two grants three days after receiving the request. Contractors were mobilized and within five weeks, the partitioning and carpet work was 90 percent completed. We delivered in-kind assistance for the renovation, carpeting, wiring, and network of the CoE's office.[31] We provided basic office furniture, equipment, and stationery. This rapid assistance was modeled after the "ministry-in-a-box" approach, which USAID had used in war-torn Iraq and Sudan between 2003 and 2007. In 2005, I had been involved with USAID's assistance to Sudan before moving to Kenya, designing grants to provide rapid, visible, tangible, and useful equipment to unfurnished South Sudan ministries. The CoE's enabling legislation required the CoE to "keep a verbatim record of the proceedings of each and every meeting."[32] USAID purchased and delivered recording and transcription equipment to facilitate the CoE's charge. Rapid, visible assistance is often a catalyst for others to act. USAID's impetus pushed Kenya's Ministry of Justice to deliver furniture while USAID was supplying computers, photocopiers, and office equipment. The office was ready before the end of June.

By July 2009, sparked by USAID's confidence, other donors stepped forward with their support.[33] While these donors, primarily European, had the funds, they had been hesitant from the outset to release them because they wanted the Kenyan government to demonstrate its good-will and commitment. At USAID, however, we were convinced that key people within the government were unwilling and, therefore, they had to be pressured into releasing funds.

Obstruction: Public Review

Thanks to USAID, the CoE could respond to the starter's gun and get to work. On November 17, 2009, they unveiled the Harmonized Draft of the Constitution of the Republic of Kenya in an elaborate ceremony at the Kenyatta International Conference Center in downtown Nairobi across from the parliament building. This draft harmonized a decade of previous drafts, including elements of the Bomas and Wako drafts. Over the next two days, the CoE released 450,000 copies in national daily newspapers. Kenya, however, had over 11 million potential voters and these voters had a 30-day period to comment on the draft. With the public clamoring to get hold of their own copy and unable to critically read the text for themselves, my colleagues and I were worried that partisan interests may use divisive political rhetoric to mislead the public and derail informed debate on the document. What easier way would there be to convince people to vote "No" if you can control their understanding of the content?

The CoE once again turned to the US government for assistance. We responded with a $550,000 in-kind grant to print and deliver 1,250,000 copies (800,000 in English, 450,000 in Swahili) of the harmonized draft. This number was driven primarily by the printing capacity of the three major newspapers. USAID also supported the transportation, labor, and advertising efforts for their distribution across the nation. The CoE also relied on traditional media, including radio and television talk shows, and social media to reach those who could not get or read a copy of the printed text.

USAID is often accused of taking too long to act. In this case, however, USAID quickly finalized a budget; secured internal approvals for the grant; authorized an exception from USAID's strict branding require-ments because a document of national sovereignty, such as a constitu-tion, cannot be branded with the USAID logo; and issued checks to the printing companies only a few days after receiving the grant concept from the CoE.

Public response to the draft was overwhelming and the CoE received approximately 1.7 million recommendations in over 50,000 submissions.[34] The CoE worked through the December holidays to revise the document and presented a new draft to parliament on January 8, 2010. USAID also supported the International Development Law Organization (IDLO), a public institution, with a grant to provide technical assistance in the form of a "selected group of international scholars to produce reports analyzing the text of the entire draft constitution at various stages for the COE."[35]

Kenya's Parliamentary Select Committee (PSC) proposed additional recommendations the CoE considered before presenting the proposed constitution on February 23, 2010, to parliament for final amendments and approval. The next mountain began to appear on the horizon. Parliament could, technically, change the document.

Obstruction: 150 Amendments

The law required parliament garner a two-thirds majority to approve *any* amendment to the draft. Members of Parliament (MPs) introduced 150 amendments and, given their strict deadline of 30 days, had to complete all debating and voting within a condensed timeframe. In the past, parliament would have been the president's rubber stamp; the Kenyan public would have not been able to witness any debates and votes. However, in 2000 when the Kenyan National Assembly secured structural autonomy, USAID and the United Kingdom began a 15-year program to modernize, reform, and strengthen Kenya's parliament. A major thrust of the parliamentary reforms was to create a more open and transparent legislative process, which the Kenyan people could easily access and understand. As part of this process, in 2008, USAID began supporting the Office of the Speaker of the House and the Parliamentary Broadcast Unit with $1 million of broadcasting equipment and technical support to enhance parliament's ability to broadcast radio and TV programs to the public. For the first time in Kenyan history, thanks to USAID, the Kenyan public could listen to or watch, firsthand, their elected officials. When I was young, Kenya's parliament was not open to the public, nor was it ever a school field trip destination. Now, decades later, I felt extremely privileged to be able to enter such hallowed grounds during the planning for former Vice President Biden's visit to Kenya in June 2010.

Serving as USAID's control officer for the vice president's visit to the Kenyan parliament was an exhausting experience. We showcased USAID's technical assistance, the broadcast equipment, and parliament's role in the constitutional process before the then–US vice president met with Kenya's Speaker of the House and other Kenyan officials behind closed doors.

Only a few months earlier, in March 2010, Kenyans were able to monitor parliament's debate and votes on their constitution through this USAID-funded equipment. Like many others, I watched the proceedings with bated breath, recognizing that many of the proposed amendments would erode some of the gains proposed in the new constitution. Given the need for a two-thirds majority and the introduction of polarizing amendments, parliament failed to agree on any one of the amendments. On April 1, 2010, thankfully defeated by their own self-serving interests, parliament unanimously approved the exact document the CoE had delivered. The document, with Kenyans watching, had overcome yet another obstacle. We thought the next one would be the referendum itself. But we were wrong.

Obstruction: Two Words

Parliament's approval of the proposed constitution passed the baton to the attorney general. He was to publish the proposed constitution within 30 days; a referendum was to follow within 60 days. But those opposed to the document had another trick up their sleeve. During the publication process, Kenyans discovered nearly 2,000 altered copies. According to *The Guardian,* a British newspaper, "To deliver Kenyans a fair constitution after more than 20 years, a committee of experts used 47,793 words. To derail the reform, someone secretly added two. The attempted sabotage occurred at the official government printer. . . . someone at the printing plant was able to add the words 'national security' to a key clause on citizen's fundamental rights."[36]

While those copies were destroyed and the words removed, the ramifications for constitutional reform were significant. According to the late Aga Khan IV, a global spiritual leader who has been deeply engaged with the development of many countries worldwide, including Kenya, "there's a recognition that constitutional issues in many countries need to be addressed. How that is addressed is very, very complex. Look at what's happening in Kenya. You have a constitutional process, the constitution was printed, and somebody, between the approval of the constitution and the printing of the document introduced two words which changed the whole nature of the constitution."[37]

USAID did not have a role in helping overcome this obstacle. No one knows who blew the whistle or why. If an investigation was conducted, the results were never publicized. But three elements are clear. First, there were three ironic facts relating to the attorney general at the time. He was the same individual after whom the Wako draft was named, the same draft Kenyans rejected at the polls in 2005. Second, he would go on to formally hand then-President Kibaki the new constitution on August 27, 2010. He stood in front of the Kenyan public and the diplomatic corps and then posed next to the smiling president, all while holding up the signed document. One result was the infamous picture of this moment being splashed across many newspapers around the globe. Third, the president's signature was placed on the document that would become both his and the attorney general's layoff letter, or pink slip. The new constitution fired three people: the attorney general and the auditor general, both of whom could continue in office for a maximum of 12 months, and the president, who would thereafter be ineligible to run again.[38]

If some of those altered copies had been distributed, two versions of the constitution would have been circulating before the referendum, and Kenyans would have lost all confidence in the fragile process.

Obstruction: Educating Voters

How does one empower voters to decide on a constitution? His Highness the Aga Khan, who had established primary and secondary schools as well as universities in Asia and Africa, noted this quandary in May 2010, a few months before the Kenyan referendum: "You consult a population that has no knowledge whatsoever about the choices of constitutional government, about the success rate of constitutional government, about the problems of constitutional governments, and you ask them to vote. Intellectually, what is the credibility of that?"[39] Many Kenyans, both urban and rural, could not internalize the intricacies of the draft document. I could engage in a critical conversation with only about 10 percent of my Kenyan and foreign staff in offices in Nairobi, Kisumu, and Eldoret. Even as late as Kenya's 2019 census, nearly half of the population had only completed primary school and a quarter had finished secondary school. Less than 4 percent had completed education beyond the secondary level.[40]

Although the lack of credibility in the results of a referendum voted on by uneducated populations is a concern anywhere, it is an unavoidable side-effect of democracy. The alternative is to take away power from the people. Referendums in the US are not necessarily better. At least once a year, I pore over a ballot and accompanying instructions as I decide on the referendum questions in front of me. The wording of these questions is extremely nuanced. I must read the opinions of both sides, do my own research, and come to my own conclusions. Most of my peers either elect not to vote on these questions or gloss over the fine print before selecting one. For example, in the United States, in Washington state during the 2020 election, turnout was 84 percent (4.12 million voters). One hundred and seventy thousand people did not vote on the only referendum question on the ballot, while up to 360,000 chose to skip at least one of five advisory questions.[41] Of those who voted, many likely simply remembered the last one-line slogan they saw on a lawn sign.[42]

In 2020, Washingtonians had six separate questions on a single mail-in ballot and could select either "Yes" or "No" for each. In 2010, Kenyans had to accept or reject a package of over 260 clauses. Approximately 24 percent of Washingtonians had a bachelor's degree or higher compared to only 3.5 percent of Kenyans.[43] How could Kenyans weigh the overall good and bad? Their decisions could not be statistical; they could not decide to vote "Yes" if they simply liked at least 230 clauses. Some clauses were much more important than others. Some example decisions included whether the president should be allowed unlimited terms in office, if the president should have power over the judiciary and legislature, or whether the chief justice should have a lifetime appointment. None of these can be taken lightly. In contrast, using the Washington state example, deciding whether a supreme court justice nominee should have 15 years of relevant experience instead of 10 or 20 is, by comparison, likely insignificant. Washington state only has one requirement for its supreme court justices. They must be certified to practice law in the state, while the US Constitution has no such qualifications for its Supreme Court justices.

My program team at USAID was concerned that individuals opposed to Kenya's Constitution would use one or two clauses to convince people to reject the entire document. Even worse, those selected clauses could have little significance in the big picture. Kenyans, like Americans, can easily be swayed to focus on one or two key issues and ignore the rest; in Kenya, the draft constitution had many key issues to choose among. Our task was to help Kenyan organizations spread the word about the upcoming constitution referendum, educate people on its content, and remind people that they were not voting "Yes" or "No" in the abstract. We explained that they were at a significant crossroads in Kenya's history: Would Kenya return to the dark 2007/2008 postelection violence, or would it change course and embrace a new constitution? We wanted people to see this referendum within the larger context of the horrific violence that rocked the nation in 2007 and 2008 and the subsequent commitments made in Agenda 4.

USAID was one of many organizations (United Nations, other development partners, and Kenyan civil society) facilitating civic education, voter registration, and get-out-the-vote campaigns. Some civic education efforts trained facilitators who traveled out to communities and led discussion groups in town halls, outdoor events, places of worship, and community centers. Other efforts focused on mass media—print, radio, television, and social—to reach a larger audience. USAID's efforts also included a third approach, directly reaching the masses through arts and entertainment. These were designed to draw large crowds across the country. USAID's *Kenya ni Wajibu Wangu* (*Kenya is My Responsibility*) roadshow series included several prominent entertainers, a theater troupe, musicians, and a traveling art exhibit, *Kenya Burning,* to evoke a reflection of the horrors of the election violence. We wanted our partners to focus on the key messages to ensure the audience focused on the big picture and could separate fact from myth. I spent many hours assisting the musicians and theater groups as they composed and rehearsed their various scripts to narrow their focus on these key messages. I even tested my staff with pop quizzes to maximize their confidence in separating fact from fiction.

But the biggest hurdle lay ahead: the voter registration and the referendum itself. Because of the disastrous 2007 election, the entire voter rolls had been deleted. The new elections commission had to start over. Voter registration was an ongoing effort we supported through mobilization campaigns and public awareness. While the media and civil society were actively calling on youth to register and get out to vote for their own futures, the elderly were being forgotten. Or, at least, they were not being actively targeted. Kenya's future was as important for them as it was for the youth, and the elderly may have held the institutional memory of the early constitutional amendments. Needing a quick and efficient tactic, I approached my own 99-year-old Kenyan grandmother in Mombasa. During one of my regular personal visits, I invited her to be a showcase for all elderly Kenyans. She wholeheartedly agreed and we organized a media-covered visit to a local voter registration center. Evening television anchors picked up the story, with one showing the video clip and acknowledging that while everyone was focused on the youth, it was as equally important to get Kenya's elders to participate. Some of my staff later commented that I would do anything for Kenya, even use my own grandmother! I saw the strategy as yet another tool in the USAID toolbox.

Obstruction: Referendum

The new Interim Independent Election Commission (IIEC) had been created after the signing of the peace agreement, as the previous commission had been completely disbanded. The IIEC had managed a few special elections, geographically limited to one or two constituencies, but the 2010 referendum was their first nationwide vote. It was their first true test. Kenyans and the international community were anxious to see their performance. USAID, along with many other donors, had been supporting the IIEC through a United Nations pooled fund. The IIEC also requested, and USAID provided, 250 smartphones (Black-Berries) to facilitate communication during the referendum and to securely transmit the results. Only the senior elections officer in each constituency could use their assigned phone, while the receiving server in Nairobi validated the transmitting phone numbers before recording the results. Paper copies then followed before the results were finalized. USAID, therefore, played a small but important role in the referendum. The Kenyan people felt more secure knowing USAID (and specifically Kenya's own Barack Obama) had donated the smartphones commonly and affectionately referred to as "BarackBerries."[44]

On August 4, 2010, the US embassy geared up with all hands on deck. Security was tight and nerves were on edge because this would be the first nationwide election since the disastrous December 2007 presidential vote. The embassy had deployed staff around the country to observe and report back to both the IIEC and the embassy's command center. My own team, comprising Americans and Kenyans, were also dispatched. Because of my Kenyan background and my ability to blend in as a Kenyan—I speak the same language and we share similar attitudes, cultures, and histories—the embassy officials assigned me to the tallying center. In other words, I could blend in and "pretend" to be Kenyan. While all my sworn loyalties were to America and its foreign policy objectives, I did not want to see Kenya fail, cheat, or lie to its own people.

The tallying center was located at the Bomas of Kenya, which had also housed the 2002–2004 National Constitutional Conferences and would later become headquarters for the 2013 election. The Bomas of Kenya is a large tourist village located six miles west of city center, adjacent to this affluent Karen area, in the vicinity of the famous Giraffe Center where my visitors could kiss a real giraffe. When I was growing up, it was a mandatory school field trip experience. When I was posted to Kenya with USAID, I made it a mandatory weekend stop for all my visitors to experience the dance, culture, and living conditions of Kenya's diverse tribes.

The facility itself appeals to organizers of conferences, constitutional conventions, and elections because it is a large, secure facility, away from dense urban areas. It also has a variety of multiuse buildings, facilities, and parking areas. Its unique auditorium can seat up to 3,000 people in a completely circular, tiered design like a circus tent. This allows participants to look down onto a large central floor. The circular design prevents any one section from being the dais or focus; no political party can claim to be in a privileged front seating area.

My experience that night was exciting, yet, in retrospect, it was relatively uneventful. Of course, there were ups and downs for both campaigns. The lowest peaks occurred when the results transmission system seemed to freeze, and 20 minutes would go by with no updates. The lagging campaign at the time would inevitably question the integrity of the system. Thankfully, the IIEC could explain how the system actually worked and others, such as myself, could understand and articulate this explanation back to our respective embassies and capitals. We would remind the campaign agents of the counting and verification processes happening overnight across thousands of polling stations around the country. Campaigns, media, and the international community all had their own staff in multiple polling stations as well as in the constituency centers. The system was built with redundancies. For example, when a presiding officer announced results at a constituency center, the formal results would then be transmitted to the Bomas of Kenya, and the media, campaigns, and international community would transmit the same results to their own third-party tallying centers around Nairobi.

Isolated reports of mistakes or fake news riled up the campaigns for a few minutes each time, just as it would in any country. Human nature drives losers to vent and winners to gloat. Throughout the night, I sent regular email reports to the US embassy and, by the time my replacement had arrived in the early hours of the morning, it was clear Kenya would be embracing a new constitution in a few days. When Kenya's president promulgated the constitution in a pompous event at Nairobi's Uhuru Park a few weeks later, the final "Yes" tally stood at 68.6 percent of voters. Kenyans had indeed heralded in a new dawn.

The next hurdle to jump was the aggressive legislative agenda needed to implement the far-reaching and visionary constitutional provisions. The constitution also had to be protected against those who would want to change it.

Obstruction: Wholesale Amendments

Kenya's Constitution identified laws that were needed, and it established a strict timetable for each one. It also identified penalties for noncompliance. Parliament, with a two-thirds majority, could authorize a onetime, one-year extension for each delayed bill. If parliament continued to delay, any individual could petition Kenya's high court for action, and the court could advise the president to dissolve parliament. This was, indeed, a visionary document; parliamentarians act when their own jobs are at stake. But parliamentarians could also attack the constitution.

As noted earlier in this chapter, the Independence Constitution was gutted by the 1964 amendments. In 2020, Kenyans feared their new constitution was going to be ravaged again. In early 2020, then-President Kenyatta and opposition leader Raila Odinga joined forces to promote a slew of amendments packaged as the Building Bridges Initiative (BBI). However, on May 23, 2021, the High Court of Kenya, operating under the new constitution, unanimously put a stop to the process. The court simply reminded Kenyans that the president did not have authority under the 2010 Constitution to initiate an amendment; these may only originate in parliament or from the public. On appeal, Kenya's court of appeal upheld this decision on August 20, 2021. The "Supreme Court judges said the president had acted unlawfully when spearheading the reforms" in its March 31, 2022, decision four months before the presidential elections.[45] The amendments were dead and BBI did not surface during the campaign season that followed. The BBI amendments would have undone many protective provisions made by the 2010 Constitution, including judicial independence and a separation between the executive and the legislative.

Internal US Obstacles

In the preceding sections, I described how reformers dodged obstacles in the constitution-making process using a variety of instruments from our toolkit, much as a Kenyan marathon runner wins her steeplechase by employing a variety of approaches to overcome each hurdle. Now, I turn to the overarching internal US government obstacles we faced as we tried to use each device in the toolbox.

American policymakers and international development practitioners may be convinced that helping countries on their constitution-making path directly contributes to stability in those countries and, therefore, depending on the country, to our own peace and security, as identified in our national security strategies. But such assistance is likely to attract attention. Those who oppose our role in such activities, especially those who do not want a constitution that protects the public instead of those who hold power, may oppose our actions. This opposition may manifest in either direct or indirect attacks on our policy or assistance. Practitioners should also be aware of internal US government obstacles (leadership, symbolism, attitudes, laws) that may unintentionally hamper or even prevent the best ideas from being implemented.

Leadership

The head of the US government's presence in Kenya, or in any country, is the ambassador; their official title is Ambassador Extraordinary and Plenipotentiary of the United States of America. This mouthful of a title is standard for many nations' ambassadors. A plenipotentiary is a diplomat who has full powers, that is, the authority to sign a treaty or convention on behalf of their sovereign. In the case of the United States, that sovereign, the president, nominates ambassadors, whom the Senate must then approve. Every time I met with the US ambassador to Kenya, whether in a large meeting or a discussion on the back porch of their official residence, I would emblaze this in my mind's eye: "I am meeting with the representative of the president of the United States of America."

The term "plenipotentiary" is rational and applicable to an ambassador. However, the other word, "extraordinary," which comprises part of an ambassador's title, causes me to ask, "But why or how does an ambassador become *extraordinary?*" This term is not unique to American ambassadors; rather, the United States adopted an older, widespread European tradition. We dropped many archaic and hierarchical European traditions when we gained independence from the British—our judges and attorneys no longer wear wigs, we do not refer to mayors as "Your Worship," and we do not have a royal family. These titles artificially bloat one's self-image. Many Kenyans have fallen into this trap, including, unfortunately, several staff, consultants, and grantees I worked with between 2008 and 2014 and who ran for office in the 2013 or 2017 elections.

My most vivid memory of this bloated self-worth came during the *Kenya ni Wajibu Wangu (Kenya is My responsibility)* roadshow we funded in the town of Naivasha, an hour away from Nairobi. With a few thousand people present, and the American ambassador on his way to speak at the event, we received an unexpected visitor. The mayor of the city of Nakuru drove up in his motorcade. Nakuru and Naivasha are two separate towns more than 40 miles apart. However, under the pre-2010 governance structure, he had authority over Naivasha. He clearly wanted to pander to the Americans. He was wearing a formal suit and his large gold chain, a symbol of his power and position. He asked to be escorted to the VIP (Very Important Person) tent. My boss and I told him politely that the event was for the public, for all to mingle, and there was no VIP tent. Surprised, he asked, "But where will the US ambassador sit?" Addressing him as "Sir," we politely told him the ambassador would arrive, mingle with the public, give a speech on stage, visit the art exhibition, and then leave.

He was offended, not only by the lack of a platform for him to sit on but also by how we addressed him. He bluntly told us, two low-level

American diplomats, to address him as "Your Worship, the Mayor." My boss and I, a Christian and a Muslim, respectively, had the same thought, namely, that we do not worship human beings. After all, we had been working closely together for two years in Nairobi. My boss turned to the mayor and said politely, "Sir, as a good Christian, I only worship God!" The mayor was speechless; he turned, strode to his car, and drove away. His bloated self-worth had popped.

But why has the United States held onto the term "extraordinary" for its ambassadors? Why has it kept other distinguishing titles? In the United States, the word "honorable" is still used for judges, US legislators, and even cabinet secretaries. The title "honorable" should not be given or inherited with a position; it has to be earned, and it cannot be earned easily. The term "extraordinary" falls somewhere in between; it is more than "honorable" and less than "your worship." But to designate someone as "extraordinary" is to put them way above all others. In other words, the United States is saying that its ambassador (to Kenya, for example) is supposed to be extraordinary and way above all Americans living and working there.

This expectation, on me as an American diplomat working in Kenya, was sometimes difficult to digest and act upon. This was especially the case when it came to Scott Gratian, the second of the three American ambassadors to Kenya I interacted with, and I was not alone. The "Ambassador's score for attention to morale is the second lowest of more than 80 recently inspected chiefs of mission, and his score on interpersonal relations is the lowest" according to the State Department Office of Inspector General's survey, conducted among the 400 direct-hire Americans in 2011.[46] The survey received a higher-than-average response rate of 72 percent, suggesting that people felt compelled to offer their feedback. Nine hundred other Kenyans and Americans who worked for the US government in Kenya, including myself, were not surveyed because of our employment status, but we all felt the same way.

At the time, my confidence in then-President Obama also became diminished because he appointed Gratian as his Ambassador Extraordinary and Plenipotentiary. The Inspector General's report reads like a work of fiction, and my Kenyan colleagues outside of the embassy, the ones we funded and worked with, were quite amused by the content. Some of the highlights that criticize the ambassador include:

- Notwithstanding his talk about the importance of mission staff doing the right thing, the Ambassador by deed or word has often encouraged staff to do the opposite.
- He subsequently sought—but did not obtain—access to individual survey responses that would have violated the anonymity of the respondents.
- He ordered a commercial Internet connection installed in his embassy office bathroom. . . . He drafted and distributed a mission policy authorizing himself and other mission personnel to use commercial email for daily communication of official government business.
- During the inspection, the Ambassador continued to use commercial email for official government business.

The story about the ambassador's internet protocol resurfaced in 2015 during the email server debacle surrounding former Secretary of State Hillary Clinton. Gratian accused Clinton of a double standard because he served under her before being pushed out of office, partly because of his email and internet behavior.[47] The *Daily Mail,* a British newspaper, played up the story, stating, "Retired Air Force General Scott Gration was US ambassador to Kenya for 13 months between 2011 and 2012, departing after a scathing performance report blasted his leadership style and determined he created security risks by running his own one-person IT department."[48]

Ambassador Gratian served from May 2011 to July 2012, resigning, unsurprisingly, before the Inspector General's report was made public in August 2012. His behavior was galaxies away from the "extraordinary" label an ambassador holds. For six months, following his departure, we had no ambassador until Ambassador Robert Godec (2013–2019) arrived in Nairobi in February 2013. He was a no-nonsense, career diplomat who had to deal with two pressing issues: his predecessor's aftermath at the US embassy and Kenya's 2013 election, the first true test of the nation's new constitution.

Two former US ambassadors to Kenya epitomized the title "Plenipotentiary," the spokesperson for American policy, position, and posturing. The first, ambassador Hempstone (1989–1993), pushed Kenya hard and has been credited for bringing multiparty democracy to Kenya. His main adversary was Kenya's former President Moi, and their vicious sparring punctuated the ambassador's four-year assignment in Kenya. Hemp-stone wrote, "Moi, his political arteries clogged with the cholesterol of old age, paranoia, and inadequacy, understood and preferred the old ways to the new, repression to reconciliation."[49] The Kenyan government tried to get Hempstone out, attacking him both in Kenya and the United States. Hempstone noted that the *"Kenya Times* advised me to 'ask to be transferred,' failing which, it declared, I should be 'recalled.'"[50] Later, "the campaign to get me out of Kenya now extended to Washington. It was now waged on a number of fronts. Moi directed two American lob-bying firms working for the government of Kenya to launch an offensive of vilification against me on the Hill; reportedly he made $250,000 avail-able to buy or rent congressmen willing to participate."[51]

But the US State Department stood by its ambassador "Extraordi-nary and Plenipotentiary." Deputy Secretary of State Eagleburger wrote to Ambassador Hempstone on October 25, 1990, saying, "The *only* danger you now face is that you will begin to second-guess yourself and your actions because of your worries about support back here. Don't fall vic-tim to that disease! Everyone else around here does. From you I expect your normal, nasty, sweet, self-effacing, modest, tough self!"[52] History has shown that Hempstone followed this advice. From the time former President Moi left Kenya's State House in 2002 until his death in 2020, he remained a powerful force behind Kenya's political structures and remained true to his autocratic ideas of governance. At the age of 85, he was a key leader of the campaign *against* Kenya's 2010 Constitution.

Michael Ranneberger, the US ambassador to Kenya during the 2007 election, postelection violence, and Kenya's recovery, reflected Hemp-stone's efforts and drive. Kenya's top daily newspapers compared the two ambassadors, with *Daily Nation* publishing an article titled "Kenya: Rogue Ambassadors—It Did Not Start with Ranneberger" on December 27, 2010, and *The Standard* writing, "Ranneberger's tenure as ambassador can be closely compared to former US Ambassador Smith Hempstone and British High Commissioner Edward Clay, who equally had their share of controversies" on April 24, 2011.[53] Reminding Kenyans of the past, the 2011 article went on to say, "Hempstone was nicknamed the 'Rogue Am-bassador' for tongue-lashing the Kenyan regime in the early 1990s."[54] The newspaper laid out the attack on Ranneberger: "[President] Kibaki and [Prime Minister] Raila took Ranneberger to task, for meddling in local affairs.... Earlier, during the constitutional campaigns in July, last year, the 'No' team led by Eldoret North MP William Ruto had demanded the recall of Ranneberger, accusing him of breaching diplomatic protocol.... The worst moment for Ranneberger, however, came during an attempt by MPs to move a censure Motion against him in Parliament."[55]

Like Hempstone, Ranneberger did not waver when faced with external pressure. He emphasized the US government's position in a speech on January 26, 2010, at the American Chamber of Commerce:

> I want to emphasize the unwavering determination of the United States to push for and support implementation of the reform agenda. Achieving implementation of the reform agenda is the central objective of U.S. policy in Kenya. Success in implementing key reforms will help ensure future democratic stability and prosperity. Failure to implement significant reforms will greatly enhance prospects for a violent crisis in 2012 or before, which might well prove worse than the last postelection crisis. Such an outcome is directly counter to both Kenyan and American interests.[56]

In solidifying the nexus among US national interests, reforms, prosperity, peace, and security, Ranneberger openly supported and encouraged USAID's initiatives to promote reforms in Kenya. In the same speech, he distinguished between diplomacy and active financial support, stating, "Specifically related to the reform agenda, we continue not simply to remind the Kenyan Government of its own commitments to change, but to work directly with the Kenyan government and people to support implementation of the reform agenda."[57]

Like Hempstone, Ranneberger did not mince words. His landmark policy and justification speech offers a practical, tangible example of the definition of peace and security. His words exemplify the nexus between stability in Kenya and US national security: "Achieving implementation of the reform agenda is the central objective of U.S. policy in Kenya."[58] He attacks the "entrenched political class" in the same vein as his predecessor, Hempstone.[59] Both recognized the devastation this political class, left unchecked, has brought and could continue to bring to Kenya. Lastly, he encouraged US involvement, promoting US support of local government and civil society in advancing those reforms and personally involving himself in activities such as the *Kenya ni Wajibu*

Wangu roadshow, the Kenya Burning photography exhibition, the El-doret judiciary project, and other US government supported initiatives helping Kenyans with their reform agenda.

The ambassador did not lose sight of the pivotal and fundamental role the constitution plays in such reforms: "President Obama and Secretary Clinton each recently called both the President and Prime Minister to urge them to reach a compromise over contentious issues surrounding the new draft constitution."[60]

Ranneberger established credibility by referring to the then–US president, Barack Obama, by name. This worked because Kenyans considered Obama the first Kenyan president of America because his father was Kenyan. I had already moved to Kenya when, in November 2008, Obama won the US presidential election. In response, Kenya declared a national holiday and billboards with Obama's name and picture sprung up across the capital. Ranneberger made it clear at the top levels of the US government, to both the president and Secretary of State, that the US Embassy staff were closely following the constitutional process. But Ranneberger also made it clear, dispelling myths and fake news, that the United States did not take a particular stand on any of the content of Kenya's Constitution.

This fine line became extremely important to USAID's reform efforts. Ranneberger articulated the delicate position the United States was in—simultaneously pushing for a new constitution, identifying the key principles the United States wanted to see, but steering clear of differences over specific content:

> Though we have not put forward any specific proposals, it is important that whatever draft is agreed upon, first, ensures a coherent government system which limits power though a system of checks and balances and, second, ensures full participation and fair representation of all the people of Kenya. . . . The President and Secretary made clear that tough compromises need to be made on the constitution and that implementation of the reform agenda must be greatly accelerated.[61]

I frequently had to explain this balance when meeting with members of Kenyan civil society. I had to make it absolutely clear the United States was not advocating any particular position. My message was direct: "We don't care if Kenyans select a presidential or parliamentary system." Former Vice President Biden had been unequivocal, speaking three months before the referendum, when addressing University of Nairobi students. He clarified, "The United States strongly supports the process of constitutional reform. . . . But, let me repeat, this is your decision, your decision alone. And the people of Kenya must make this choice—a choice for Kenya by Kenyans."[62]

The US ambassador was more specific in his 2010 speech: America wanted checks and balances, participation, and fair representation of *all* Kenyans, not a winner-take all solution, and measures to deemphasize ethnic-based alliances.[63] These ethnic-based alliances percolated to the top of the Kenyan political system with the introduction of multiparty elections in the 1990s. In this regard, then-President Moi was right, given the entrenchment of ethnic politics, multiparty democracy could devastate Kenya.

But Moi was relating to Kenya's conditions under its old constitution. The measures in the new constitution will prevail over the ethnic divides Kenya has experienced over its first half-century. Indeed, the early years, the first decade, have proven this belief is true. The key provision in the constitution resembles the much-criticized US electoral college system, although it is much simpler. It encompasses constitutional devolution (multiple counties, each with its own legislative and executive bodies), a minimum threshold for electing the president (the winner must secure at least 25 percent of the votes cast in each of more than half of the counties), and protection against haphazard constitutional amendments (at least 25 percent of registered voters in each of at least half of the counties must participate in a constitutional amendment referendum).

Lastly, Ambassador Ranneberger offered the only carrot he had at hand, the hint of more aid: "Thus, taken together, the development of a consensus draft and the holding of a successful referendum would constitute a very significant watershed for reforms. My government, at the highest levels, would respond very positively to this."[64]

A note about sources is important at this juncture. The extracts from *The Standard,* the *Daily Nation,* and the Ambassador's speech at the American Chamber of Commerce articulate the importance of the constitution process, USAID's support of reforms, and the roles of American ambassadors in our foreign policy. As a former embassy official, with access to classified information, I was privy to other material and even contributed to some of the sensitive reporting. There are other sources, positive and negative, available on the internet that criticize and praise Ranneberger and USAID's roles in Kenya. They cite classified information. Some have been leaked to the public; some are simply false or have been significantly altered. As a former USAID staff member, I cannot use this material in my book; nor would I want to.[65] Doing so could threaten the safety and lives of American diplomats and their sources. The proliferation of leaked classified information across the internet makes America weaker because reliable sources of information are less forthcoming, and people are now less willing to talk to American diplomats. I experienced this myself; my own sources were hesitant to discuss local, antireform, or extremism-related topics after sensitive and classified information was spread via WikiLeaks.

The overarching message here, to all ambassadors, US government diplomats, and development officers, is if you speak out for what you believe in within the confines of US foreign policy and for what is best for US national security, you will face strong opposition and personal attacks. Two critics of US ambassadors, both of whom used public and subversive tactics to discredit the United States, were William Ruto (since 2022, Kenya's president; at the time, however, he was Kenya's minister for higher education) and former President Moi. Unsurprisingly, they were the most vocal members of the "No" campaign trying to get Kenyans to reject the new constitution. In fact, Ruto, before becoming deputy president in 2013, was one of the six Kenyans indicted by the ICC Pre-Trial Chamber II on March 8, 2011, on charges of crimes against humanity for his alleged participation in the postelection violence of 2007/2008.

The inherent weaknesses of some of America's ambassadors constitute one obstacle that America's foreign policy and international development specialists must overcome. These weaknesses may manifest in unprofessionalism, which brings down the entire US embassy, or the absence of people taking a strong stand, which leaves little in the public domain for historians to reflect on. Both would leave the United States weaker in its quest for peace and security. Had Ambassador Ranneberger not been in a leadership position when Kenya sought its new constitution, KTI and its partners could not have implemented creative solutions to address each obstacle in our path.

Symbolism

Leadership weaknesses can be addressed: People can be encouraged to resign, or they can be replaced. A more subtle obstacle, one that the tools are powerless against, is the mighty semantic symbolism America's foreign assistance uses. USAID's presence in Kenya, or in any country with a USAID presence, is known as "The Mission." In 2010, USAID had over 60 such missions worldwide, and over half were in Africa. The head of USAID's presence is the mission director. This term both baffles and bothers me. Why is USAID referred to as a "mission"? I had a lot of time to reflect on this, as I was constantly exposed to the term between 2008 and 2015; my office was based at the USAID mission in Nairobi.

I have two separate but related hypotheses about the use of the term. The first relates to a missionary: a Christian-specific evangelical effort attempting to spread the faith across the globe. Christian missionaries from Europe are well traveled across North and South America, India, and Africa. They are still active and widespread across Africa. Ambassador Gratian told those of us at USAID that his parents had been missionary teachers in the Belgian Congo. Was the United States using its development arm to spread Christianity?

Few Kenyans were concerned about the term "mission," perhaps because most of them are Christian. However, I was concerned, as were some of the Kenyan Muslims I interacted with during our programming and US embassy outreach efforts that focused on Muslims. Perhaps I was privy to discussions my other American colleagues were not, including questions around the term "mission" and, specifically, whether the United States was trying to promote Christianity in Kenya. The American wars in Afghanistan and Iraq (2001–2021), and the public's attitude toward Muslims in post-9/11 America, did little to dispel this myth.

I did not find a single shred of evidence for this theory during my deployment. Nor did I see even a hint of it in any other country I went to on behalf of USAID. That list is not short: It comprises Colombia, Jordan, Zimbabwe, Côte d'Ivoire, Chad, Sudan, South Sudan, and Pakistan. Therefore, to reconcile the use of this term, I must separate "mission" from "missionary." A mission is a task, vocation, or purpose.[66] The United States has a mission, or a task or purpose in Kenya, and USAID constitutes the actors trying to execute that mission.

Attitude

Overarching every government employee's experience is the dreaded bureaucracy. This is another internal obstacle to America's success in advancing peace and security using the instruments in its toolbox. This is because the bureaucracy, while well-intentioned, can stifle creativity. Ambassador Hempstone captured this problem quite succinctly and appropriately: "Dealing with most of the rest of the bureaucracy was like wrestling in a bathtub of jello [*sic*]. There was always a regulation, cited gleefully, why something needed to be done couldn't be done and if it could be done, it was bound to take ten times as long to do it as it should have taken."[67] The USAID's OTI, where I worked, was an exception. During my onboarding in their Washington, DC, office, three years before I moved to Nairobi, I was told the word "No" was inappropriate. If someone asked for something, you had to find a way to get it done! Unfortunately, this guidance was not widespread across USAID and the State Department. During my decade with USAID, I saw many dejected USAID professionals simply deflated by the bureaucracy.

My most vivid memory from that time is of a foreign service officer working down the hall from my cubicle in Nairobi. He had recently received an award for completing 25 years of service. I had missed the award ceremony because I had been out of town working on one of our projects. Later, when I congratulated him, his reaction stunned me. I was sincerely portraying admiration for someone who could dedicate 25 years to the US government; I believed he should be respected for his sacrifice because US foreign service officers must move around a lot and sometimes live in dangerous and inhospitable places. However, he shook his head, frowned, and glanced down without making eye contact, as if he were embarrassed to have been with USAID for 25 years. He muttered, "I hate it here, the bureaucracy is stifling."[68] No device in the toolbox can deal with this sort of internal obstacle. Only a shift in individual and collective attitude can change it, the type of attitude OTI instilled into each one of its staff and contractors.

KTI's efforts to help Kenya secure a new constitution faced many internal USAID bureaucracy obstacles. Most notable was our proposal to deliver 1,250,000 copies of the new document, funded by a $550,000 in-kind grant. OTI's internal policies, designed to provide accountability and avoid misuse, allowed the in-country staff to approve activities up to $100,000 and the Washington, DC–based OTI Kenya employees to approve activities up to $250,000. OTI had little experience with larger activities and the initial reaction I received was an overwhelming "not possible" when I tried to gain approval within the 48 hours we had. Nevertheless, we prevailed, with sheer determination and a couple of very late nights.

A second example pertains to the difference in attitude between OTI and the rest of USAID. As discussed in the introduction, we were the "Cowboys in the Basement," seen as having special authorities and exemptions. However, when overseas and, therefore, under the authority of the USAID mission director, we had to abide by both the mission's and OTI's rules. The US government requires all staff to have preapproved travel orders, known as a travel authorization. Given the three to four different approvals required for each authorization, and the need to commit funds specific to the travel, missions would generally require at least a week for the approval process. That delay did not fit KTI's approach, and I spent time and effort establishing a blanket travel authorization for limited in-country travel with no advance notice. It was all in the attitude with which I approached this hurdle; a few conversations with the mission's management and the creative addition of parameters to offset their concerns got me a signed document. Other non-OTI colleagues at the mission were appalled; they thought I had used OTI's authorities to secure the authorization. I had not; I had simply followed the mission's own policies and procedures. The most dejecting moment, unfortunately, came when I explained this to others. Instead of wanting to learn and mimic my strategies, they simply waved me off and grumbled. One cannot blame the bureaucracy, only our own attitudes; we must be vigilant, understand why the bureaucracy exists, and work within it to accomplish our goals.

Other US Laws

Leadership flaws, semantic symbolism, and bureaucracy are three types of internal obstacles to successful programming. United States agencies sometimes must operate under conflicting domestic laws, presenting a different internal challenge. Although each law, by itself, has a particular purpose, it can unintentionally hamstring programming and operations overseas. For example, the basic function of the Freedom of Information Act (FOIA) is "to ensure informed [American] citizens, vital to the functioning of a democratic society."[69] Those opposed to the new constitution and USAID's efforts in Kenya to promote the reform agenda attempted to use the FOIA process to slow us down. They requested copies of all documents pertaining to KTI, our program, hoping to find something to smear us with. This strategy of attacking US efforts overseas was not new; in his book, *Rogue Ambassador,* Hempstone alluded to an effort by then-President Moi to discredit Hempstone by attacking him in Washington, DC.

The most surprising attack USAID endured was one we never anticipated. It harnessed the antiabortion movement in the United States, using a topic Americans are led to believe fundamentally polarizes them. Even worse, because of America's system of federalism, which emphasizes state rights, antiabortion advocates cannot succeed in restricting abortion nationwide. Instead, they try to impart their position to the rest of the world. As USAID was trying to help Kenya move forward with its reform agenda and educate Kenyans on the content of the draft constitution, we received an inquiry from the US Government's Accountability Office (GAO). They wanted to initiate an audit.

As detailed in the GAO's public report, the Siljander Amendment in US appropriations law "prohibits the use of certain U.S. assistance funds to lobby for or against abortion."[70] When I saw the initial request, I was baffled. How were we seen as lobbying for or against abortion? The word "abortion" had never come up in all our years of programming on the reform agenda. The GAO's 2010 desk study morphed into a field visit with interviews in 2011. Specifically, as noted in the report, Congress asked "about the extent and nature of U.S. support and assistance regarding the abortion-related provisions in Kenya's constitution."[71] I saw this as an interesting, multipart puzzle that could have only one outcome: collecting overwhelming evidence that KTI's support for Kenya's constitutional process had nothing to do with abortion.

First, we were trying to get Kenyans to understand the new draft constitution and to get out and vote. We were not lobbying. Second, the draft explicitly prohibited abortion, except in certain cases. Was this "for" or "against" abortion? It was neither. Third, while USAID had provided the CoE with both an office and its equipment, and had funded international experts to advise the committee, USAID neither controlled any of the advice nor directed the experts on what to say (or not to say).

I interpreted the congressional request, likely flagged by someone from the "No" campaign in Kenya, as a direct attack on the US government's efforts to contribute to peace and security in Kenya and, by extension, to America's own peace and security. Luckily, the attack failed. The GAO concluded, much to the chagrin of our anonymous accusers, that USAID had done nothing wrong.

The report went further, coming to an unusual conclusion that stepped beyond the specific case of Kenya. The auditors used the opportunity to discuss the bigger picture, the nexus among constitutions, US foreign policy, US assistance, and peace and security within the context of the 2010 Arab Spring. They noted:

> The United States has long determined that it is vitally important to support nations in undertaking democratic reforms, such as Kenya's constitutional reform. With the current political upheavals in parts of the Middle East and Africa, it is likely that several nations will either establish new constitutions or revise existing ones in the near future. . . . However, constitutional reform can involve a wide spectrum of issues, including abortion and its corresponding U.S. legal restrictions, which are unfamiliar to some U.S. officials who deal with democracy and governance issues.[72]

I was elated when I read the published conclusion. I had purposely and carefully brought up this issue with the audit team when I had been interviewed in Nairobi. I had articulated this angle, one more important than naval-gazing on USAID's efforts in Kenya. The Kenyan Constitution had become law; it could be neither undone nor discredited by an audit on USAID's efforts. I was more concerned about the future, especially about future constitution-making efforts in the Middle East and Africa. My points resonated with the audit team, and they incorporated them into the report's conclusion.

The auditors raised an important issue for US policymakers and development experts. It is easy to get lost in restrictions and to miss critical opportunities to help advance US peace and security interests overseas. They stated, "U.S. officials and implementing partners . . . risk becoming involved in activities that may be interpreted by some as lobbying for or against abortion. Similarly, they may miss appropriate opportunities to provide assistance for fear they may potentially violate this prohibition."[73]

This threat of attack was another incarnation of the ones made on Ambassadors Hempstone and Ranneberger. Following the publication of the inspector general's final report, one of our attackers, the congressman Chris Smith (New Jersey), published a scathing press release that stated the war against USAID in Kenya was far from over. He claimed that "The Obama Administration basically hired surrogates to do its dirty work of abortion promotion in Kenya."[74] Such obstacles to peace and security initiatives are not intentional attacks like those on Hempstone and Ranneberger. Rather, unintentional, unclearly negotiated, and bipartisan language from Congress can hamstring diplomats and development professionals as they attempt to advance peace and security overseas.

The US Constitution

A chapter about US efforts to promote a new constitutional era in Kenya under the rubric of peace and security, and a summary of external and internal obstacles to promoting such programming, must end with the impact of the US Constitution's reach. This 200-year-old document about America interjected a perspective into the Kenyan context that altered elements of USAID's efforts there.

The First Amendment of the US Constitution, ratified in 1791, states, "Congress shall make no law respecting an establishment of religion, or prohibiting the free exercise thereof; or abridging the freedom of speech, or of the press; or the right of the people peaceably to assemble, and to petition the Government for a redress of grievances."[75] While this clause is often debated by USAID and Defense and State Department officials working on countering violent extremism across the globe, we at KTI assumed, incorrectly, that the First Amendment had nothing to do with our reform efforts in Kenya.[76]

Because we were running a nimble, tactical, politically astute program, our team had to keep an attentive eye on potential roadblocks or speed bumps the constitution process may encounter. One topic beginning to bubble up was the Kadhi courts—religious courts in Kenya that address social issues pertaining to Muslims only and have jurisdiction only when both parties voluntarily go before the court. These courts

preexisted Kenya's independence, were enshrined in the 1963 constitution, and did not affect anyone other than Muslims, who represent less
than 20 percent of the population. Yet, opponents of the constitutional
reform process wanted to use the Kadhi courts to fervent opposition.

In response, we planned on offering a rapid response grant to a neutral community group to bring together a variety of community leaders,
politicians, and religious leaders from all faiths to discuss the issue.
The grant was summarized in the weekly update we provided to our
Washington, DC, office. I responded to an inquiry about this summary,
explaining the purpose, amount, and scope, and describing the grantee
and participants in the proposed activity. Thereafter, I was cautioned. I
was informed that I could not invite religious leaders to a USAID-funded
event, even if the topic at hand was the Kenyan Constitution and even
if those leaders represented all faiths. This interpretation of the First
Amendment left me dumbfounded. How could the United States help
Kenya with its reforms if it did not facilitate a dialogue with religious
leaders of all religions?

I wondered why other branches of the same US government, operating under the same US Constitution, could have a radically different
interpretation of the implications of the First Amendment. I had just
attended a US-government-funded *iftar* program (a gathering to break
the daily fast during Ramadhan, the Muslim month of fasting) at the
US ambassador's residence in Nairobi. The ambassador wanted to
respect Kenyan Muslim leaders and their traditions while showing US
support for their efforts in Kenya's postelection recovery. The US State
Department incurred costs related to a large tent and carpets for the sole
purpose of allowing those who wanted to perform their evening prayers.
Since the mid-1990s, all US presidents have hosted at least one similar
event at the White House. A few days after the Nairobi *iftar* event but
before the warning from Washington, DC, I wrapped up a meeting between a Department of Defense colleague and a Kenyan Muslim Imam,
who worked at the Kenya Prisons Division. The Imam was asking the
Defense Department for an extension of funding to conduct moderate
radio programming targeting Muslim youth. With these State and Defense Departments examples fresh in my mind, the USAID effort to bring
religious leaders together to talk about the draft version of the Kenyan
Constitution seemed extremely mundane. Yet, it represented another

internal series of obstacles US development experts and policymakers face: How does the executive branch of the US government apply domestic constitutional law to its activities overseas? Why do different agencies, all operating under the authority of the same US ambassador, interpret US laws differently? Coupled with another internal obstacle, attitude toward innovation and getting to "Yes," a narrow approach to the First Amendment does not help the United States promote peace and security among America's allies overseas.

The ability of a constitution to withstand attacks, provide for the public's needs and wants, protect and promote democracy and democratic structures, and establish a vision for the future are hallmarks of an outstanding document. The more visionary a document, the more it can promote peace and security for the country.

A Visionary Document

The 2010 Kenyan Constitution is the most comprehensive attempt to reverse half a century of colonial history and oppression, fight the power-hungry, and overcome antireformers. Kenya's first chief justice under its new constitution, Chief Justice Mutunga, stated that adopting the constitution in 2010 "is a story of ordinary citizens striving and succeeding to reject or as some may say, overthrow the existing social order."[77] Kenyans outsmarted the existing social order; they steered their own course and played within the rules established by the peace agreement, Agenda 4, the Constitution Reform Act, and the new constitution itself. Former Chief Justice Mutunga captured this choice succinctly: "The Kenyan people chose the route of transformation to end their poverty and deprivation and regain their dignity as well as sovereignty. To this end, Kenyans deliberately steered away from the path of revolution."[78] This demonstrates that the 2007/2008 postelection violence was not the revolution. It was the impetus to a peaceful transformation anchored in a new constitution.

With 264 carefully crafted clauses, each with up to a dozen subclauses, the 2010 Constitution was a valiant (and perhaps successful) attempt to undo, avoid, and prevent past mistakes or weaknesses. It addresses human rights, security, economics, governance, elections, administration, and justice. Chapter 5 of the CoE's final report describes the agreed-upon issues in the harmonized draft constitution while chapter 6 describes the areas of contention.[79]

The CoE did its job, drawing on the experts who worked on the 2004 and 2005 drafts as well as other countries' experiences with constitutional reform. That is what constitutional experts do. They learn from past mistakes. Former US Supreme Court Justice Marshall reflected on his role in drafting Kenya's Independence Constitution in the *Reminiscences of Thurgood Marshall:* "That, to my mind, is really working toward democracy, when you can give to the white man in Africa what you couldn't give the black man in Mississippi. It's good."[80]

The 2010 Kenyan Constitution itself is extremely visionary. For example, it explains how Kenyans should interpret it, it sets a high and necessary standard for gender balance in representatives, and it is only one of three constitutions specifically mentioning abortion (as of 2021).[81] Other countries can only desire constitutional protection for these issues. Instead, they must rely on legislation or case law that can easily be altered.

However, in some cases, it was too visionary, or at least too far ahead of itself. By containing principles Kenyans cannot implement, the constitution weakens itself. One example is the provision for gender representation. The constitution requires "not more than two-thirds of the members of elective or appointed bodies shall be of the same gender."[82] On the surface, this is simple, noble, and unambiguous. It is also extremely futuristic. Today, the intent behind gender-equality measures is to ensure that women, who in 2010 constituted only 10 percent of the parliament (the only elected body under the old constitution), would have a seat at the table. But the framers of the constitution envisioned a future in which women may one day dominate elected bodies and men would need special protections. Therefore, the framers used gender-neutral language to serve both purposes.

Why is this clause ahead of itself? Because for over a decade, Kenyans have failed to actualize this clause. In September 2020 Kenya's chief justice advised the president to dissolve parliament for its failure to comply with this requirement. Perhaps the president ignored the advice because he knew the next parliament would not fare much better. How does one actualize this requirement? When considering every individual's right to run for elected office, to vote without impediment for their preferred candidate, and to run as an independent candidate or with a political party, as well as ensuring the fixed number of elected positions in a body, one can appreciate the impossibility of a graceful solution. Simple innovative clauses such as this can, unfortunately, erode confidence in the government's sincerity to implement the constitution. As exacerbated by the chief justice's advice, a constitutional crisis continuously looms over Kenya over this one issue.

Unfortunately, no constitution expert can forecast these difficulties, especially when they have an extremely compressed and strict timeline to develop such a document. But this is an extreme example; the constitution contains many other clauses designed to mitigate against political interference, clauses that have already withstood the test of time. In 2024 the Kenyan Constitution took to the international stage. The High Court of Kenya temporarily blocked the government's deployment of police to assist with the managing crisis in Haiti because, according to Justice Mwita, "the effort, and in particular the attempt to deploy police officers to Haiti, must fall for lack of constitutional and legal foundation."[83] The case was filed by the director of the CoE on the constitutional review team; the same director had been KTI's lead counterpart in our support to the CoE in 2009. Kenya would later solve this problem by signing a reciprocal agreement with Haiti on March 1, 2024.

Closer to Kenyan politics, one test came in 2020 in the form of wholesale amendments, as discussed earlier, which all three Kenyan courts threw out after reprimanding the president for his extraconstitutional move. However, the visionary document's first test, probably the most difficult, materialized in 2013 during the aftermath of the general election, as discussed below.

The 2013 Election

The March 4, 2013, election was the first comprehensive test of the new constitution. Kenyans had to complete six different ballots for the president, senators, the lower house representatives, governors, and county assembly members. This secret-ballot election, with independent and political party candidates, was the opposite of the rubberstamping 1983 election I witnessed as a child. My parents lined up behind a poster of their candidate of choice, the person with the longest line won, and all candidates were from the same party. All other parties were banned. The 2013 logistical requirements were dumbfounding; they included tamperproof ballot boxes, redundant observers, ballots and pens, a results transmission system, and helicopters to get equipment to remote areas. Many polling centers lacked electricity, but poll workers and organizers garnered generators and gas lanterns for the voting and counting, which had to start before dawn and end late at night.

As with the 2010 Referendum, the US embassy ramped up security measures, increased the number of observers, and established a command center. I had been fully credentialed by the election commission to observe the polls, but my assigned duty, once again, was to be at the Bomas of Kenya at night. I chose to start my day, however, at a local school at 5:30 a.m. because I wanted to see the entire process unfold. I observed the setup of the polling station, talked to several people lined up around the block in the predawn hours, and observed the first few voters cast their ballots in the light of a fuel lantern. Later that night, I returned to the same polling station and observed the sealing of the ballot boxes and the late-night counting (and recounting). Kenyans were patient, calm, and followed instructions. The polling station officials were equally patient, professional, calm, diligent, and thorough. During the counting process, behind closed doors, I accompanied observers from the major political parties, civil society, and the media. Each ballot was checked, held up for all observers to see, and placed in an appropriate pile. The ballots were then counted aloud and then recounted, and multiple officials signed the final forms.

I was extremely impressed. Even questionable ballots, incorrectly filled, were scrutinized and discussed. If all observers agreed on the voter's intent, the ballot was counted. If anyone disagreed, it was set aside for subsequent scrutiny at the Constituency Center. Not one ballot from the box was set aside. I doubt this level of human, multiparty scrutiny took place in Florida in the contested 2000 election of Bush and Gore.

After several hours, having observed the complete processing of one ballot box, I decided it was time to go to the other end, the election headquarters. It was after 10 p.m. and the streets were empty, but I armed myself with my embassy-issued emergency radio, extra clothes, food, and a sleeping bag in case there was trouble the next day and I could not get home. The night was long; people were more agitated than during the 2010 Referendum, partly because there was more at stake for the individual candidates, and I witnessed brief periods of tension and frustration. During the night, it was not lost to me that this election, Kenya's first under the new constitution, was being held on a day with a unique and symbolic name, a day when all Kenyans could unite and move forward together: March 4th or March Forth. I hoped the country, my place of birth, could march forward.

By dawn, there was a long lull as I handed over the baton to my replacement. This was the quiet before the storm. Either the situation would deteriorate, or the storm would blow over. Kenyans were relatively patient, as had been proven repeatedly during past elections. Based on history, there would be no violence, protests, or trouble until after the results were formally announced. Yet, the international media and cynics circled anxiously, like vultures waiting for the kill. The losers would complain; they always do. That night, things were not looking good for the opposition party, which was led by Raila Odinga. He was behind in the vote tally as it was reported live at the Bomas of Kenya. The media were broadcasting the same results on television and radio. The elections commission was publishing a live stream on its website and on Twitter. The results could change as the hours ticked by because early counts came from densely populated areas with electricity and internet infrastructure. Rural results took much longer, and Kenya was 73 percent rural. Having witnessed the long, diligent process associated with only one ballot box, I knew the ballots and outcomes would be checked and then double- and triple-checked before being transmitted to each constituency center, reviewed again, and then sent on to Nairobi.

The Brookings Institute published an article appropriately titled, "Kenya: A Country Redeemed after a Peaceful Election," stating: "Kenyans turned out in large numbers with over 80 percent of registered voters coming out to vote. There were no serious incidents of violence, and the electoral process was deemed by many international observers as free, fair, and credible. Although the IEBC faced challenges in the tallying process because of the technological failure of the data transmission system, the reversion to manual tallying did not compromise the integrity of the process."[84]

The peaceful election, the smooth handing over of power, and the public's response marked the end of USAID's political transition program. Although I later returned to the United States, I tracked Kenya's 2017 election and its unique and fascinating outcome grounded in its new constitution. Former Ambassadors Carson and Bellamy inappropriately equated the events following the 2017 election with the 2008 postelection violence period: "As was the case during the horrendous postelection violence of 2007, Kenya today needs outside assistance to help it alter course."[85]

Perhaps they were thinking of the old Kenya, the one that existed when they were ambassadors. Or it may have been that they had not recognized the new constitution's power. They overlooked one significant difference between 2007/2008 and 2013/2014: Kenyans now had their own constitution, replete with established institutions, administrative and judicial structures, and a cosmopolitan ethic. In 2007, the losing candidate, Raila Odinga, chose to bypass the old legal system. He did not trust it. In 2017 when he lost again, he trusted the new legal system. Kenyans trusted their Supreme Court. Their constitution had established a strict time frame for the courts to address election disputes and criteria for a reelection. The court made a landmark and unprecedented decision, invalidating the election and sending Kenyans back to the polls. The politicians obeyed and the world watched, fascinated. As the British Broadcasting Corporation (BBC) reported, "Chief Justice David Maraga said the 8 August election had not been 'conducted in accordance with the constitution' and declared it 'invalid, null and void.'"[86] Kenya's 2013 election was the first real test of its visionary 2010 document. In passing the test, the constitution demonstrated it could now give Kenya the peace and security they needed and under which to develop their own PARADISE.

Conclusion

The previous chapter wove together a complex tapestry encompassing why the United States believes stability in some foreign countries is vital to its own national peace and security and, therefore, why it provides a significant amount of foreign assistance to countries such as

Kenya. I also introduced the meaning of the compound phrase "peace and security," which I argued denotes "secure peace." Then, I presented this term within the larger context of an ideal state, represented by the mnemonic PARADISE.

This chapter has focused on a single topic from the global political spectrum, the story of Kenya and its quest for a new constitution, to demonstrate one approach to achieving a secure peace. USAID, through KTI, worked to assist Kenyans in making their own choice about their country and government and securing their new constitution. We at KTI overcame internal and external obstacles, materializing from as far afield as the government of Kenya's printing press staff who tried to insert two words into the new constitution all the way to Washington, DC, where an American senator tried to block USAID under the spectra of abortion rights.

The new constitution and Kenya's efforts to secure it encompass all aspects of my PARADISE mnemonic and has sustained peace in Kenya since Kenyans embraced this document in 2010. The Bill of Rights in Kenya's Constitution established a foundation for Accepting Kenyans' diversity, equality, and pluralism; the Bill of Rights and the new structures, including Kenya's new Supreme Court, has improved Rule of law and human rights. The Administration of government services and responsibilities has significantly improved with new or revised bodies and devolved structures. Democratically elected leaders include county governments, a new bicameral house, and an effort to ensure a gender balance. Innovation is strewn throughout the constitution, some achievable (e.g., dual citizenship) and some remaining for future generations to implement (e.g., two-thirds gender rule). The constitution dedicates a chapter to land and the environment, bringing Stewardship and environmental responsibility to the forefront. Lastly, Economic rights are enshrined in the constitution and the words "economic rights" occurs at least 20 times in the document.

I have also outlined the history of Kenya's relationship with its constitution and the numerous opportunities we interjected in its development, beginning with former Supreme Court Justice Marshall and punctuated by Ambassador Hempstone's successes in reintroducing multiparty democracy to Kenya. I described the obstacles Kenya faced between 2008 and 2010 before it succeeded in promulgating a new constitution. I also identified some ways the US government positioned its foreign assistance program to help Kenya overcome these obstructions. I have opined on the strength and vision within the constitution, proven by the court's landmark legal decisions following both the 2013 and 2017 election as well as the most recent frontal attack in 2020, an attack reminiscent of the wholesale amendments Kenyan politicians made in the 1980s.

Former US Ambassador Ranneberger underscored the link between a constitution and the quest for PARADISE in Kenya: "The constitution is, in many respects, the *sine qua non* of the reform process. Without a new constitution, implementation of other reforms will not prove sufficient to steer the country in the right direction. If a new constitution is put in place, then implementation of other reforms along with the new constitution, will help ensure future democratic stability and prosperity."[87]

Mwangi S. Kimenyi, writing for the US-based Brookings Institution, agrees: "Over the [past] five years, Kenyans have made significant reforms in their institutions that in part contributed to the violence in 2007. Kenyans now have a new constitution that not only creates lower-level county governments but also reduces the powers of the presidency and establishes many independent institutions that are not subject to manipulation by the executive."[88]

Under Ambassador Ranneberger, the US government's agencies focused on the goal of a new constitution for all Kenyans. As a key member of the implementation team, I understood both the strategy and tactics we used. Strategically, we did not focus on the text itself. Instead, we knew the text was important for what it represented, a new dawn or a new Kenya, one Kenyans would be proud of. We also knew the text needed to speak to and for the individual, and that it would establish the foundation for all other reforms promised in Agenda 4 of the peace agreement. Furthermore, it had to withstand the pressures and manipulative tactics that Kenyan politicians had mastered since independence in 1963. We concentrated on the entire process, or what became an 18-month gestation period. Tactically, we tried to preempt or respond to attacks and obstacles with a plethora of tools from the US foreign assistance toolbox.

The tools the United States uses in any specific situation will depend on the level and types of funding available, the personnel and operational capacity on the ground, the windows of opportunity, competitive advantages, and areas in which the United States can leverage other domestic and international financial and moral support. The American decisionmaker must not overlook the simple needs (e.g., the CoE's basic needs) or downplay potential Washington, DC-based attacks.

But US development professionals and diplomatic corps must understand that the instruments in the toolbox only work if they know which one to use and when; they must understand both the local context and the synergies at play. Ambassadors Hempstone and Ranneberger were successful because they took the time to understand Kenya. As the late Dr. Joel Barkan stated, "If the United States wants to secure Kenya's engagement in the war on terrorism it must develop a more nuanced understanding of Kenya's domestic situation."[89] Having served as a political officer in Kenya in the 1990s and as the lead evaluator for the KTI program in 2013 and 2014, Dr. Barkan knew Kenya, like many countries, is complex. To help make a positive difference, practitioners must hone a nuanced political, historical, and cultural understanding of the country they work in. In the unpublished final program evaluation, Barkan stated, "the heads of the program's field offices and supporting personnel must be smart and knowledgeable about the country's political economy and confident in their work. They must also be imaginative and think strategically as well as possessing insight, political acumen, and high integrity."[90]

CHAPTER FOUR

Mother Earth

"Kenya also has a long history of insecurity and conflict driven by ethnic intolerance, disputes over land and natural resources, marginalization, patriarchal structures, poverty, and, in recent times, violent extremism. Kenya's society has deeply entrenched negative ethnicity, toxic masculinity, and nepotism due to systemic inequalities which have enabled Kenya's leaders to block others from the benefits of political and economic opportunities."
  —USAID, *Country Development Cooperation Strategy (CDCS) October 2020–October 2025,* September 2021

Bottom Line Up Front (BLUF)

At some point in the careers of those involved in international development—specialists, policymakers, security experts, diplomats, consultants, or implementing partners—some may be asked to recommend, design, or implement a program related to Kenya's interminable land question. As Ambreena Manji, Professor of Land Law and Development at Cardiff University and previously director of the British Institute in Eastern Africa, wrote, "Indeed, land has often been the lens through which historians, political scientists, and latterly lawyers, not to mention economists and students of development, have sought to understand the country's fraught politics and to propose solutions to its perceived ills."[1]

Peace and security experts and development specialists alike portray land reform as the perfect programming opportunity. According to them, it should meet three design requirements: (1) a well-documented connection between land issues and conflict; (2) grassroots demand for interventions from the Kenyan public, civil society, environmental groups, human rights groups, and reform-minded Kenyan officials; and (3) requests from US government policymakers in both Washington, DC and Nairobi. I was quickly swayed that they were correct as I began my tenure as the deputy country representative for USAID's KTI program, following the 2007/2008 postelection violence.

Early on, I received written or verbal concepts from a diverse spectrum of Kenyans, including Kenyan governmental staff, civil society leaders, representatives of churches and mosques, business leaders, and youth activists for funding land reform activities. I was intrigued. The current US ambassador to Kenya at the time emphasized "the unwavering determination of the United States to push for and support implementation of the reform agenda" and KTI was one of several tools that the US government had to advance its interests in Kenya.[2] Land reform was one of the long-term issues that all parties had agreed to address during the Kenya National Dialogue and Reconciliation process that led to the February 2008 peace agreement. Therefore, we had to put land reform on KTI's programming agenda.

This chapter reflects on this decision and offers a retrospective. After defining the intractable land question and discussing the successes and failures of past donor programming, I offer a recommendation. Land issues are frequently blamed for localized insecurity, especially during election seasons. Since secure land tenure is a prerequisite to stable income, investments, and infrastructure, land reform is undoubtedly important for Kenya. Development specialists are right to focus on it. But land reform should not be part of the US peace and security programming toolbox. It is extremely complex, can easily be misdirected, and does not meaningfully contribute to US peace and security objectives.

Introduction

Agenda 4 of the 2008 peace agreement, entitled "Statement of Principles of Long-Term Issues and Solutions," negotiated by former Secretary General Kofi Annan after the 2007/2008 postelection violence, concluded, "the issue of land has been a source of economic, social, political, and environmental problems in Kenya for many years. We agree that land reform is a fundamental need in Kenya and that the issue must be addressed comprehensively and with the seriousness it deserves."[3] All of us, Kenyans and foreigners alike, agree that land reform is a fundamental need. Unfortunately, we cannot agree on its definition or scope; sometimes we call the matter "issue of land," the "land question," or "land reform." Yet many of the people I worked with—members of advocacy groups, lawyers, representatives and employees of the Kenyan government, and international donors—disagreed with me because they considered the issue crystal clear. But it was murkier than the heavily sedimented Mississippi River in the United States and the Tana River in Kenya.

The United States is no stranger to, nor shy about, Kenya's land woes. A 1978 CIA report, written soon after Kenya's first president died and declassified in January 2002, confirmed the Kenyan government's efforts to protect the elite's accumulation of land by blocking parliamentary attempts to reform land ownership.[4] Forty years later, USAID published provocative terms in a formal US government diplomatic report, as shown in the quotation at the beginning of this chapter. The terms "negative ethnicity" and "toxic masculinity" are harsh, and they relate to a score of problems in Kenya, including land. This formal US government diplomatic report was the 2020–2025 Country Development Cooperation Strategy (CDCS), America's formal collaboration strategy for a given country.

A CDCS document articulates a results-oriented strategy that fosters partnerships "with host countries to focus investment in key areas that shape countries' overall stability and prosperity."[5] In developing a CDCS, USAID embarks on a long, consultative, and elaborative process that includes data collection, surveys, analyses, and multiple workshops with host country government and civil society representatives.[6] I participated in some of these workshops during a previous CDCS development cycle in Kenya. USAID senior staff and State Department officials scrutinize the interim drafts before the USAID mission director and the US ambassador approve the document. Everyone is on their best behavior during the workshops; no rogue text or inflammatory language can be used because diplomatic reports and strategies are meant to be polite and vague, with lofty language that tiptoes around any offensive discussions.

How do I, with my multiple personas, react to the provocative vocabulary (e.g., "negative ethnicity" and "toxic masculinity")? As a third-generation Kenyan, with Kenya in my blood, I find it insulting. I cringe. As a former US diplomat, with the United States in my heart and mind, I grimace with a hint of amusement because I recognize it as particularly poignant. As an international development specialist, interested in the quality of life of all humans, I see it piercing the heart of a fundamental problem in Kenya. These three competing personas play the rock, paper, scissors game. In this iteration of the game, as the author of this book, I embrace the quotation but recognize I would never have drafted it when representing the US government. Diplomats do not point fingers at their allies, accusing them of having negative ethnicity and toxic masculinity. Our elected officials get upset when non-Americans use the phrase "Death to America" and burn the US flag in protest, or even call the United States a racist country because of a US Soccer Federation social media post during the 2022 World Cup.[7] How would Americans respond if one of our allies published similar formal statements about us in their diplomatic documents?

Negative ethnicity and toxic masculinity are not unique to Kenya's problems. My grandparents were born in India; their forefathers were likely lower-caste Indians born into a degrading caste system that epitomizes negative ethnicity, underpins inequalities, and exacerbates the burgeoning wealth gap in India. I have served America, my country of adoption, for two decades. Yet, I am appalled by America's collective form of negative ethnicity, from the treatment of Native Americans or Alaskan natives, which has forced them into a quality of life that is worse than what I see across rural Africa. The media highlight some of today's urban forms of negative ethnicity, namely, discrimination against blacks, much more than against browns, of which I am one. I can safely water my neighbor's garden or take a run in New York's Central Park while my fellow black Americans cannot.[8]

Yet, an undercurrent of negative ethnicity permeates a much wider swath of individual Americans. Let me point fingers only at my own circumstances and behavior. I subconsciously live in a relatively monochrome community, like many others across American metropolitan areas. I retrospectively lambast myself for making monolithic, ethnic-based judgments about others. On the behavior side, I avoid going to the Washington State Fair because the fairgrounds were an American Japanese internment camp during World War II. Perhaps negative ethnicity is subconsciously and universally prevalent in each one of us, just as I see it in myself. Like the constant struggle between right and wrong, we win some and lose some.

Toxic masculinity is also a significant undercurrent in many nations. India acquits rapists who prey on young women while US, male-dominated legislative bodies and courts prohibit women from having control over their own bodies.[9] A US politician can get elected to the country's highest office after making lewd, horrific, and degrading comments about women.[10]

In addition to using inflammatory language to define the root causes of Kenya's problems, the CDCS also establishes the goals for the United States in Kenya. Land reform is not explicitly mentioned. But the 2020–2025 CDCS does define the root causes of Kenyan violence, something that KTI refrained from doing; the latter simply adopted the root causes from Agenda 4 of the peace agreement. If donors decide to define root causes or priorities, even after a consultative process, they will often differ from the host country's stated causes and priorities. For example, a chief goal for the UK's Department for Foreign International Development (DFID) in Kenya was "to improve government systems and accountability, tackle corruption and reduce conflict and the risks of radicalisation," while Kenya defined "strengthening food security, housing, health care and manufacturing as its primary goals."[11] Both countries are playing to a particular audience but there is also a question here about sovereignty. One country should never try to speak for another. Consider the opposite scenario: If Kenyans tells the United States what it thinks its priorities should be, America's national discourse, led by social media and rambunctious elected officials, would generate a plethora of negative remarks about their audacity!

Westerners have discarded colonialism but have held onto the Western notion of dominance, underscored by both the 2020 CDCS and a 2022 headline in *The Guardian*. Excited to see an opinion titled, "The climate is already collapsing in Africa—but its nations have a plan" on my news feed, I clicked on it and started reading.[12] I quickly stopped in horror. Two of the three authors were heads of Western countries, France and the Netherlands, and the article focused on the need for the rest of the world to support Africa. This was far different from what the headline implied. The newspaper had conveniently forgotten Africa's own solution-finders, for example, Kenya's own Dr. Wangari Maathai, an environmental activist and the first African woman to win the Nobel Peace Prize. We had children's books in our house about her Green Belt Movement, founded in 1977, and her determination to save Nairobi's version of Central Park from greedy developers.

In the 2008 peace agreement, Agenda 4 identified land, the focus of this chapter, as a paramount issue. The agenda was the outcome of negotiations between both political parties during the postelection violence. At our first KTI strategic planning session, both Kenyan and American experts highlighted land reform as critical to our strategic plan. Although we had no idea what it meant, what we would do, or how we could contribute to it, we inherently knew it was critical. Everyone— the Kenyan public, government, academia, and foreign experts—widely believes that resolving the land question in Kenya is a paramount prerequisite for peace, prosperity, and security. Like the wider Kenyan public, KTI's Kenyan staff proclaimed this as an unambiguous fact; but they were also realists, they were international development profession- als who forecasted that KTI would grapple with the land question for the duration of the program and that Kenyans would struggle with it for generations to come. They knew this because they could not define the land problem adequately and comprehensively, let alone solve it in their short professional lifespans.

Kenya's land question is extremely complex; it is a complexity exacer- bated by the politicians and elite who use it as a political weapon to stoke frustration and violence. Alongside "toxic masculinity," women's owner- ship of land, especially in terms of inheritance, is frowned upon in some Kenyan cultures.[13] As for "negative ethnicity," it pits one tribe against another in the fight over productive land. The government, which is run by the elite, will never want to truly resolve the land question because members of government are the biggest beneficiaries in social, political, and economic arenas. Yes, they have always paid lip service to reforms or approached reforms from one of many different sides; however, they know that a single focused approach will not resolve it. No one I talked to, Kenyan or foreign, recognized that the historic underpinning of the land problem is based on a decision (discussed in detail later in this chapter) made by Kenya's first president, Jomo Kenyatta, before independence, in response to the Cold War and the global financial standings. Importantly, this was a decision that can never be overturned.

In hindsight, after running a six-year USAID program and spending years reflecting on my experience and writing this book, I acknowledge that when we launched KTI, I was probably as naive about land issues as other Western donors and experts often are. Of course, I did not believe that at the time; I had a unique background, having spent 16 years as a third-generation Kenyan Asian and then returning, decades later, as a US diplomat. I believed I was more informed than other diplomats and international development specialists and led everyone around me to believe that too. But the first indicator of my naivety was that I could not articulate the complexities of the land question. The second was believing that foreign powers should attempt to tackle the land issue because of its intractable nexus with peace and security, as highlighted during the 2007/2008 postelection violence. Perhaps an alternative perspective is that foreign powers helped create the problem and, today, one can only nibble around the edges and achieve nothing of significance. Worst still, foreign actors may do more harm than good, or, at the very least, unknowingly promote inequalities and the status quo—just as I may have done in retrospect. As discussed in this chapter, there is a lot I will never know about the outcome of our interventions. But there is one silver lining: The three renowned experts on Kenya, who evaluated the program, only referred to one set of our land interventions as "experiments, albeit successful ones."[14]

The Elusive Problem

My understanding of the land problem in Kenya is shaped by considerable thought and analysis, grounded in my interpretation of systems, and I do not mean computer systems. My undergraduate degree in systems engineering taught me to consider everything within a system. We modeled the human heart, traffic lights, ecosystems, and municipal garbage collection systems with similar methodological lenses. Each system has complex inputs, outputs, influencers, and obstacles. Such is the land question in Kenya. Land ownership is a complex system analogous to the Eastern parable of the three blind men and the elephant. Each man had to describe the elephant after touching only one body part. Since the tusk, ear, leg, tail, and head are all different, none could identify or describe the whole animal.

I was like the author of the parable during my initial years with USAID in Kenya as I grappled with the definition of the land question. Everyone I spoke to portrayed a different blind man, offering me their perspective of the whole problem without acknowledging their singular, biased lens. I kept my systems engineering focus and tried to develop a comprehensive understanding of the land question as a complex system before weaving it into our KTI implementation plan. This chapter is based on my discussions with a wide spectrum of Kenyan practitioners, those who live with or deal with the land problem on a daily basis. This spectrum includes Ministry of Land officials, attorneys, high court judges, developers, rural and urban homeowners, landless youth, media, and civil society. I interrogated the diplomats and international development experts. I pored through government publications, investigative reports, journal publications, and books.[15] As a USAID official, I had access to other diplomats and development experts and a formal seat in the Development Partners Group on Lands, a donor coordination effort led by the United Nations Human Settlements Programme (UN-Habitat).[16]

Don't get me wrong; I unequivocally believe that land in Kenya *is* intricately tied to Kenyan peace and security. But depending on one's perspective, anything can be used to both undermine and promote peace and security. A gun is a great example; depending on who is wielding it, a gun can be an offensive weapon that makes a situation less secure or a defensive weapon that restores peace. A group of people who oppose a current government are called rebels—until they oppose a foe's government and magically become freedom fighters. The United States trains Kenyan troops and sells weapons to Kenya under the peace and security umbrella.[17] Kenya uses those troops and weapons to promote national peace and security but inevitably harms people in another country or a specific group of Kenyans.

Consider the US National Guard as something that can both undermine and promote peace and security. Comparing two very different events, in different states and different decades, the National Guard both promoted peace and shattered lives. In 1957, then–US President Eisenhower nationalized the Arkansas National Guard to enforce the Supreme Court's landmark decision to allow nine black students to enter the all-white Central High School in Little Rock, Arkansas. Yet, in 1970, the Ohio National Guard killed four Kent State University students and wounded nine during a First Amendment–based assembly to protest the US invasion of Cambodia.

The 2008 Kenyan peace agreement recognized the role of land reform in helping Kenya move toward peace and security. Yet, Jomo Kenyatta, an activist and politician, brandished land reform as a weapon to mobilize his tribe, the Kikuyu, against the British in the 1920s.[18] One hundred years later, politicians continue to follow in his footsteps. In 2003 the Ndung'u Commission was established; it was one of many government efforts initiated to investigate patterns of corruption and unfair allocation of land and to propose remedies. According to its 2004 report, "most illegal allocations of public land took place before or soon after the multiparty general elections of 1992, 1997 and 2002."[19] In the runup to the 2013 election, Raila Odinga's plan promised to address injustices, "including, but not limited to, squatters' problems, displacement of indigenous communities, and involuntary resettlement of populations."[20] However, Odinga's opponent, Musila Mudavadi, tied land to peace, security, and prosperity in a rally by pledging to "provide proper funding for county land boards and other institutions in order to accelerate reforms."[21] Six weeks before the 2022 election, President Kenyatta waved land titles as an election enticement by launching another phase of the national land title deeds issuance program.[22] At a formal ceremony at the Kenyatta Conference Center in Nairobi, he handed over a token 200 titles and promised 1 million more.[23] Lost to many Kenyans was the repetition of history; his father had also launched a million-acre scheme for small landowners in 1962, a scheme that contributed to the historical land injustices that Kenyans lament today.

Many Kenyans across generations fail to see beyond these purposely staged political weapons because of their entrenched yearning for land. This desire derives from the social construct of land that I saw deep in the eyes of many Kenyans of all tribes and economic standing. My Kenyan housekeeper was saving to buy her own small plot in Western

Kenya, where she wanted to be buried. The wealthy Kenyan business-
men I knew talked endlessly about the nefarious land transactions they
had recently completed and the ones they were planning.

Since land is intricately tied to peace and security in Kenya, US development and security specialists must include the land question in their
development menu. But before selecting it from that menu when crafting
multiyear strategies and determining how to provide land reform assistance, development specialists must understand and be able to articulate
the land problem. My articulation takes the form and flavor of an avocado.

The Avocado Analogy

The land question is like an avocado. First, there is the skin or the
outward manifestation of the problem. This is what everyone, Kenyan
and foreign, sees and experiences across generations. Its color, texture,
and smell may be appealing or abhorrent. It may also change relatively
quickly. The current pleasing elements include land tenure for squatters,
security for agriculture, improved management information systems,
and the 2010 Constitution's treatment of community land. Abhorrent
manifestations include political manipulations, gender intolerance
over land ownership, widespread landlessness, unproductive land, and
almost daily headlines about stealing land (land grabbing).

Below the avocado's skin is the fiber of the problem, or the underlying issues, that stem from the historical context in which the British
colonialists play a significant but not unique role. The avocado fiber can
be tasty or rotten; one can savor it alone, garnish it, or mix it with other
ingredients, which in this analogy, could be the judiciary, parliament,
constitution, gender imbalances, and economics. This fiber includes
land administration, the regulatory regime, and corruption. Finally, at
the core of the avocado is the seed, the root causes of the land problem,
the very things that Kenyans rarely describe, discuss, or dissect. The few
who do recognize the seed, or the root causes, see it as one solid mass.
But it, too, is made up of different components, including capitalism
and world markets, privilege, nepotism, tribalism, and class.

The avocado is more than an analogy for the land problem in Kenya. It is a real symbol of climate change, adaptation, and conflict in

Kenya's Highlands. The Highlands in the central part of the country around Mount Kenya are extremely important in understanding the nation's land woes. They hosted the beginning of Kenya's struggle for independence, equity, and freedom from the British. It is this fertile land, with a climate conducive to agriculture, that Kenyans lost to the British settlers. These areas evolved from subsistence farming before colonialization to market-based cash crops during British rule. When I was growing up, coffee farms would stretch across the hills and over the horizon. Now, avocados are replacing coffee. In 2021, avocado farms moved Kenya into eighth place among the top exporters of avocados, and first place in Africa.[24] Kenya is capitalizing on a demand driven by health-conscious diets, climate change, and China's economic growth.

Conflicts multiply as farmers contend with avocado thieves, fueling an underground economy that had no appetite for coffee.[25] But for Kenya to continue moving up this global avocado ranking and remain diversified, farmers, transportation networks, and ports all need access to suitable land that can be developed. For that to happen, Kenya needs better adjudication of land, a free market for land transactions that allows unused land to be harnessed, and land to be a security that can generate capital.

The avocado analogy represents the internal components of the land problem. The coffee-to-avocado transition portrays the external relationship of the land problem to real-world problems of development. Kenyan and foreign experts must understand both the internal and external aspects of the land problem. But they must also appreciate, internalize, and factor in the nation's psychology and history before considering targeted assistance. The psychology is manifested in the social construct of land while the history unravels with the three distinct land scrambles in Kenya.

The Social Construct of Land

Most large cities in the world are experiencing a rapid development of high-rise buildings. The definition of "high" is contextual; my small city of Redmond, Washington, home to Microsoft, has replaced most of its one-story, downtown commercial buildings with new developments consisting of a retail ground floor and four stories of residences. That's high for Redmond, but approximately 15 miles away, Seattle residents in the urban core embrace living on the fortieth floor of a new high-rise building. Across the globe, vertical micro cities sprout up into the clouds, providing housing for millions of people. These communities find it economically, socially, and culturally acceptable to own air instead of owning a patch of dirt. In the United States, we treat air rights like any other finite resource and fight over it when threatened. In 1978, after a ten-year journey through the US legal system, the Supreme Court upheld New York City's decision to restrict developing a building that reached into the air above the historic Grand Central Station.[26]

Americans also get creative about building vertically while maintaining smaller historic buildings. While Redmond, Washington, demolishes its one-story buildings of little historic value, other American communities maintain their historic facades. They remodel the insides or build modern high-rise buildings above or adjacent to smaller historic structures. The result could be that an old historic church, for example, is now towered over by a new glass high-rise, resembling an exquisite, tall, buff, and shiny torso of a person whose feet remain hidden behind an historic pair of shoes. I helped secure the permits needed to construct Atlantic Wharf in Boston in 2004; its twin buildings representing the interplay between the traditionalist and the modernist, a way of preserving Boston's past while building for the future. The US National Historic Preservation Act (NHPA) of 1966 requires every federal agency to evaluate this interplay before proceeding with its proposed projects, permits, or funding.

I spent many childhood days in a historic building in downtown Nairobi, the Ismaili Jamatkhana, which celebrated its one-hundredth anniversary during the COVID pandemic. A comparable building in downtown Seattle would likely be redeveloped with a high-rise hotel and condominium tower above or around it. But Kenya's social construct of land mandates ownership of a physical plot of land. Despite the need for more building space in Nairobi, I cannot envision the Jamatkhana in the shadows of a high-rise residential building in the coming decades.

While people around the globe embrace the reality of finite resources and construct building high up into the clouds, develop new islands in the middle of the Arabian Gulf, exhibit creativity in historic preservation, and fight over air rights, Kenyans remain literally entrenched in their soil. Many Kenyans, whom I met over cups of boiled milk tea in meeting rooms and living rooms, alike expressed a deep-seated inherent belief that to be successful, to be a real person, they must own their own patch of land.

At least once a year during my tenure in Kenya, acquaintances would approach me with a proposal to invest in a high-value property. I always declined, finding an easy way out by mentioning a US government restriction on diplomats investing locally to prevent conflicts of interest. Many were surprised that, as a former Kenyan, I did not own land. In the words of Caroline Elkins,

> To be a man or woman—to move from childhood to adulthood—a Kikuyu had to have access to land. A man needed land to accumulate the resources necessary to pay bridewealth for a wife or wives, who would in turn bear him children. Land and family entitled him to certain privileges within the Kikuyu patriarchy; without land a man would remain socially a boy. A woman needed land to grow crops and nurture and sustain her family; without it in the eyes of the Kikuyu she was not an adult. A Kikuyu could not be a Kikuyu without land.[27]

Land is as important for the herders of cattle as it is for the tillers of the soil; all Kenyans, including the pastoralists, attach significant social importance to access to land.[28]

Not everyone will be able to own their own land. Estimates show that there are 11 million titles of land for a population of 55 million, and many of those 11 million titles, as discussed later in this chapter, are tiny, unproductive parcels of land that cannot sustain a family and its livelihood. According to the Kenya Land Alliance, only 12 percent of Kenya's land is classified as high-potential, agricultural land with adequate rainfall. Even less, only 8 percent, is deemed of medium potential. The remaining 80 percent is arid or semiarid.[29] The youth, the majority of the population, have dreams and aspirations of their own, but not the capital to invest in land. Access to land will continue to be a driver of poverty, as 85 percent of Kenyans in 2010 relied on agriculture for their primary livelihood.[30] People in US metropolitan areas are having similar realizations today, as there is not enough land for every American family to own a home.

The social construct of land in Kenya is a relic of the colonial period. But it only explains part of the nation's land problem. To grasp the next aspect of the problem, we have to turn to the three historic scrambles for Kenyan land.

Three Scrambles for Kenya

According to former Chief Justice Mutunga, "it is impossible to envisage the present-day economic structure of Kenya without acknowledging its roots deep in regimes of land ownership that were facilitated first by a settler political economy and then, postindependence, by an elite that reserved for itself access to and ownership of land on a massive scale."[31]

Historians point to the scramble for Africa to explain the relationship between the colonial powers and today's independent nations.[32] Knowing about one scramble is not enough to understand Kenya's land problems; Kenya has been scrambled over three different times. This chapter does not attempt to detail the history of Britain's rise and fall in Kenya's Highlands. Ambreena Manji's *The Struggle for Land and Justice in Kenya* and others provide a much deeper dive.[33] My presentation is simply a broad perspective, one that is a prerequisite to understanding the multiple interpretations of the land question in Kenya.

The First Scramble

The Europeans were the first to scramble Africa between the late 1800s and the end of World War I. At the 1885 Berlin Conference, they carved up central Africa, giving the Congo to the Belgians and dividing Africa into multiple annexes, colonies, or territories without respect for traditional tribal boundaries, culture, natural features, or human migration.[34] The last African countries to gain their independence from colonial shackles were Djibouti from France in 1977 and Zimbabwe from the British in 1980. That is 200 years after America broke away from British rule. Today, the illogical shapes of these African countries resemble gerrymandered constituencies in the United States. The 1885 conference established a precedent for European powers to establish and modify these random borders. As a teenager growing up in Kenya, one ramification of these random borders was that my scout troop could not climb Mount Kilimanjaro, Africa's highest peak, which stood a mere 150 miles from my house. At 19,341 feet high and 200 miles from the equator, the mountain was snow-covered year-round, home to numerous glaciers, and taller than any peak in the continental United States. But the mountain is in Tanzania, international travel required dollars, and dollars were a scarce commodity in Kenya in the 1980s; in essence, Kenya restricted international travel for those who did not pay bribes to get dollars.

According to prevailing legend, Queen Victoria gave the mountain to her nephew, the Kaiser of Germany, as a birthday present.[35] The border jogs around the mountain as it transcends from the coast to Lake Victoria. This folktale is most likely untrue, as recent analysis finds that Tanzanian ownership of the mountain was probably an outcome of agreements between the British and Germans when carving up East Africa and not, specifically and somewhat maliciously, a birthday present.[36] Nor was Kilimanjaro the only victim of European artistic powers and gentlemen's cigar-and-whisky-infused agreements. In 1925, the British and Italians traded the Somali port of Kismayo giving Jubaland to Italian Somalia and dividing the Somali people between an arbitrary Kenyan–Somali border.[37] The British also established a line west of the city of Garissa in eastern Kenya as the official boundary for Somali people within Kenya. This was not an international border but an internal boundary to prevent the movement of one group of people. When I crossed that line from east to west on my way to a USAID event in Garissa, it felt like I was leaving Kenya even though I wasn't. The prevailing question for visitors crossing from west to east, including development workers, was *How is Kenya?* The question itself implied that east of the line was a completely different country.

This first scramble for Africa mimics the European scramble for America a couple of centuries earlier as the French, British, Dutch, Spanish, and Russians carved up North America. One group of territories became the original 13 colonies represented by the 13 stripes on today's US flag. There are several similarities between Britain's departure from the 13 colonies and its retreat from Kenya. Although almost 200 years apart, both groups of settlers used trickery and force to evict the local populations from their own lands, conducted mass killings, and established farms and plantations that contributed to the Crown's economic might. Both used African slave labor to further economic growth, albeit American plantation owners benefitted personally while, in Kenya, the British used incarcerated Mau Mau laborers to build public infrastructure, including Nairobi's Embakasi International Airport. The most telling similarity is that in both Kenya and America, the British suffered humiliating military defeats in their own colonies.

But there are substantial differences between these two former colonies. In the United States, the settlers cut off ties with England and permanently settled in the new land. After all, they had decimated a large portion of the Native American population and made the rest powerless and landless. The way they took native land, by forcing written agreements that the natives could not understand, or using European-style land laws, echoed how the British stole Kenyan land 200 years later. In Kenya, large areas of land quickly changed hands in this first scramble because the elite settlers established power, became landowners, and grew in strength and numbers.

The Second Scramble

Only British lunacy can explain the second scramble for Kenya, which established the foundation for today's inequitable concentration of land in the hands of wealthy Kenyans. In 1896, the British extended the Indian Land Acquisition Act to its East Africa protectorate, including Kenya, permitting land to be appropriated for public purposes such as building a railway. They then embarked on the construction of the *Lunatic Express,* a 600-mile railway from the port of Mombasa to the shores of Lake Victoria. I have many fond memories of train trips to the coast. Each one began with an evening train safari through Nairobi National Park; a white tablecloth three-course meal in the dining car; cabin service that pulled out the hidden bunk beds and who made them up with pillows, bedsheets, and blankets; and breakfast the next morning in the dining car accompanied by a vivid sunrise as the train approached Mombasa. My last memorable moment of this narrow-gauge railroad that served Kenya from 1901 to 2017, when it was replaced with a Chinese-built standard gauge system, was a family trip I took in 2002.

We had been warned by the train staff about thieves who come in the middle of the night. Adults lying on the roof of the moving train would hold the children by their ankles as they looked for an open window to rob an unsuspecting tourist. Sure enough, over the clatter of the train tracks and in the dark of the night, I saw a child's hand working its way down the outside of the window. Because our window screens were locked, the hand and its child quickly moved to the next cabin. When I returned to Kenya in 2008 to run KTI, I could not share my magical train experiences with my children because the embassy's security rules prohibited us from traveling by train.

One early justification made by the British to begin a multimillion-pound project was that the railway would "improve the moral and material conditions of existence of the native races," a requirement of the Brussels Anti-Slavery Act of 1980.[38] Others say it was to access natural resources in Uganda and beyond. More farfetched theories include access to the River Nile, running from Lake Victoria on Kenya's western border to Egypt in the north. The Nile is the longest river in the world and the lifeline of Egypt, which was also a British colony. Did the British want to control the Nile to prevent the French from establishing an east–west corridor across the continent?[39] Did the British want the ability to transport troops to the Nile to prevent the Germans from damming it and cutting off Egypt's lifeline or establish a Zionist state for persecuted European Jews?[40] Perhaps it was simply an economic effort akin to an infrastructure project to invigorate the Kenyan economy and attract additional investments. Henry Du Pré Labouchère, a British author and politician, "went lyrical when debate for its funding came up in Parliament in 1896. [He said,] 'The railway starts from nowhere and nobody wants to use it. It goes nowhere and nobody wants to come back by it.'"[41]

Regardless of the original purpose, the British needed a return on their investment. They encouraged white farmers, from both England and South Africa, to settle in Kenya. This economic purpose is not different from the current Chinese investments in Africa. The Chinese build ports, railways, and roads across the continent that help expand Chinese power. The West thinks that China is building this infrastructure to expand its long-term economic and diplomatic relationships.[42] But like the British 100 years earlier, the real reasons go deeper. Chinese companies sometimes offer a better competitive price or hinge their bids on Chinese loans. These contracts and loans force African nations into more and more debt and, when these countries default, as Sri Lanka did in 2016, China takes over the ownership of the infrastructure.[43]

For the construction of the *Lunatic Express,* the British imported tens of thousands of Indian indentured laborers who had helped build the British railway system in India. Many of the workers who survived the five-year grueling work and the man-eating lions of Tsavo settled in Kenya. They encouraged other Indians to join them. My grandparents were among these early economic migrants, looking for a better life in Africa. In the same way, I would migrate further west, across the Atlantic, looking for a better life in America. There, I would find an echo of my grandparents; tens of thousands of Chinese immigrants had built railways in America's Pacific Northwest.[44] In 2022, Kenya celebrated Rishi Sunak, Britain's new prime minister, who claims Kenyan, Tanzanian, and Indian descent. Like my grandfather, his was born in India and migrated to East Africa in the early 1930s. His grandfather worked as a clerk, mine in a grocery store. While the British needed both office clerks and grocery store workers, they needed the *Lunatic Express* to make money by transporting agricultural goods. The Indian immigrants to Kenya were interested primarily in professional jobs and small businesses, not in largescale farming. The British had succeeded in enticing Indians to Africa to build the railway; now they had to entice white farmers from England and South Africa to farm Kenya's most productive lands and provide goods for the railway to carry. History often repeats itself. In 2019, Kenya's former President Kenyatta mandated that goods from Mombasa to Nairobi be transported by the new Chinese-built railway instead of by truck.[45]

The 1902 Crown Lands Ordinance, passed by British colonists in Kenya, offered land grants to settlers. Doing so involved evicting agrarian Kenyans already on the land, in much the same way that American settlers had evicted Native Americans. As David Anderson writes,

> Many squatter families were in their second or third generation of settlement in the Rift Valley by the end of the 1930s. Though few squatters could have been aware of it at the time, a judgement handed down by Kenya's High Court in 1925 had, in effect, already sealed their fate. The ruling of Justice Barth established that resident laborers on European-

owned farms were 'tenants at will' under the law and could therefore be
evicted on order of the landlord without the right of appeal.[46]

By 1915, the British had successfully created African reserves for each of
Kenya's tribes. Elkins compares these reserves to today's Native American reservations and white-only settlements in South Africa during
apartheid.[47] This effort left the productive highlands white-only. In a
few years, the Crown had taken over control of land in Kenya and could
allocate it to settlers while disinheriting Africans from their own soil.[48]

The British approach mirrored the US's reliance on the doctrine of
discovery to expand west in North America. This doctrine was a "legal
principle [that] was created and justified by religious and ethnocentric
ideas of European and Christian superiority over the other cultures,
religions, and races of the world. The Doctrine provided that newly
arrived Europeans automatically acquired property rights in native
lands and gained governmental, political, and commercial rights over
the inhabitants without the knowledge or the consent of the indigenous
people."[49] In the United States, the state of Oregon, for example, was
carved up and distributed like the Kenyan White Highlands, with the
US government giving away 320-acre parcels of land to white settlers
under the Oregon Donation Land Act of 1850.[50]

In 1920, the British also instituted a requirement for all black African
men leaving their reserves to carry a pass, which recorded their name,
fingerprint, ethnic group, past and current employers.[51] Such measures
were later echoed by Nazi Germany in the 1930s and 1940s when all Jews
had to wear the Star of David. While the demarcation of Kenyan reserves
was based on ethnic groups, in Nairobi, it was based on the color of one's
skin. Neither my parents nor my teachers ever mentioned the vivid demarcation of Nairobi into areas reserved for people of a particular color. I
grew up in Parklands, a neighborhood north of Nairobi's railway station.
It is still predominantly a brown neighborhood because the ramifications
of British racism a difficult to undo. Schools, community centers, and
hospitals serve distinct communities and are not easily moved.

Land tenure documents are also stuck in the past. While working in
Kenya, a colleague of mine showed me a current, valid, long-term lease
for a property in the affluent neighborhood of Karen, an area southwest

of Nairobi's railway station and home to the popular Giraffe Center and Elephant Orphanage. The document restricts leases to whites only. Today, no one obeys it; Karen is like Manhattan's Upper West Side. Kenya's black and white elites live side-by-side in their large Karen homes.

Nairobi cannot undo the racial zoning inherited from the British. Americans cannot either. In 1917, the US Supreme Court overturned well-established city ordinances that adopted racial zoning ordinances separating blacks and whites, but many communities continued the practice racial segregation, unhindered by city governments. For example, in 1919, the Realty Board in Portland, Oregon, adopted a rule declaring it unethical for an agent to sell property to either "Negro" or "Chinese" people in a white neighborhood. This language was not removed from the board's Code of Ethics until 1956.[52]

The Waki Commission, which investigated Kenya's 2007/2008 post-election violence, "expressed grave concern at what it saw as both overt and covert policies to encourage ethnic homogeneity in land allocation and in the acquisition of land."[53] It found that this "had led over the years to 'residential apartheid,' for example in urban areas where concentration of ethnic groups together had become commonplace."[54] What it failed to mention was that the British had first sowed the seeds for this residential apartheid in Kenya and one cannot fail to notice it walking around Nairobi today.

The land scramble continued during World War II, as the British war machine turned to Kenya to increase both agricultural production and the supply of soldiers. The British manipulated the markets to promote white farmers. They prohibited Africans from growing the most profitable cash crops such as tea, coffee, and sisal (often used for manufacturing rope, mats, and bags). They later required Kenyans to sell all maize, a staple crop, to the marketing boards at a set price.[55] Today, the maize boards continue to play a substantial role in Kenya's market and food economy.

But World War II perhaps played the greatest role in Britain's downfall in Kenya: its independence in 1963; the second scramble for Kenya; and the current manifestation of the land problem. Both white settlers and black Kenyans were recruited and mobilized in the Southeast Asian Theater, or the Burma Campaign. This theater (1944–1945) included American troops and British Commonwealth land forces comprising these Kenyan soldiers. As both Manji and Elkins explain, after serving together as equals, these black and white Kenyans returned after the war to ongoing discriminatory practices.[56] According to Elkins, black "veterans found many of their British counterparts receiving demobilization support from the colonial government in the form of land, low interest loans, and job creation programs."[57] These black veterans, as many as 75,000, were given nothing. Black Kenyan soldiers did not come home with only physical fighting skills.[58] They returned with knowledge about other oppressed peoples. They were inspired by their commonwealth counterparts, learning about ongoing violent and nonviolent movements against the British in Asia. Only a few years later, they would hear about successful independence movements that freed British colonies, including Pakistan and India (1947) and Burma (1948). Native Americans who also fought for the United States in Asia also returned with the same lessons, which they applied to their movements.

The British not only took Kenyans into the war theaters; they brought the war to Kenya. During my tenure in Kenya, I would surprise visitors, both family and other officials, with two popular tourist attractions. The first was a tiny church, built in 1942 by Italian prisoners of war whom the British had captured in Ethiopia. Today, that church lies on the last hairpin bend in the road from Nairobi before one arrives on the floor of the Great Rift Valley, en route to the junction that splits off to the west to Masai Mara National Park and to the north to the 9,108-foot Mount Longonot. The British had forced the prisoners to build the road and the church.

The second tourist site is the Nairobi War Cemetery, near the Ngong Racecourse, another British relic in Kenya and one that mimics the Aston Downs. The cemetery houses the remains of Kenyan soldiers killed on the front lines of the two World Wars. In the early 1900s, British Kenya lay nestled between German Tanzania to the south and Italian Ethiopia and Somalia to the north. My parents, both baby boomers, would relate tales of air raid sirens, blackouts, bunkers, and errant troops—not in Europe but in their hometown of Mombasa.

The British government's postwar promises were racist, benefiting only the whites in Kenya, conceiving the Mau Mau movement, and driving the demand for the return of Kenya's land to black Kenyans.[59] The British mounted a multipronged defense against the Mau Mau and rising anticolonial sentiment. But it was an exaggerated war. Elkins concludes, "officially, fewer than one hundred Europeans, including settlers, were killed and some eighteen hundred [black Kenyan] loyalists died at the hands of the Mau Mau. In contrast, the British reported that more than eleven thousand Mau Mau were killed in action."[60] Elkins' research, however, shows "there was in late colonial Kenya a murderous campaign to eliminate Kikuyu people, a campaign that left tens of thousands, perhaps hundreds of thousands, dead."[61] The end of British rule was inevitable; the second egg had been broken and scrambled, land had been stolen, and British atrocities were unforgivable. Kenyans mobilized against the British and, within a few short years, Kenya gained independence.

The Third Scramble

The immediate years before and directly after Kenya's 1963 independence constituted the third scramble for the nation's land. This one is perhaps more complicated than the first two because, contrary to public perception, the enemies were united. The British government, with assistance from the World Bank and the blessing of Kenya's future leaders, began different types of massive resettlement schemes, which continued to evolve postindependence. It was a well-planned land distribution scheme "designed by the British colonial administration and the international lending agencies—influenced by European settlers and not the African political leaders."[62] The British and new Kenyan government did not, as many Kenyans believe, buy large tracts of land from white farmers and redistribute them to black Kenyans. Land was never given back to Kenyans for free. USAID acknowledged this façade in its analysis of the draft National Land Policy of 2009, stating, "the repeated references to resettlement as part of the solution is unsettling, as badly planned or executed settlement schemes have been a large part of the problem."[63] More than half a century later, Kenyans must refrain from calling these settlement schemes "land reform." As Francesca Di Matteo, writes, the "Africanisation of the White Highlands followed neither the logic of restitution to the first occupants (land to the "natives") nor that of redistribution (land to the landless). The state orchestrated both sales of the old White Highlands and their financial conditions without any restructuring of the property system."[64] Kenyans had to use their own money or borrow money that had to be repaid either to Britain or the World Bank.[65]

The colonial powers and the new Kenyan politicians endorsed this approach together, driven by international capital markets, agricultural experts, and public relations. Even in the early 1960s, Kenya's new western educated leaders were concerned about the country's credit rating. They did not want to start off in debt. Neither did the British want to leave Kenya saddled with additional debt or burden British taxpayers, having spent millions on local administration, infrastructure, and the *Lunatic Express.* Agricultural experts drove the settlement schemes' designs, including locations, type of crops, and parcel sizes. Public relations responded to internal pressures, "intensive lobbying by European farmers with significant illegal assets," and external pressures to fix the impressions of both Britain's colonial failure and Kenya's looming independence.[66]

Kenyan leaders were not unanimous in their endorsement; a small, powerless opposition movement unsuccessfully "opposed the very principles of land reform as presented by Kenyatta, chiefly the requirement that the landless raise deposits and loans to reacquire property which was theirs."[67] Most leaders, comprising the elite, promoted the British plan. They wanted to underscore the idea that any land title was indefeasible; it could not be voided, canceled, or revoked under any situation or condition. They claimed that the opposite, a defeasible title, would threaten the security of tenure. The British plan "proposed that giving African farmers security of tenure through providing 'indefeasible title' would provide both an incentive for investment of labour and effort in farming and also enable the land to be used as security to raise financial credit."[68] Both the British and the ruling black elite loved it. In 1959, just four years before independence, the Native Lands Trust Ordinance was passed. It was based on the British model of registering a title, codifying the indefeasible title practice that underscores many of today's land concerns, which are not exclusive to Kenya. Some Americans have asked the same question; given that land was stolen from Native Americans, how can we now make reparations when private individuals and companies own the land?

A second undercurrent separated the haves and have-nots. Those Kenyans who could afford to pay for the land or underwrite a loan were the salaried middle class. Kenyatta's own Kikuyu community "was more able to command access to finance with 'better access to loans and better protection from default.' This meant that the first wave of land purchases and thus the first transfer of land ownership from white owners in the Rift Valley was marked by class and ethnicity" with competition for the best land.[69] Readers familiar with Kenya's history will appreciate how this class and ethnic conflict manifests in each of Kenya's election cycles. The white power holders were replaced by black ones. In Ambreena Manji's words, "the colonialists had succeeded in their primary approach to systematically diffuse political nationalism by creation of a social class within the African ranks having similar interests, aspirations and ideals as those of the ruling colonial elite."[70]

The Land Question

Having understood the context for Kenya's land concerns, the social construct of land, three scrambles, and two undercurrents—the indefeasible title and a new black social class—we can now turn to the land problem itself. Kenyans interchangeably use the terms "land problem," "land question," "land reform," and "land issue." Dr. Willy Mutunga, a former university professor, activist, and the first chief justice of Kenya and president of the Supreme Court under the new constitution (2011–2016), describes it as "our seemingly intractable land problems."[71] Mutunga doesn't explain the overarching problem, instead he delineates a non-exhaustive list of the manifestation of the problems, or the outer skin of the avocado. Specifically, he identifies "inequitable concentration of land in the hands of the wealthy, a propensity for land grabbing, unresolved historical land injustices, and landlessness."[72] But what constitutes the flesh and seed of the avocado?

USAID goes to the other extreme, identifying the sum of the root causes of Kenya's development woes. In keeping with its brazen tone in the quotation at the beginning of this chapter, the 2020–2025 CDCS concludes that *all* of Kenya's problems have "enabled Kenya's leaders to block others from the benefits of political and economic opportunities."[73] The end of that sentence explains why both development partners and Kenyans are obsessed with the land problem in Kenya; it is because they want the public to have equal access to political and economic opportunities.

Unfortunately, development partners (donors and their implement-ing partners) are simply a reflection of the people that work for them, and people, across cultures, seek out short, easily defined, tangible solutions even when faced with complex, system-based problems. They don't ask why Kenya's leaders have blocked others, been allowed to block them, and continue to block. The international community, encouraged and led by Kenya's vibrant civil society, made a similar mistake in Kenya after the 2007/2008 postelection violence. As His Highness the Aga Khan told the Canadian Parliament in February 2014, "at a time of extreme danger in Kenya a few years ago—the beginnings of a civil war—the former Secretary-General of the United Nations, Kofi Annan, led the way to a peaceful solution which rested heavily on the strength of Ke-nya's Civil Society."[74] That peaceful solution, an agreement signed by all parties, took the overall problem of election-related violence and broke it down into its individual manifestations to explain why Kenya flirted with civil war. The fourth agenda of the agreement, the "Statement of Principles of Long-Term Issues and Solutions," was a noteworthy at-tempt to identify what had to be corrected under each of the issues to prevent a future crisis.

The second of the six issues in Agenda 4 was "Land Reform." The document states that "the issue of land has been a source of economic, social, political, and environmental problems in Kenya for many years."[75] The sum of the individual land-related issues constitutes a whole that is greater than the individual parts. In this case, the sum is all-encompass-ing, namely, all economic, social, political, and environmental problems. The wording is too vague for the Kenyan government, the nation's civil society, and the international community to grasp. I prefer focusing instead on USAID's conclusion that land issues, like other development problems in Kenya, have "enabled Kenya's leaders to block others from the benefits of political and economic opportunities."[76]

Only after understanding these matters comprehensively can we then ask why this block happened, has been allowed to happen, and continues to happen. What roles have land issues played in this block-ing strategy? In this section, I peel back the avocado skin, examine the different tastes, textures, and temperatures of the flesh, and break open the seed of root issues for the Western reader. I address four issues that constitute my articulation of the land question, beginning with the first two components that former Chief Justice Mutunga identified: (1) concentration of land in the hands of the wealthy and (2) land grabbing.[77]

Issue One: Land Concentration in the Hands of the Wealthy

In the United States, one's elite status derives from a variety of total assets, including physical (land, equipment, and infrastructure), financial (stock, futures, investments), businesses (physical or virtual), power, or influence. Driven by the social construct described earlier in this chapter, wealth in Kenya is synonymous primarily with land ownership and land is concentrated in Kenya's wealthy elite. The elite may be found among politicians, dynastic families, and businesspeople. However, ministers were politicians and not bureaucrats as they are in the United States because prior to the 2010 Constitution, Kenya followed Britain's parliamentary system with ministers drawn from parliament. The wealthy elite, today, also include powerful civil servants and those in the military and judiciary. The Ndung'u report identifies these elite individuals as beneficiaries of illegal land awards.[78]

Most of these elite go unnoticed. Like many of my brown Kenyan counterparts, they accumulate wealth outside of the public spotlight. I have no idea how many malls, office buildings, hotels, industries, and tourist lodges they may own. Some have their moment of fame when the media, or civil society, highlight their wrongdoings, or when they are caught red-handed as a middleman in an illegal scheme. But they are quick to fade back into the shadows.[79]

Other members of the elite—presidents, ministers, and other politicians—cannot evade the public spotlight. The 1978 declassified CIA report detailed Kenya's first president and first lady's land holdings (over 280,000 acres including a ranch, two tea plantations, and three sisal farms). In 2013, *Forbes* published the article "Kenyan Millionaire Uhuru Kenyatta Officially Wins Presidential Election," which placed a spotlight on this dynastic family stating, "the Kenyatta family land holdings alone are worth over $500 million."[80] In 2021, Kenya's former interior minister, Fred Matiangi, provided a parliament committee with a list of the land holdings of then–Deputy President Ruto, including 18,000 acres in three farms, two hotels, and three residences.[81] Right before the 2022 election, the media also published a report of Ruto's opponent, Raila Odinga, stating, that the former owns "multimillion homes in Karen, Mombasa, Siaya and Kisumu."[82]

These political and economic elites use land as a weapon, fueled by the social construct discussed earlier. Politicians win votes by promising the return of grabbed public land, offering new title deeds, or initiating new settlement schemes, just as American politicians use guns, immigration, and abortion as political weapons in the United States.

In Kenya, the economic elite use land to expand their own wealth, and as USAID identified, block others from economic opportunities. Kenya's Supreme Court recognized this in a 2014 advisory opinion: "Land title, by its singularity as the mark of entitlement to landed property, is the ultimate expression of a vital property right, quite apart from being the very reference-point in numerous financial and business transactions-national and international."[83] The indefeasible land title, even if fraudulently obtained, is a security that can be traded; the land it protects can be developed or mortgaged for significant economic gain.

The Kenyan elite first started amassing this weapon during the third scramble for Kenya, when they took over from the white British elite. According to the 2009 National Land Policy, "it was expected that the transfer of power from colonial authorities to indigenous elites would lead to fundamental restructuring of the legacy on land. This did not materialise and the result was a general re-entrenchment and continuity of colonial land policies, laws and administrative infrastructure. This was because the decolonisation process represented an adaptive, co-optive and preemptive process which gave the new power elites access to the European economy."[84]

These power elites are experts in deflecting attention and blame, protecting each other, and thwarting public attempts for change. As the declassified 1978 CIA report stated, "to protect the holdings of its members and the family, the government blocked every parliamentary attempt to limit land ownership."[85] Members of the elite have managed to uphold the status quo since independence by playing the long game, continuously using defensive and offensive tactics to entrench their rights. For example, in the mid-1970s, President Kenyatta verbally decreed that no first- or second-line beachfront plots could be bought or sold on the Kenyan coast without presidential consent or approval from the powerful provincial administrator. This decree, in effect, ensured that valuable coastal waterfront land would only be available for the elite and their cronies, or the foreign corporations that they had established to hold such land at arm's length.[86] The 2010 Constitution listed at least 48 new laws to be passed within five years, including new legislation on land within 18 months (Fifth Schedule). The first Land Act (No. 6 of 2012) did not mention beach front property, likely because there was a significant amount of domestic and international scrutiny of these new laws. Nevertheless, the government continued to enforce Kenyatta's verbal restriction on coastal land until 2014 when Kenya's court of appeal sided with the Law Society of Kenya to end this "unlawful, nonexistent, and opaque" practice.[87] The first round goes to civil society.

Four years later, after the first presidential election under the new constitution, when public and international scrutiny had waned, and following the court of appeal's 2014 decision, which found no legal basis for the restriction on beachfront property, the power elite struck again. This time, parliament passed the Land Laws (Amendment) Act (No. 28 of 2016), enshrining, for the first time in law, the first president's decree on first- and second-row beachfront land. The elite take round two.

Once again, the Kenyan public, through its civil society, had to react and fight back. In October 2021, Kenya's land and environment court concluded that this requirement, in the 2016 amendments, was unconstitutional. Does this decision mean that the elite will rest? No, not by a long shot. The decision could always be appealed, the law revised again in a different bill, or, at the very least, the land administrative system can be further weakened or at least blocked from being improved, as I will discuss under "Issue 4" in this section. Sometimes the elite will win; other times, with the courts' support, they will lose a battle but not the war. When public sentiment swings the pendulum too far against the elite, they find creative ways to push back.

The elite also know when to put the land weapon down and try something else. In 2020, *The Star* stated that Odinga is, "damned if he does, damned if he doesn't" regarding his position on land.[88] This is similar to the position that Kenyatta found himself in before the third scramble for Kenya: "As Raila seeks their support for 2022, the land disinheritance proposal puts him in a fix. Do the right thing for needy landless people or satisfy the influential landowners/occupiers whose help he needs? At a time when Raila has been enjoying strong national support . . . stirring up the controversial and emotive land issue, experts warn, could deal him irreparable damage."[89] But while the elder Kenyatta took a stand and sided with the British land occupiers, Odinga waffled. In the runup to the 2022 election, Mugai reported, "for the first time in decades, Kenya's leading presidential candidates are skirting around the explosive issue of land justice—instead of exploiting it as a way to mobilise voters to their campaigns. Both candidates—for different reasons—have chosen to accept the status quo on legal regime on land rights."[90]

Not only will members of the elite stand up and protect each other but so will those who are in their debt. If someone accepts a title for a parcel of land from a power-wielding elite, they cannot blow the whistle on their benefactor. Youth gangs are often bought out to do the elite's dirty work, including forceful evictions and the destruction of property. Professionals do the elite's bidding by influencing, coercing, or forging documents. Three commissioners of the Truth, Justice, and Reconciliation Commission published a statement of dissent that "reveals the cloak-and-dagger environment that prevailed at the Commission, and how some commissioners were coopted into downplaying, changing or deleting certain sections of the TJRC's final report that mentioned the Kenyatta family adversely."[91] Unstated in the dissent is that the individuals who pressured the commission were likely not members of the Kenyatta family but rather hired or coerced by them.

The elite are also extremely tenacious. Consider a 2020 mainstream newspaper report about an interview on Nation Television (NTV) with Kenya's former deputy president, William Ruto. The article compared Ruto to Donald Trump, who was then serving his first presidential term: "In the much anticipated NTV interview of Deputy President William Ruto, he once again demonstrated something few politicians—including the most loathed by many like U.S. President Donald J Trump—are able to do: Creating an aura of invincibility that many buy hook, line and sinker when in reality, they're men and women under siege."[92]

Can Kenyan civil society, backed by the international development partners, counter this power? They think they can. USAID's 2020–2025 CDCS includes the following intermediate result: "Accountable, ethical, and effective leaders who drive change increased." Most of the proposals I received for KTI fell into one of two themes pertaining to the elite's power over land: litigation and public shaming. I would discuss the proposals with the applicants and explain why neither was in the US government's interest to fund. First, the US government cannot fund one group to sue another party. Second, litigation in Kenya, as I discuss later under this chapter's "Issue 4" section, has not accumulated enough positive momentum to check elitist power. Third, shaming the elite, whether formal or informal, is like using a water gun to put out a forest fire; members of the elite have no shame when it comes to their land holdings and wealth in Kenya. The nation has a whole collection of formal government investigative commission reports (e.g., from the Njonjo Commission, Ndung'u Commission, and Truth Justice and Reconciliation Commission) and civil society studies (e.g., from Kenya Land Alliance) that identify specific land barons and their legal and il-legal holdings. These splash newspaper headlines, feed Kenya's vibrant traditional and social media, and then are quickly forgotten, or they are used only by researchers or officials to inform subsequent investigations.

Nevertheless, KTI did support a few creative approaches, probably inconsequential in the larger scheme of land reform. One series of grants enabled local youth and women's groups to research myths about land ownership and to disseminate those findings, thereby facilitating a shift from myths and hearsay to fact. After KTI's assistance, other groups tried to use that information to attempt to shame the elite but those efforts did not achieve anything, positive or negative.

A second soft grant was extremely subtle; it was an injection of ethics and rationale, meant to enter the system and diffuse over a long-term period. In early 2010, over cocktails at the US ambassador's residence in Nairobi, I engaged with the British principal of one of Nairobi's elite private British schools concerning the upcoming constitution referendum. He was concerned and frustrated with the lack of engagement by senior Kenyan students on the nation's crisis and crossroads. He wanted assistance in developing and disseminating age-appropriate information about the reform agenda, constitution, and the impacts of the 2007/2008 postelection violence. Although unsaid, we both realized the significance of such assistance, namely, that the students at the school were the sons and daughters of Kenya's elite, the same elite who, according to USAID, block *others from the benefits of political and economic opportunities.*[93] Could we infuse ethics and a democratic rationale into these future hereditary elite? Could they, in turn, influence their parents?

The principal had already initiated new mandatory classes on civics, and KTI then entered into a grant agreement with a civil society group to provide technical assistance, lesson plans on reform and the constitution, guest speakers, and an interschool forum that culminated with a discussion with the media houses. Other schools expressed interest, but KTI could not follow through because by then all US efforts were focused on get-out-the-vote campaigns for the August 2010 referendum (see chapter 3). There was no feasible way to measure the grant's impact given that the grant period was one semester. No one from the outside ever saw our work in this domain and, the impact, if any, would not be felt for a generation. After all, this was not an activity one could evaluate by assessing changes in attitudes among the very parents we were trying to target.

USAID's global reporting structure monitors the funding to grantees and contractors, measuring the work that they do within their respective scopes of work. For example, the number of youth networks were strengthened, classrooms renovated, or farmers equipped. USAID programs may consolidate those numbers and discuss the overall contribution to the country's leadership, education, or agriculture. However, program evaluations cannot attribute changes to specific interventions because there are too many other variables to consider. For example, youth networks strengthened by USAD funding could also be coopted by the elite to engage in violence; classrooms may be renovated but teachers may not be performing well; and farmers may be equipped but products may linger due to a lack of markets or transportation. In the end, development partners, like USAID, only *hope* that their contribution will result in improved development indicators. For example, the 2020–2025 CDCS states, "to engage and cultivate youth leaders, USAID will prioritize strengthening local youth-led organizations and networks as well as leverage its regional Young African Leaders Initiative (YALI), including its trained alumni, to provide leadership and life skills training."[94] On the surface, KTI's initiative was no different in that engaged and cultivated youth leaders.

Americans may never have expected that one Kenyan who received a scholarship to study in the United States would later become the father of our first black president. The result, or outcome, of an intervention can never be predicted. As KTI came to an end following the 2013 election, and in the decade that has followed, I have remotely tried to track the staff, consultants, grant recipients, and program beneficiaries that have run for and even succeeded in being elected to office. I know for sure that the KTI extended family has or has had, since 2013, at least one governor, senator, member of the National Assembly (the lower house of parliament), deputy speaker, commissioner, cabinet minister, and high court judge. Former members of the KTI family are now scattered across Kenya and the globe working on other development partner projects. KTI's evaluators noted, "perhaps [what is] most significant.... [is that] KTI has contributed to the formation of social capital in Kenya by incubating current and future civil society leadership. . . . As KTI winds down in Kenya and its Kenyan staff move on to new positions, this asset is one that will continue to impact the country in the years to come."[95]

Issue Two: Land Grabbing

Kenyan media references to land grabbing are as frequent and sensational as a 2 percent swing in the Dow Jones Industrial Average (DJIA). Both are societal jolts that happen about once a week. Many, Westerners, like me, puzzle over the phrase "land grabbing." The term "grabbing" refers to taking personal or moveable items. One can grab a purse or wallet, clothes or furniture, an exotic pet, or, unfortunately, a child. Grabbing a permanent fixed asset is counterintuitive; I did not use the term when I first moved to Kenya because it was an enigma to me.

A valid land title proves ownership of a parcel of land. It is a security that can be bought, traded, or used as collateral. When I bought my home in the United States, I had to order a title search to ensure the seller was indeed the owner and that there were no claims, liens, covenants, or other encumbrances on the property. My mortgage lender also required that I buy title insurance to cover my lender in cases of title fraud, mistakes, or undisclosed heirs to the property. This level of protection is not the norm in Kenya, probably because the risk of fraud is too high for any insurance company to underwrite.

I define "land grabbing" as illegally taking land by fraudulently obtaining a title. How do Kenyans do this? One way is to make or buy a counterfeit copy of the title. Like anywhere in the world, the more you pay for a counterfeit, the better the quality will be. In this case, this means superior replicas of security features, which the Ministry of Lands, Public Works, Housing, and Urban Development (hereafter: Ministry of Lands) uses on its legitimate titles. What systems are in place to prevent or catch counterfeit titles? A title search is meant to compare the title, or its information, that a seller provides alongside the official information recorded with the government. In the United States, a title could be stored in a physical form at a county registry of deeds. Larger towns may make this registry available online but the official version, in the case of discrepancies, is the paper version in the physical registry. A Kenyan registry uses the same theory. A paper title may be issued (or forged) and a digital copy may or may not be available in the ministry's new web-based system, but a conclusive search must be conducted at the registry. Kenya's registries also maintain an official green card, a large index card that records each transaction for a particular property.

Because KTI staff visited district registries in an official capacity, the registrars in several towns were proud to show us the inside of the registries, behind the counter where the public cannot go. These areas include their file rooms; we were shown them because employees wanted to demonstrate their dire need for basic assistance in the form of workspace, shelving, files, and lighting. In one registry, I randomly selected a folder that prominently displayed the parcel number on the file label. There was no surprise there; the folder likely mirrored billions in land registries across the world. What was unusual in this registry, that someone unfamiliar with local land administration problems could latch onto, was the adjacent folder to the one I randomly selected. It was a different folder but had the same parcel number as the one in my hand. I looked at the land registrar with a huge question mark on my face. He shrugged, looked at me not as an American official but as a Kenyan who should understand the reality of bureaucracies and fraud, quietly took the folder from my hand, put it back on the shelf, and ushered us along.

With more than one official record, a single parcel of land has more than one legal owner and the possibilities of fraud become endless. A friend of mine fell victim to a fraud scheme when buying land in Nairobi. He inspected a property that a realtor had advertised in the newspaper, made a verbal offer to the realtor, and began his due diligence. He ordered a title search at the land registry by providing the parcel number and seller's name. The official search results came back; the owner's name and property description matched what he believed he was buying.

Therefore, it appeared legitimate. He met with the sellers, realtor, and lawyer at the law firm, signed an agreement, and paid the deposit. By pure luck, he took his own contractor to the property and the contractor had actually worked for the property owner and knew that they did not match the sellers in the lawyer's office! These were legitimate lawyers and realtors, but the seller was fake. By the time the word got out, the fake seller had disappeared and, most likely, the duplicate fake record at the ministry would have quickly disappeared. With no evidence of fraud, police or Kenya's Ethics and Anti-Corruption Commission (EACC) can do little to investigate and prosecute fraudsters or those who facilitate fraud within the administration.

Land grabbing schemes also focus on public land, which, like in the United States, comprises more than parks, schools, and road reserves. Such land includes property held by public entities, including transportation authorities, port authorities, utilities companies, and the local government. These may be set aside for future use, leased out to businesses or industries, or developed by the public owner. With the help of officials inside a land registry, wealthy and well-connected individuals can "purchase" a duplicate file or subdivide a public parcel and then transfer the ownership to themselves or a holding company. In 2011, a KTI grant to a youth group in Kisumu uncovered an example of this approach. The youth proved that, with help from an insider at City Hall and the Ministry of Lands, a well-connected, private developer fraudulently secured the title of the beautiful, 1.6-acre downtown Taifa Park. The municipality had a 99-year lease, effective from 1961, for the parcel from the government of Kenya. But in 2008 a new certificate of lease was issued and four days later the property was transferred to well-connected individuals. Forty-three days later, the lease was sold to a local businessman. The district lands registrar updated the green card in 2009. Further investigations showed that a town clerk had declared the old certificate lost, obtained a new certificate of lease in 2008, and then authorized the 2008 transfer. The Kisumu council claimed ignorance over the matter, the town clerk and registrar had already relocated when the investigations began, and the file was never found in the registry. Such a transaction requires the paying and receiving of bribes and acts of collusion among multiple people within industry, city administration and the land registry.[96] According to the Ndung'u report, "the extensive complicity of professionals (lawyers, surveyors, valuers, physical planners, engineers, architects, land registrars, estate agents, and bankers) in the land and property market [is] key to the process of land grabbing."[97]

This type of narrative is not unique. Consider a different incident, reported in the mainstream Kenyan media after the KTI program ended. On July 3, 2018, *The Star* published the following: "Former Nakuru land registrar charged with fraud, freed on Sh2m bond."[98] This came out after a former member of parliament in Kenya and the land registrar staff were found guilty of land grabbing. Justice takes a long time (see chapter 1). Four years later, *The Star* published an article titled, "Court postpones MP Arama's sentencing."[99] The piece explained that the Kenya Railways Corporation (a public company) leased two plots of land in Nakuru to a private company in 1996. The company then sold the land to a businessman in 2011. In 2015, the businessman investigated unusual construction activities on his land. An MP had colluded with the land registrar in Nakuru and issued a new certificate of lease to the MP in 2015. An internet search of images that match the phrase "land grabbing cartoons Kenya" will demonstrate the insanity and depth of this problem. The scale of the problem is unknown but the Ndung'u report conservatively estimated that 200,000 illegal titles were created between 1962 and 2000, 98 percent of those between 1986 and 2000; moreover, those who benefited included ministers, senior civil servants, politicians, businesspeople, churches, temples, and mosques.[100]

Many of Kenyan administrations are no longer embarrassed or worried about the publication of civil society or government investigative reports of public land grabbing and corruption. The N'dungu report; Njonjo Commission report; Truth, Justice and Reconciliation Commission (TJRC) report; and multiple publications by the Kenya Land Alliance all offer extensive details of land grabbing. Some explain the mechanics of *how* land is grabbed, others list tables of data showing land concentrated in a few hands, while other reports the detailed methods and specific names of people and organizations that grab public land.[101] The information in these reports could easily feed an entire, captivating reality television series. But, at the end of it all, it doesn't matter. As discussed in the section on ineffective judicial systems, evidence is almost nonexistent and the number of people successfully prosecuted and sentenced for land grabbing is negligible when considering the scale of the problem. The Kenyan public quickly forgets today's headlines about land grabbing as other scandals or news distracts them. Consider the tenacity of the former deputy president: "Ruto and his co-accused were acquitted [in 2011] of selling the land to Kenya Pipeline Corporation, which the government argued was hived off Ngong Forest. The three were let go due to lack of evidence. For anyone who knows anything about justice and law in Kenya, 'lack of evidence' is code terms for the acquitted bought 'justice' they wanted, not that there was no evidence to convict."[102] In 2020 the Kenyan Directorate of Criminal Investigation reopened the old case but, in 2022, Ruto won the 2022 presidential election and the investigation was terminated.

The Kenyan government, with support from various aid agencies, especially those originating from Sweden, has embarked on many efforts to digitize or automate its land administration systems, believing that technology and the transformation from paper into digital files would solve the problem. One USAID administrator, Rajiv Shah, believed this. On July 13, 2010, he gave a speech entitled, "Transforming Development Through Science, Technology, and Innovation."[103] He made no reference to sociology, anthropology, or psychology. Two parcel numbers can look identical to the human eye but not to a computer; the latter would readily accept 53045-029, 53O45-029, and 53045-O29 as different codes because of the interplay between the number zero and the letter O. In Kenya, such games will go on, irrespective of technology, if the elite wants them to. If the numbering system is fixed, another loophole will be found. As Ambreena Manji writes, "The Ndung'u report found that surveyors employed by the Ministry would survey a piece of land 'from their desk' without ever visiting the site and subsequently issue two title deeds to the same parcel of land [under two different valid land acts (1963 and 1982)]. The double issuance of titles was meant to facilitate the illegal allocation of land."[104] One can only wait to see if Kenya's future efforts to clean up laws, digitize, and automate will be incrementally smarter than their predecessors' efforts.

As with the first issue, concentrating land in the hands of the wealthy, the proposals KTI received to try and address the problem of land grabbing relied either on more litigation or shaming, both of which we rejected. We did fund some logistical and operational startup costs for the TJRC, which would eventually split on the issue of land. At the request of a coastal civil society group, we funded research into land grabbing and historical injustices surrounding a factory on the coast. Like many others in Kenya, this group had a narrow understanding of the real story behind the factory's ownership and activities. As a result, the subsequent research allowed them to see, firsthand, that the case was not as clear cut as the public had believed and that blame was to be shared among the government, company, and public. But one of the real reasons we funded that particular research was because the lead researcher, Muhammad Swazuri, would soon be named as the first chairman of the newly created National Land Commission. The grant gave KTI an opportunity to establish a relationship with the new commission and to focus its attention on the coast. Later, we would capitalize on that relationship when we were asked to become the first international donor to fund the commission's startup.

The *Nairobi Law Monthly* offered its own verdict on the performance of the first commissioners, including Swazuri, whose term ended in 2019: "The commission has achieved great strides in recovering illegally acquired public land[,] especially in riparian lands and along railway lines in areas such as Kisumu, as evidenced by the recent demolitions. However, this is a drop in the ocean as the commission has miserably failed to go after the real beneficiaries of irregular allocation of public and community land, namely politicians who own large tracts of land."[105] After the former chair was accused of impropriety on more than one occasion, former Mombasa senator, Emma Mbura, defended him saying, "no one is perfect in this world, but Swazuri has tried. . . . These people, some of whom got into Ardhi House illegally, will always have something bad to say about him. From where I sit, he has tried. Swazuri helped communities at the Coast get title deeds for the first time in their history."[106] It sounded like our efforts were not in vain. But the former chairman's downfall, including an August 2022 report of a case against him at the anticorruption court, emphasized the hopelessness of the land grabbing problem. Whether the accusations are true or false, he is yet another Kenyan reformer who has either succumbed to Kenya's undercurrent of corruption and fraud or been accused by member of the same elite group he was trying to rein in. *The Standard* article echoed how I felt when hearing about the charges against him: "Those who knew the professor from years back say they struggle to recognise the man now."[107] Development partners, including the United States, are powerless against this monumental and deeply anchored practice.

Since this is the only section in which I address Kenya's infamous corruption pertaining to facilitating the transactions needed to grab land, I must address two important aspects. First, many Western donor staff members forget that corruption exists in the United States. In 2022, the US ranked twenty-fourth in Transparency International's corruption index: "[The] U.S. still has a corruption problem, and it's one that we need to take seriously. We're by no means the world leader in clean government."[108]

Second, while "corruption" is synonymous with "Kenya" in that it underpins almost every segment of society and most service and procurement transactions, it is also something that Kenyans likely inherited from the British. David Anderson details the level of British corruption associated with constructing massive housing estates in Nairobi before independence at the same time as the third scramble over Kenya. The colonial government awarded contracts to smaller "Asian one-job-at-a-time companies" for 13,000 new bed spaces per year. "The scale of corruption unearthed by the Rose Commission surprised even Kenya's most cynical observers." One contractor "had no experience of largescale contract work, and was badly undercapitalized."[109] Anderson explains the Rose Commission's findings:

> European officials had accepted 'gifts' from building contractors before and during the contracts. Malpractice was found to be widespread in every aspect of the tendering and management of the Council's building contracts. The whiff of corruption also tainted the reputations of the highest aldermen of the Council: the Mayor of Nairobi, Israel Somen . . . was also accused of using council workers for his own enterprises, including the construction of a private swimming pool. Even in the City Fire Brigade, a group of senior European officers were involved in a longstanding scam to 'sell' city property, and then have it bought back at a margin. At the city market, corruption was rife in the allocation of licenses and plots, senior African clerk taking bribes as a matter of course from all the traders, and the European Market Manager, Mr. Burton, abusing his position to secure unpaid labor from the stallholders to work his own farm on the outskirts of the city.[110]

According to Anderson, the Rose Commission "reached the unequivo-cal conclusion that bribery and corruption were 'by no means uncommon' among city office holders at 'all levels and in all departments'; that the scale of cash inducements involved to secure services or preference from the Council was often significant; and that such behavior was accepted as the norm and widely tolerated."[111]

The commission's report would echo the findings of dozens of future Kenyan corruption investigation reports; the only difference among them is that, in the subsequent reports, the term "European" would be replaced by "Kenyan." Not much has changed in 70 years. Corruption thrives, bribes, abuse of power, and scams to sell public property and buy it back at a margin are common in current-day Kenya. The concentration of land in the hands of the wealthy, facilitated and exacerbated by the scale of corruption and the ease of land grabbing, are important issues. Knowing about such matters is necessary but insufficient to understand the land question. Two other important factors require analysis, that is, weak administrative systems that the donors tend to focus on and the unrealistic and untouchable expectation of reparations.

Issue Three: Weak Administrative Systems

The US government is one of the largest employers of civilians in the world and many of its employees are bureaucrats. Government bureau-crats have a bad reputation among the wider public because they appear slow, inefficient, bogged down by administrative details, and sticklers for processes and regulations. I have spent almost two decades working with federal government bureaucracies on international development, transportation, fishery management, environmental compliance, and hazard mitigation. I often find myself explaining and defending govern-ment bureaucracies.

The US Congress passes laws that the agencies of the executive branch must interpret and execute. Then, US agencies must promulgate complex regulations that detail the processes that the agency will use to execute the laws and that the public must use when trying to comply. For example, the Endangered Species Act of 1973 refers to "critical habi-tat," or areas that a threatened or endangered species occupies or that contain features essential to the species. The entire act is 44 pages.[112] The implementing agencies have had to develop policies and regulations that comprise several hundred pages. For example, the procedures for completing a consultation on critical habitat with the Federal Government under just one section of the law is 315 pages.[113]

Congress has established processes for agencies to develop these regulations and policies. These cannot be changed easily; it can take a couple of years to make a simple change because the agency must develop, draft, review, seek input from other agencies, and analyze the potential impact on the public, businesses, and the environment. The agency must publish the proposed changes, solicit public input, analyze that input, and then develop and publish a final notice to explain what comments it received and how it addressed those comments. Only then can the new regulation or policy be put into effect. A similar process covering legislation, regulations, policies, and procedures applies at the state and local governments levels.

American states require that their cities and towns establish land use plans and development zones. If a city wants to change its zoning, it must go through an elaborate analytical and public process that identifies the proposal's pros and cons and ensures that landowners will not lose their property development rights. Changes are generally not retroactive. In other words, a landowner cannot be required to comply with a new requirement or zoning restriction unless they later develop their property. For example, if my house were built when the city required a 50-foot buffer from any stream or wetland, the city cannot require I demolish part of my house if it later changes that requirement to 75 feet. However, if I were to rebuild my entire house, I would have to comply with the new requirement. As discussed above, changing the requirement from 50 to 75 feet can take many years because the process involves analysis, notifying the public, a public hearing, a committee decision, and an appeal period.

Why do Western governments require this level of bureaucratic effort for simple changes? Because a bureaucracy is designed to provide a buffer between an idea and its implementation such that haphazard or harmful ideas will be discarded. Each proposal must be analyzed to minimize its economic, social, and environmental impacts. American federal law, the 1946 Administrative Procedures Act (APA), determines the way federal agencies develop and issue regulations. The National Environmental Policy Act (NEPA) requires that the federal government analyze, disclose, and consider the environmental impacts of every single federal action it takes. That law has been in effect since 1970 and, in most cases, despite perennial grumblings from elected officials, works well for what Congress intended it to do.[114] State and local laws may have similar requirements for their proposed changes. A bureaucracy therefore protects the public from changes that unnecessarily impact society and its members. It also prevents politicians from waving a magic wand to make an instant change or overhaul a process simply to win electoral favors.

Kenya, however, does not have a developed, robust bureaucracy capable of withstanding such shocks. A politician or new department head with an idea may want an idea implemented instantly, without any studies, reviews, analysis, or opportunities for public input. I grew up 400 feet from the Nairobi River but never saw it or heard the water flowing. I knew it existed, out there somewhere, as a constricted, dirty waterway. It was not something I would venture down to, even as a teenage boy. Like most Kenyans, I did not understand the relationship between construction along the river, reduction in the floodplain capacity, and flooding we all experienced during the rainy season. In 2018, Nairobi's rivers made the international headlines as the city council embarked on a massive demolition program with little or no warning. Private property walls, buildings, a gas station, and even a multilevel shopping mall were torn down because they were illegally built in the riparian zones along rivers. According to the media, property owners had shown their building permits to a parliament committee and were told that their properties were safe. Yet the executive branch had given them only a few weeks of warning to vacate and, in some cases, the excavators arrived before that period expired.[115] Who was at fault? Was it the earlier government officials who accepted bribes to issue building permits? Or was it the developers who had built the buildings with fake or illegally obtained permits? Or, perhaps, those at fault were the unknowing buyers who had purchased properties with valid building permits.

In the example described earlier about development along the coast, the elite lose battles but not wars. They bounce back. This resilience is national. In Nairobi,

> after exactly four years, the Shell petrol station demolished in August 2018, is currently under reconstruction in exactly the same location

with permission and licence from the necessary agencies . . . During its demolition the official statement by the environmental management body was that it was encroaching on riparian land and was also on a road reserve. Its reconstruction demonstrates the recolonizing nature of demolitions in Nairobi: when they are enacted against the working class they are permanent but when carried out in affluent areas they are only temporary with loopholes that the elites can exploit to rebuild or receive compensation.[116]

Weak administrative systems hurt a country by making it impossible to criminalize perpetrators. There are just too many perpetrators in the entire cast of characters responsible for an unethical or criminal act. These weak systems result in damage, destruction, death, and disability. The media consistently report on building collapses stemming from corruption, fake engineers and architects, or a lack of inspections. A Kenyan police inspector was quoted in a report published by Voice of America, a US-funded international broadcaster, concerning two separate building collapses within a month that resulted in nine deaths. The inspector was reported as saying, "the big issue, the big elephant in the room, is corruption. . . . Even when [regulators] are there, they are able to allow a whole lot of substandard practices, a whole lot of illegal practices, because of course they're able to extort bribes and are not serious about doing their work."[117]

These weak systems enable the elite to prevent changes that they don't want, either because those changes would hamper the further expansion of their fortunes or, worse still, reclaim their illegal spoils. I saw this firsthand in Kenya. Progressive midlevel government officers approached me with great ideas for change that had been blocked from implementation. Those who had a vision and a will to change took a risk—we signed more than one grant agreement with government officials across ministries outside of Nairobi. Each one wanted to sign the agreement locally because they knew it would be blocked if they took it to their headquarters in Nairobi.

Field office staff in the United States often complain about headquarters. Regional administrators in the United States, or mission directors and ambassadors overseas, make as many local decisions as they can because they know that the officials in Washington, DC, would not understand the local dynamics or would have too many other pressing priorities to act in a timely fashion.

Why do Western and international development partners believe improvements to these administrative systems are simple and could be the silver bullet for solving land problems? Because they do not appreciate that personal gain through corruption trumps Western ethics and morals. Donors, including USAID, tend to focus too much on the laws and policies. Like politicians everywhere, including in the United States, they believe that improving an overlying law or developing a better policy automatically trickles down to changes on the ground. Not really. According to one Kenyan judge, "general prepositions of law did not solve concrete cases."[118]

One example from both Kenya and the United States demonstrates the reality of the disconnect between laws and implementation. In 2010, two in three Kenyans voted to approve the new constitution, an act which, among many other things, required that every elected or appointed body be constituted by not more than two-thirds of people of the same gender. This progressive, gender-based requirement was aimed at increasing the number of women in Kenya's government. At the same time, it ensured that in the future, men would never account for less than one-third. It was a noble attempt at gender equity but one that had not been thought through. A dozen years later, Kenya's parliament has been unable to pass legislation to effectuate this requirement for elected bodies because there is no viable and graceful solution. Kenya allows candidates to come from political parties or be independent. Without violating other laws on equality and the right for anyone to run for office, laws cannot require the public to vote for a person of a particular gender, nor prohibit a certain type of person from running for a particular office. One of the analyses on the attempts to implement this visionary constitution clause summarized, "lessons from 2010 indicate that the Constitution, however eloquent and well-articulated, is not self-executing. It requires and relies on key pillars to enable it to germinate, grow and flourish. The Constitution presupposed that its transformative potential would be implemented in the context of a matching culture of compliance."[119]

Nine thousand miles away from Nairobi, former US President Biden was visiting Portland, Oregon, to announce a $25 billion bipartisan infrastructure improvement law. The members of Congress who spoke before the president implied that they had played a key role in ensuring that money for seismic upgrades to a runway at Portland Airport (PDX) were included in the law and that the project had already been implemented. The president stated, "Folks, but your senators and congressmen are looking out for you. They fought to dedicate $3.75 million in the last month's omnibus bill to build a resilient runway here at PDX."[120] A law that sets aside money for a study is not self-executing; it cannot rebuild a runway. The $3.75 million was only for design; the actual project would cost $140 million.[121]

Laws and policies are necessary but not sufficient for change. With buy-in and patience, changemakers can alter an administrative system in a US government agency. This would be unlikely in Kenya, especially for land reform. The Ministry of Lands, in partnership with one or more development partner, has tried to automate or digitize land records on more than one occasion. Such significant efforts are bound to fail because those in opposition, the powerful elite, are too great a force; corruption is too widespread; and human nature drives one's desire to want more money, irrespective of one's individual salaries. Members of the elite know where the pressure points are and are not afraid to manipulate them. A study of UK's Department for Internal Development (DFID) projects in Kenya found that, "the lack of support from key Kenyan ministries undermined DFID's long-term strategy for public-sector reform in Kenya."[122] Additionally, "more broadly, in both Kenya and Nigeria, projects aimed at improving the accountability of institutions often wrongly assumed that formal oversight bodies would act as DFID's allies in the fight against impunity—but party allegiances and self-interest generally prevented this."[123] I had thought I was taking the higher ground by securing local ministry buy-in for land reform in Kenya. Yet, I, too, may have fallen victim to Kenya's underlying corruption and ethic of self-gain.

During my factfinding trips around Kenya's postelection violence hotspots, I kept in mind potential future flashpoints. One of these was the Mau Forest resettlement plan. One of my interlocutors introduced me to the chief registrar of the Ministry of Lands registry in Nakuru. A humble, well-spoken, and polite officer greeted our team; together, we engaged in formalities, including introductions, and an explanation of USAID, KTI, and our team. Thereafter, he gave us a tour of the registry. We saw the customer area, the filing rooms, files, and the green cards.

Everything was paper-based; I saw only one computer in the entire building. Light fixtures were broken, shelves were overflowing, and stacks of papers occupied every available desk and floor space. It was a mess; I would never want to work in such an environment. I also realized how easy it would be to lose files, misplace documents, and maintain duplicate files. The registrar himself led me to believe he stored some of the more delicate or susceptible files in his own office.

Back in Nairobi, I discussed the registry's physical problems with my colleagues, both USAID and at the US embassy. I also brought up the issue and showed pictures at the Development Partners Group on Lands, chaired by UN-Habitat. Everyone was appalled, yet every organization was helpless. Most donors channel funding through the central government and hope that it trickles down to the regions. Much of the emphasis on improving administrative systems is centered around Nairobi. As the Nakuru registrar had told me, his staff cannot even get the folders needed to store documents because those must be requisitioned from Nairobi. How could the development partners, led by Sweden, fund the digitization of land records when the records themselves were in such a mess? One thing I had learned from my first job in information technology was garbage in equals garbage out.

In typical KTI style, consistent with our sister programs around the world, we decided to institute a pilot, hands-on demonstration program in the Nakuru Lands registry. Our program team consulted with the registrar and his staff, observed employees in their daily routines, and designed and budgeted a small grant that ended up supplying in-kind goods and services worth $95,000 over 15 months. Although the registrar himself was unable to sign the grant agreement, KTI entered into an agreement with the commissioner of lands in Nairobi. The registrar oversaw the contractors and interns to rebuild shelving, fix lighting, paint the building's interior, fix floor tiles and doors, purchase and deliver folders and labels, organize files, and create a digital file inventory on computers that the ministry then delivered from Nairobi. This entire process was a prerequisite to any future digitization of land records.

The registrar told me how surprised he was to see the commissioner sign the agreement and provide regular support staff from the ministry's office in Nairobi, a two-hour drive away. I did my part to showcase the effort by organizing a site visit for other Development Partners Group on Lands members, many of whom rarely left the capital for site visits. They were clearly impressed but noted that the project did not fit their *mondus operandi* of international development work. The visit, however, did underscore my approach to analyzing problems and land reform matters in Kenya. Our evaluators noted, "essentially, once [KTI] arrived with your new political economy framework of the country the donor group could become more focused and agree on how to move forward."[124]

The project gained national recognition as land registrars and organizations using the registries networked. The Law Society of Kenya documented the transformation of the registry from being "historically fraught with challenges of poor record keeping and missing files" to being a "well-organized registry."[125] Based on demand, KTI supported its replication in other towns. The final evaluation team noted, "some of KTI's most impressive interventions, for example . . . the land registries in Kilifi, Kitale, Nakuru, Kajiado, and Thika, appear to be experiments, albeit successful ones."[126] By design, no two solutions were the same. Sure, all registries needed files, interns, shelving, improved customer reception areas, and training, but the solutions were customized for each location. In Kilifi, on Kenya's coast, land grabbing had resorted to the stealing of physical files from the registry. On more than one occasion, people had broken in through the dilapidated registry roof to steal records. Therefore, our support in Kilifi included a new, 40-foot secure, and weatherproof storage container, outfitted with locks, shelving, lights, and workstations. The contractors creatively managed to connect it to the registry file room, much like a vault in a bank, thereby ensuring the staff did not have to leave the public-restricted area to access the records in the container. Another registry team planned an exchange program between its registry and Nakuru to identify both successes and mistakes before implementing its own program. In a postimplementation survey, Kilifi Lands Registry staff, noted, "we are now able to meet our service charter goals . . . before we [had] improved our filing system, we could never locate files."[127] They also noted that "the fencing and strong room have increased our confidence and improved our morale."[128] An independent review team wrote in December 2012 that "KTI's work in several Land Registry offices in the Nakuru area has led to localized cases of increased citizen trust, evidenced by an increase in requests for documentation and, reportedly, a decrease in requests for bribes/manipulation of the system."[129]

The pilot in Nakuru evolved in 2010 and was completed in 2011. Over the past decade, I have always wondered about the success, sustainability, and shortcomings of the program. Did it help in the big picture? Did it help reduce fraud and legitimately misplaced files? How did it tie into the latest donor-supported initiative for digitizing land records and making them available online to landowners?[130] I never imagined that we at US-AID may have facilitated more efficient fraud. Perhaps we didn't. Years after the program ended, I did learn that, in 2018, a former Nakuru land registrar with the same name as the registrar I had worked with a decade earlier, was charged with land grabbing and, subsequently, in 2022, was found guilty alongside a former MP.[131] Perhaps there are two people with the same name and each has been the registrar of lands in Nakuru. Or, like the former chair of the National Land Commission, Swazuri, whom I discussed earlier, perhaps the registrar was set up because he had been unwilling to accept bribes and facilitate fraud. Or perhaps he, himself, had succumbed to the innate human desire to make a tradeoff between one's ethics and improving the quality of life for oneself or their family. I am neither judge nor jury, and I will not venture a verdict.

Perhaps I should have appreciated a tradeoff, rather than a silver bullet. The impacts of the land registry projects were clearly beneficial; there were, nonetheless, unanticipated adverse effects. I do not know if KTI's project facilitated fraud by making it easier, or whether fraud continued to happen at the same rate, or if was fraud reduced by US efforts. Nor will I ever know. What I can conclude, however, is that the social construct of land and the ingrained nature of corruption and personal gain far exceeds any effort that reform-minded people within Kenya's government and its development partners can execute. Improvements to administrative systems are not sufficient, in and of themselves, to address the land question.

Issue Four: Expectations of Reparations

Many studies on land reform and conversations that I have had over endless cups of Kenyan milk tea focus on only one element of the land question—reparations for injustices. Kenya is intricately tied to British and Indian culture, law, and traditions; like the British, Kenyans drive on the left side of the road, their police do not carry guns, and the courts cite British common law. As for the medical system, it is British based. I was amazed at the stark differences between the cut-and-fix approach of my American doctors and dentists compared to the wait-and-see approach of my Kenyan ones. Indian samosas, triangular-shaped, savory, fried snacks, and chapatis, thin unleavened flat bread, both originate in the Indian subcontinent and are staples at every Indian event I attend, whether in South Asia, East Africa, Europe, or America. But I could find these two items in any small village or roadside truck stop across Kenya. I often had to survive on these two items, along with cooked Kenyan milk tea, during my travels with KTI. White and brown Kenyans are part of Kenya. Kenya decided not to follow Uganda's example when Idi Amin evicted all Asians in 1972. White and brown Kenyans serve in parliament, run businesses, are corrupt, grab land, run charities, donate to the needy, and are inherently Kenyan. On the July 21, 2017, former President Kenyatta formally recognized Asians as one of Kenya's tribes. *The Gazette Notice* stated, "WHEREAS, Kenyans of Asian Heritage have been an integral part of our National fabric since the Dawn of our Nation" and "THAT Kenyans of Asian Heritage constitute a Community that is one of the Tribes of Kenya."[132]

When in the cities and towns, no black Kenyan would give me a second look as I went about my days. I could be standing in line at a government office or doctor's waiting room, buying a newspaper or cup of coffee, or riding a public bus. The same would apply to any city and large town in the United States. However, in the rural south in the United States, I may stand out in a sea of black and, in northern New England, in a sea of white. In the mid 1990s, my presence in a rural town in western Maryland once caused consternation in a local restaurant and I was politely asked to leave. In Nairobi, I could walk around Kibera, one of the largest and oldest slums of the city, without raising an eyebrow. Kibera is famous; it lies in the same constituency as former prime minister Odinga. Tour groups organize walking tours of Kibera, and it attracts many foreign charities and volunteers. However, this openness to Asians (and all nonblacks) does not apply to the entire city. I remember pausing and turning around while walking through a different slum, Kawangware, on the western edge of Nairobi. I heard a small boy, perhaps 10 years old, shout "*mzungu*" as I walked by. While the term technically refers to any foreigner or wanderer, it is used in Kenya to refer to a white person. The boy was technically correct, but culturally off. But to him, I was indeed a foreigner because of the color of my skin.

A more vivid experience took place over 150 miles away on the edge of Mau Forest. Along with local government and nonprofit officials, I was participating in a tree-planting effort that KTI was funding. A couple of my white female colleagues were visiting us from Washington, DC. As we wrapped up the tree planting and headed back to the vehicles, a local black official asked us if he could take a photo with us. After taking the first picture, he invited a few local teenage girls into the picture and then politely gestured for the two men to step aside. I obliged and the girls posed with my colleagues. Later, out of earshot of others, I asked him in Swahili what that was all about, hypothesizing that the girls simply wanted to pose with visiting women, as most of the Kenyan government officials were male. He smiled at me and whispered in Swahili, "They have never seen a white person before." I was initially shocked. In retrospect, this was understandable, as we were in a remote area; the girls had probably never ventured into a neighboring city or town, just as many Americans in the rural south may never have traveled outside of their county.

Within this overall assimilation of white and brown Kenyans in some segments of society, and their foreignness in other areas, the notion of historical land injustices can be dissected. The prevailing sentiment is that all Kenyans have suffered significant historical losses of their land, and that that land needs to be returned to them. This is the only commonality that exists among all Kenyans when it comes to explaining these injustices. The environment and land court in Malindi, Kenya, put it succinctly in October 2021:

> With the arrival of the settlers, many indigenous people were displaced from their original homes as the Colonial Government systematically put in processes that took away huge chunks of land from the residents. That fact saw the beginning of a vicious war pitting the indigenous Kenyans on the one side and the colonial administration on the other. After Kenya gained independence from the colonialists in 1963, it was felt that the atrocities committed against the indigenous people in as far as land was concerned would be remedied.[133]

If one asks, "What land?," "What losses?," or "How does one return the land?," the answers one gets depend on the respondent's tribe and age. Americans will never solve the problems of reparations to the descendants of Native Americans or black slaves. At least one American tribe, the Onondaga, has recognized this dilemma. In March 2024, their lawyer stated that without admitting the truths of the past, people cannot move forward together. Yet, he underscored the serious legal and practical implications of these land grabs, stating, "the problem is that all of the land in New York, in the United States, is stolen Indian land . . . What does that mean in terms of U.S. property law?"[134]

Likewise, Kenyans will never figure out who should get what land. Brian Green has conducted an in-depth discussion of reparations in the United States, noting that "restoring land and land rights to Native Americans is a complex issue because unlike stolen money, stolen land is not fungible and cannot always be replaced."[135] Regarding Kenya, some would blame the British, who took land for their own settlers, primarily in Kenya's White Highlands, and subsequently sold it back to Kenyans after independence. But those who own these parcels today are not the people who took it between the 1920s and 1950s.

Other respondents might posit that far worse injustices were perpetuated by the elite Kenyans after independence. This ties back to the first issue ("Land Concentration in the Hands of the Elite") under the land question, as discussed above. A third group of respondents, those outside of central Kenya or the White Highlands, would point fingers at those Kenyans who moved to other parts of the country and legally or illegally appropriated land that is perceived as belonging to a different tribe. While examples can be found all over the country, the Kenyan coast presents a poignant example. The local Mijikenda tribe claims to have been victimized by a wide swath of outsiders, including the Omani Arabs before the British, Asians, and the Kikuyu, who come from Central Kenya. The underlying sentiments are so toxic across the country that we at KTI were careful about the tribal ethnicity of those we hired and posted to our different offices so as not to upset local sentiments. This idea is foreign to many American companies and individuals; in the United States we generally try to hire the best person for the job, regardless of where they come from within the country.

Kenya's 2009 National Land Policy defines "reparations" as the solution to the problem of "gross disparities in land ownership."[136] It presents three possible types of reparations: redistribution, restitution, and resettlement. USAID's comments on the draft best conclude why no legitimate solution to the problem of reparations will likely ever emerge: "The author's concern is that there is a danger in a policy paper promising these measures without providing a clearer roadmap as to how they will be implemented. Otherwise, they may prove empty promises, causing popular disappointment, and providing fodder for politicians more interested in exploiting these issues than resolving them."[137]

All countries, including Kenya, have an elite. As long as the social construct of land in Kenya remains unchanged, these elites will continue to undermine improvements in administrative systems and to grab more land to enhance their own wealth. They will also avoid any form of reparations.

Donor Initiatives

The KTI final report, available between 2014 and 2019 on the now-retired website (www.kenyati.com), contained a fact sheet describing $1.8 million in land reform interventions between 2009 and 2013. Some interventions focused on research and advocacy, including one grant to a legal nonprofit to document examples of successful public-interest litigation completed under the new constitution. KTI also supported meetings and consultants to assist parliament in reviewing the draft land bills that were required by the new constitution. While USAID Mission's Democracy and Governance (DG) groups tend to focus on this type of activity, the DG office and OTI often leveraged each other's strengths and competitive advantage when needed, given that we were all part of the USAD mission to Kenya. OTI's advantage was speed and flexibility because of the type of contract and subgrants that OTI relied on. DG's strengths were designing and patiently playing the long game.

KTI also funded the new National Land Commission (NLC) with a global OTI hallmark approach known as a "ministry in a box." This means providing basic office renovations, furniture, equipment, salaries, and supplies for new institutions or government offices that have been destroyed by war or looting. This was not KTI's first ministry in a box. We had also supported the Commission for the Implementation of the Constitution (CIC) that drafted the new constitution, as described in chapter 3.

The third category of grants were for supporting local land registry offices, as discussed earlier in this chapter. The fourth category of grants, and probably the most problematic in retrospect, were designed to bring diverse stakeholders together and help them see the land problem from a different perspective. Examples included bringing land attorneys together with Ministry of Land officials to work together on a common cause, for example, cleaning up and organizing the registry's files; jointly training civil society and local government on land management and land legislation; and jointly led information campaigns targeting the public. A fifth category focused on mobilizing activists to return grabbed public land, such as Taifa Park in Kisumu.[138] My role as a member of the Development Partners Group on Land (DPGL) constituted another type of intervention.

While the scale and duration of each KTI intervention were smaller than that of other development partners, the overall objectives remained consistent. All tried, in their own way, leveraging their own strengths and falling within their own processes and limitations, to chip away at one or more issues that constitute the land question. But while KTI's underlying objective for each intervention was peace and security, other parts of USAID and other development partners tended to focus on agriculture, natural resources, and poverty alleviation. Sweden, for example, in a 2010 report, prioritized the issue of weak administrative systems to "reform the administration of land and land use planning, improve the productive use of land, address land tenure issues and result in the protection of natural resources."[139] Throughout my tenure in Kenya, Sweden was focusing on modernizing Kenya's land information and management systems for these distinct purposes.

The British, in contrast, initially focused on the land policy itself, but withdrew their support to the Kenya Land Alliance (KLA) before the 2007 Kenyan election.[140] Their withdrawal was justified by an unavoidable historical fact. DFID was most likely responding to a May 2006 UK parliamentary report, which found that "there are sensitivities around DFID engagement in a politically sensitive sector in which there have been colonial (and post) interests in land. This was one factor in DFID withdrawing from the provision of direct [Technical Assistance] into Government."[141] Read between the diplomatic lines. The Crown is being accused of creating the land issue in Kenya 50 years ago; they should not be at the forefront of advising Kenya's government on land issues and helping Kenyans develop a new national land policy. The UK parliamentary report turned toward a solution: "One strategy to counteract this has been to establish and work through a wider land sector development partner group, which is chaired by UN-Habitat. Whilst DFID play a key role in the group, this enables us to present views and dialogue with [the government of Kenya] as a donor group, rather than as DFID."[142] The phrase "rather than as DFID" is extremely blunt. It was this group, chaired by UN-Habitat, that I served on behalf of USAID and that I have discussed above.

USAID's primary land investment focused on other aspects of the land problem, including advising on the draft National Land Policy, assisting parliament subcommittees, or engaging with local farmers and communities on communal land right issues. Like the United Kingdom, the United States must also be careful when taking a position on land issues in Kenya. First, this is because of America's unfortunate history of colonialism at home. Like the British stealing Kenya's land, the United States also stole land from the Native Americans, who preceded the first white settlers. Kenya's colonialists also took the reservation approach, forcing some Kenyan tribes into reservation-type areas. The parallel ends there. The British colonial force in Kenya eventually left the country. However, on the other side of the Atlantic, the colonialists settled and pushed the Native Americans into reservations and eroded their culture, language, and traditions.

The second reason the United States needs to be careful is because of its emphasis on capitalism and free markets. According to Kenya Land Alliance, "the intentions of USAID were at variance with civil society and academia group of the stakeholders of policymaking process. The main concern of USAID was that the policy would interfere with operation of the land market."[143] This opinion was grounded in the US policy on Africa. According to the former assistant secretary of state for African affairs (1989–1993), Hank Cohen, "we want to see human rights, democracy and free markets. But if you get the last one right, we give you a discount on the other two."[144] The audacity of these types of US government positions statements is reprehensible. Kenyans, according to Lumumba, do not have such a trump card that discounts other factors. They see "land not just as a commodity to be traded in the market, for it represented multiple values, which required to be protected in the land policy."[145] Can American development and policy professionals have an unwavering foundation upon which to provide assistance that serves both Kenyan and American interests concerning land under a peace and security umbrella?

Conclusion

Local peace and security in Kenya are closely and undeniably intertwined with land issues. The Commission of Inquiry into the Post-Election Violence (CIPEV) found "a feeling among certain ethnic groups of historical marginalization, arising from perceived inequalities concerning the allocation of land and other national resources as well as access to public goods and services. This feeling has been tapped by politicians to articulate grievances about historical injustices which resonate with certain sections of the public. This has created an underlying climate of tension and hate, and the potential for violence, waiting to be ignited and to explode."[146]

This unequivocal nexus among land, violence, economies, and stability inevitably leads international development experts toward further assistance in land reform. However, in the 2020–2025 CDCS, the US government concludes that "root causes are complex social issues that might not be directly tackled through the CDCS, but these will need to be taken into account throughout the strategy."[147] For three main reasons, the US government cannot and should not attempt to play a role in the complex land issue from a US peace and security perspective.

First, Kenyans can neither define land reform nor articulate what successful land reform looks like. As discussed above in the sections concerning the four issues comprising the land question, success is multifaceted and requires long-term interventions that are beyond the funding and planning cycle of the US government. Goals and objectives must be measurable and implementable. Land reform fails at the outset.

Second, success requires a complete cultural shift, as Kenyans would have to deconstruct their social construct of land. Likewise, development partners would need to deconstruct their approach to development planning by jettisoning the requirement of log frames or results frameworks, which want specific outcomes in a relatively short period of time. A 2022 study on DFID's attempts to improve the link between UK national security concerns and its development assistance found that the "second common issue hindering the effectiveness of DFID's interventions was the organization's excessive optimism. Numerous DFID projects in the three case-study countries were described in their final reviews as having been overoptimistic in their initial ideas about how the proposed outputs would lead to the anticipated outcomes."[148]

Third, and probably the most amorphous, is that a successful resolution of the historical land injustices would require some form of land reparations or reallocation of land. This would undo Kenya's firm entrenchment in the sanctity of titles and wreak havoc on Kenya's standing in the global financial market. Former President Kenyatta realized this before independence. But it also flies in the face of the United States' primary requirement of promoting a capitalist society. Should the US disregard land issues completely? No. As the CDCS states, American foreign policy needs to take it into account. As discussed in chapter 2, in the section on domestic affairs and thinking globally but acting locally, America has its own land issues that we cannot resolve. We may provoke, push, or try lighting a few occasional sparks in Kenya but, in plain English, land reform is a Kenyan problem, to be defined, addressed, and solved by Kenyans alone—if, indeed, it can ever be defined and solved.

This chapter presents an overview of Kenya's extremely complex land issues, emphasizing the four elements of the overarching land question—the concentration of land in the hands of the elite, land grabbing, weak administrative structures, and expectations of reparations. These four matters must be understood within the backdrop of the social construct of land and the three scrambles for Kenya. The donors' initiatives, including those that KTI implemented, may be noteworthy in and of themselves and may contribute in their own individual way to addressing a particular problem. Land issues are reflected in the some of the mnemonic, PARADISE, in terms of the *A*dministration of government services and responsibilities, *R*ule of law with Kenya's new land and environment courts, and *A*cceptance of Kenya's diversity by reserving the right for anyone to own land anywhere, not just in areas historically reserved for one's tribe. Land, as demonstrated, is essential to *E*conomic growth in Kenya. The absence of successful land reform can threaten local peace.

While the land issue is linked to conflict in Kenya, this is an internal struggle stirred up by past generations of the elite for their own political and economic gain. The two main candidates for the 2022 election, surprisingly, stayed away from the issue.

Land is not a matter of *international* peace and security that, unchecked, will result in Kenya's failure as a nation-state. Nor are foreigners going to be able to address it. The sum of the solutions within the United States's manageable interest, as presented in this chapter, is never going to add up to any meaningful solution to Kenya's complex land question. To capture USAID's own analysis of the 2009 draft National Land Policy, justice and solutions are out of reach: "The concerns expressed in the policy regarding inequitable distribution of land in Kenya are legitimate and the historical injustices real. Their reality is reflected in the current ethnic violence over land. There are layers of injustices, however, beginning in the colonial period and extending into the present. Disentangling them to achieve 'justice' will be difficult and complicated by the fact that a part of the land has moved through market channels to good faith purchasers, often small and medium Kenyan farmers."[149]

Development partners vested in Kenya's peace and security should focus on other sectors; those that want to address other development issues concerned with economics, agriculture, governance, and women's rights should ensure that they understand the overarching land complexities before designing any intervention. Land reform is tied to these development issues, but a holistic solution is not feasible. Petrikova's conclusion on the United Kingdom's securitization programs echoes this conclusion: "In view of our empirical findings, the UK government needs to be more aware of the limitations of development interventions undertaken in the name of security and consider other means of enabling development."[150]

CHAPTER FIVE

Countering Violent Extremism

"[We must understand] who our worst enemies are, and how we can support the majority of the world's Muslims—ordinary, normal people who desire to live in a safe, secure, and stable environment—in their own effort to defeat terror. In the end, Islamist terror must be defeated, to a significant extent, within Islam, by Muslims themselves."
—Senator Jon Kyl, *Two Years After 9/11: Keeping America Safe*, Senate Subcommittee on Terrorism, Technology, and Homeland Security, March 2004

Bottom Line Up Front (BLUF)

America's national security hinges on countering violent extremism (CVE). Although USAID has a CVE mandate, its CVE efforts overseas have tended to focus only on areas of basic education, jobs, and good governance, factors already being addressed by conventional development programs. The agency is guided by an unfortunate interpretation of the US Constitution's First Amendment, an interpretation not shared by USAID's sister agencies. Its staff are largely ignorant about Islam and what it means to be a Muslim. They maintain the ludicrous belief that USAID can help counter extremism without changing perceptions or attitudes about the interpretation of religion. After summarizing USAID's nexus and the history of terrorism in Kenya and its impact on the United States, I describe the innovative and idealistic program we attempted to implement in Kenya to stymie violent extremism despite the agency's internal and external constraints.

Context

In 2005, I interviewed with USAID for a program manager role on the agency's Iraq team. My friends thought I was crazy, but I assured them the position was based in Washington, DC, and that traveling to Iraq was unlikely. I did not tell them the position required Arabic, which did imply some travel in the region. Three years had passed since a coalition led by the United States invaded Iraq in 2003 and now, in 2006, things were a mess. I thought I could do my piece to help the United States, the country that had adopted me less than two decades earlier.

But paths meander, and I ended up not on the Iraq team but on the Africa team within the OTI, working first for the Democratic Republic of Congo, where my French and Swahili proved useful, especially as I traveled to Kinshasa and Kisangani during my first few months in that role. Six months later I was transferred to the Sudan team and less than a year after starting with USAID, I transitioned again, this time to OTI's Program Office. The transitions did not bother me, after all, I was working for OTI, the Office of *Transition* Initiatives. The Program Office suited me because I got to see more of the proverbial forest instead of only a few trees. I began to understand more of USAID's thinking and programming across sectors and continents.

My Africanness, Muslimness, and natural curiosity pulled me into a thinking vortex. Almost none of the senior policymakers at USAID, Department of State, and Department of Defense whom I ran into were Muslim. In the mid-2000s, they believed the underlying cause of violent extremism by Muslims was idleness, poverty, and an absence of democracy. This thinking drove some of USAID's programming in Africa and the Middle East. I looked for written evidence that such absurdity was systemically embedded and found proof in the 2006 US National Security Strategy.[1] It stated that "because democracies are the most responsible members of the international system, promoting democracy is the most effective long-term measure for . . . countering terrorism and terror-supporting extremism."[2] The theory trickled down. A Department of State planning document claimed, "through development, we seek to invest in countries' efforts to achieve sustained and broad based economic growth, which creates opportunities for people to lift themselves out of poverty, away from violent extremism and instability, and toward a more prosperous future."[3]

USAID's policy documents dive deeper into specific issues and provide evidence-based approaches for its development practitioners. The agency's 2011 policy, "The Development Response to Violent Extremism and Insurgency," at least introduced the concept of pull factors for violent extremism, deviating from the simplicity of the other documents, which only addressed push factors. Push factors are those that policymakers think "push" people to violent extremism—governance, poverty, corruption, and marginalization. Pull factors, according to USAID, are those "that have a direct influence on individual level radicalization and recruitment . . . social status and respect from peers; a sense of belonging, adventure, and self-esteem or personal empowerment . . . and the prospect of achieving glory and fame."[4] This better aligned with my thinking but was missing a vital component, faith.

I was appalled by the inability of US policymakers and development specialists to talk about religion. A 2021 Gallup Poll[5] found that three in four Americans identify with a specific religious faith and 76 percent said religion was either very important (49 percent) or fairly important (27 percent). While the majority (69 percent) of Americans are Christian, one in a hundred are Muslim. I ran into many self-labeled experts in countering violent extremism who were advising senior officials and developing strategies or programs to address violent extremism among Muslims globally but knew next to nothing about Islam. Wikipedia probably has more in-depth information about Islam than some of these professionals. I can understand one's lack of knowledge about a particular, important topic. But I cannot grasp the absent yearning for new knowledge and comprehension about the topic. Nor was anyone willing or able to consider the nexus among Muslim people, anti-American sentiment, and US foreign policy as manifested in our approach to Palestine; our cozy relationship with Saudi Arabia; the United States–led invasion of Iraq, with its holy cities of Najaf and Karbala; or our failure at Guantanamo Bay. USAID self-proclaimed CVE experts could not articulate the significance of March 3, 1924, as cited by Osama bin Laden in the opening of Al-Qaeda's own training manual and in bin Laden's November 3, 2001, statement to the American people.[6] America's strategies and programming would have been significantly enhanced had they understood Islam's history and appreciated that Islam is inherently a way of life, one in which spiritual and material worlds are very closely intertwined.

I often felt alone, the sole Muslim in these discussions. I knew that faith, US foreign policy, and the constant erosion of cultural and religious diversity within Islam have exacerbated the pull toward violent extremism. However, I could not academically or scientifically prove my hypothesis. Being a Muslim, having a bachelor's degree in Islamic studies from an Ivy League university, and having worked in Pakistan for two years were not enough to influence foreign policy for US peace and security.

Violent extremism is undoubtedly a threat to American peace and security. We have seen how the 1998 US embassy bombings in Nairobi and Dar es Salaam, as well as the events of September 11, 2001, have altered our sense of security. The 1998 bombings accelerated the transformation of embassies from welcomed wonders of architecture to walled fortresses, and 9/11 will forever be blamed for the hassle of air travel today.

Many, but not all, violent extremists in the first two decades of this century were Muslim. Throughout history, every group of people has had and will have a segment of its respective population thinking and acting differently. A subsect of these will turn to violence to advance or protect its cause.

I cringe whenever my smart speaker interrupts my day with news of another violent extremist. Like Muslims across America, whether the story unfolds of a gunman in the United States opening fire on a crowd, someone mailing pipe bombs, or someone bombing a building, I hold my breath, hoping the perpetrator is not Muslim. If they are, the media and local law enforcement generally reveal that fact and start to use the "terrorism" label. If the perpetrator is not Muslim, their religion is not mentioned, and the term "terrorism" is avoided. While it cannot be denied that many acts of violent extremism committed worldwide over the past 20 years have been perpetrated by Muslims, Muslims do not have, nor have they ever had, a monopoly on international terror. At the same time, one cannot deny the fact that, today, a significant threat to the United States comes from Muslims.

Why is a mall shooting in the United States significantly different from a mall shooting in Kenya? Both are acts of violent extremism. Why are Ukrainian defenders against Russian invaders considered war heroes but Iraqi defenders against American defenders are considered violent extremists? Ted Kaczynski and some of the 9/11 hijackers were both educated, holding PhDs, so why does the United States posit that poor, uneducated youth are the most at risk? And why were at least fifteen 9/11 hijackers from Saudi Arabia but USAID focuses on Sudan, Nigeria, Pakistan, and Afghanistan? None of this made any sense to me, and each published US government document I read further amplified my frustration with America's approach to addressing global violent extremism. I was powerless as a tiny cog in USAID's Washington-based capital machinery, but I did have an opportunity to pivot others' thinking when I became a senior official at the US embassy in Nairobi. My move to Nairobi brought back old memories and added new experiences of terrorist attacks in my hometown.

Terrorism in Kenya

Former Vice President Biden told students at the University of Nairobi in 2010, "Kenya is situated in a very tough neighborhood. Somalia's decades of instability have generated human tragedy and global threats. We recognize the burden it's placed on Somalia's neighbors."[7] My memory of terrorism in Kenya actually predates Somali instability. The Lord Delamare Terrace, a restaurant at the Norfolk Hotel in Nairobi, is across from the Kenya National Theater and the University of Nairobi. It has always been a wonderful place for brunch. The Norfolk was Nairobi's first hotel, built in 1904 as the gathering place for British colonialists. Today, it attracts international tourists. Its well-manicured grounds provide a haven from Nairobi's bustling traffic and air pollution. I treated many US government visitors to brunch at the hotel, brunches that were always accompanied by a history lesson.

I remember one day in particular: December 31, 1980, the night of a terrorist attack at the Norfolk. My parents had originally planned on attending an event there to usher in the new year, but they decided to cancel their plans. My mom had worked late at the downtown art gallery she managed; she had been packing and delivering chic African art to American customers who happen to be staying at the Norfolk Hotel. My parents chose to stay home with their two elementary school children. At the time, I was only a first-grader, so I do not remember the aftermath of the event; I can recall only the repeated family stories. Police investigators contacted my mother because they found her art gallery's business card on the bodies of some of the victims. They had been shopping in the art gallery only a few hours before being caught in the first terrorist bombing on Kenyan soil. It had been their art she had delivered. The New Year's Eve bombing of the Norfolk Hotel in Nairobi killed 20 people, including some Americans. Like all global terrorist attacks, internet searches of the cause will generate a complex word cloud that includes the terms "Jewish," "Israel," "Entebbe," "Hijacking," "Palestine," and "Saudi Arabia."[8] In 2013, terrorists killed over 60 people at the Westgate Mall in the Westlands, a suburb of Nairobi. At the time, I was living in US government housing less than two miles from the mall. As the attack, counterattack, and aftermath unfolded, we remained under an embassy-ordered lockdown under a blue sky, punctuated by attack helicopters and plumes of black smoke. Soon after the attack, *The Telegraph*, a British newspaper, published a timeline of all attacks in Kenya since 1980, stating, "Kenya is no stranger to terrorist attacks, most of which have been carried out on its soil by Islamic extremists linked to al Qaeda."[9]

Between the Norfolk and Westgate incidents, the most important to US foreign policy was the 1998 bombing that destroyed the US embassy in Nairobi and killed over 200 people. That embassy had been my gateway to America; in 1977 my parents had applied there for immigration to the United States and, a decade later, we got called in for an interview for permanent residence. Since the Westgate attack, Kenya has had to deal with two other prominent attacks and several smaller ones. The year 2015 brought the Garissa University attack and the killing of over 140 people. As I read about the gruesome violence, I recalled my official USAID visit to the university only a couple of years earlier. The second was the attack in 2019 at the Dusit2 complex in Riverside, near the Westlands District, that claimed the lives of over 20 people. One of my childhood homes was across the Nairobi River, less than a mile from that complex.

Nairobi's metropolitan area is home to about four million people, roughly the same as the Seattle metropolitan area. But the city occupies approximately 250 square miles or one-twentieth of the Seattle metropolitan area. It is, therefore, small and dense. My spatial connection to every major attack in Nairobi is understandable, and not attributable to bad luck. These attacks targeted Westerners; they occurred where Westerners worked or frequented, the same places where my parents worked and the middle class lived.

I have no spatial connection to a more recent attack. In January 2020, a US Army facility came under attack, claiming the lives of six people, including a US Army specialist and two pilots. Six US aircraft lay among the destroyed property. This incident did not occur in Afghanistan or Iraq; it was not an attack on US forces in West Africa or South America. It was an attack on Camp Simba, in Manda Bay, a few miles from the historic and quaint city of Lamu on Kenya's coast.[10]

Many American citizens have been killed in terrorist attacks in Kenya, starting with the 1980 Norfolk bombing and, most recently, the 2020 Manda Bay attack. Every morning, in Nairobi, as I would walk between the US embassy's security checkpoint and the USAID building, I would pass a memorial to those killed in the 1998 bombing. Combining my hypothesis that US foreign policymakers and development specialists were misguided in their ignorance of pull factors, with life in Nairobi surrounded by the constant memories and threats of terrorist attacks on Kenyan soil, I wondered if I could change USAID's approach to CVE.

The Challenge

I sure felt like a winner on a *Shark Tank*-type investment idea reality TV show. In January 2010, USAID's Washington-based Africa Bureau staff organized a training in Nairobi to integrate CVE programming into the USAID Kenya, Somalia, and East Africa strategies and programs. The training also offered an opportunity for USAID to roll out its two new policies on the drivers of extremism and development strategies.

USAID was increasing the flow of money for CVE programs to more than one USAID mission. With more money, USAID staff turned to the spigot of CVE funding to plug gaps in other types of more conventional development assistance. At the training, I asked one of USAID Washington's CVE experts what constitutes a CVE program; in other words, I asked, "What does it look like, and what distinguishes a CVE program from a non-CVE program?"

I experienced this gap plugging firsthand. After temporarily leaving USAID and becoming the startup deputy chief of party for the Kenya Devolution Program as KTI was closing down, I was surprised to learn that USAID was planning to provide the devolution program with CVE funds. Nowhere in the solicitation or our proposal was there a reference to CVE. Nor did I believe that the proposed devolution programming would be able to address, even at the periphery, violent extremism. I believe that it was simply a way for USAID to get the devolution program more funding.

A senior official with whom I had worked in Washington, DC, provided the most straightforward, albeit blunt, response to the question about what distinguishes CVE programming. This official knew me well enough to know they could not sidestep my question nor fill me with bureaucratic nonsense. I was disillusioned with the answer: The only defining criteria is the location, not the type of programming or the stated objectives. For example, a school construction program in one part of Kenya would be an education program and would need education funds. But the same school built in a different part of Kenya, one that served people who were historically marginalized or who could become extremists, would qualify for CVE funds.

During the 2010 Nairobi workshop, I asked challenging questions about the new policy. I asked why religion, as a driver of extremism, was not discussed and why pull factors were missing from the menu of development programming interventions. During a breakout group task, I sketched an intervention approach that focused on pull factors in Eastleigh. The Eastleigh area of Nairobi was originally set aside by the British as an Indian neighborhood; some of my family still lived there when I was a kid. By 2010, it had become a predominantly Somali neighborhood; the Indian community infrastructure had been sold and turned into businesses and bakeries. The US embassy security office occasionally declared Eastleigh a no-go-zone for American officials because of Al-Shabaab recruitment. Al-Shabaab is a Somali terrorist group responsible for the multiple attacks in Kenya.

My breakout group's presentation must have won the first *Shark Tank*-type prize because USAID's Washington office transferred funds to KTI through USAID's mission in Nairobi. We conducted an assessment and put together a program design based on my emphasis on pull factors. I pulled together a credible team comprising a Kenyan Muslim religious scholar; a Kenyan religious studies professor from the Muslim-dominated coast; a University of Nairobi philosophy and religious studies professor; and a Moroccan international development and youth specialist, who had designed USAID programs in West Africa. Using USAID's policy terminology, religion was front and center of the assessment. The assessment team concluded that pull factors accounted for 60 percent of the drivers of violence and extremism among youth in Eastleigh, and that "although some of the youth recruited into Al Shabab are attracted through financial incentives . . . the main method used is distorted religious ideology."[11]

A year later, we had a credible program design based on the assessment. We had also gained USAID's Kenya office and US embassy support, including $4 million worth of funds from the Africa Bureau for a CVE program in Eastleigh and on the coast. We also included a robust monitoring and evaluation component to substantiate or disprove the design hypotheses. I oversaw the recruitment, activity design, stakeholder identification, and program implementation in my capacity as KTI's deputy country representative. I took a keen interest in the program, especially the monitoring and evaluation components, spending a considerable amount of time in Eastleigh with program partners. The program ran from 2011 to 2014 and generated substantial interest across USAID employees, among other development partners, and researchers. Multiple USAID and non-USAID publications, including evaluation reports, have been published online.[12]

Programming Hypothesis

What type of local government and civil society group activities should the United States support to address violent extremism under the peace and security umbrella? In 2007, before moving to Kenya, I was sent to Peshawar, Pakistan, to help start USAID's Pakistan Transition Initiative. I had not been involved in the program's design; I was simply asked to temporarily fill in while a fulltime country representative was recruited.

I was a good fit for a temporary position, given that I had gained work experience (prior to my time with USAID) in Pakistan.

One of the program's objectives was "to help extend the writ of civilian authorities into ungoverned tribal areas along the Afghan border where violent extremist organizations controlled territory."[13] The focus was on the Federally Administered Tribal Areas (FATA), which, at the time, was a semiautonomous tribal area on Pakistan's western boundary with Afghanistan. The program justification reflected America's national security strategy and USAID's thinking in Iraq and Afghanistan, namely, that "lack of confidence and trust in government institutions could fuel violent extremism."[14] The development response in Pakistan was to partner "with nascent government agencies to implement small-scale service delivery projects, such as drinking water systems, vocational training, and school rehabilitation."[15] The prevailing logic was that if youth are engaged in building small projects and interacting with local government, their confidence in the local government will increase and they will be less likely to be drawn towards extremism.

I thought it was a farce. An individual's living or working environment, or their contributions to developing a local community, are not the primary drivers of a behavioral decision. Cultural traditions and provocation by distorted religious ideology play a more significant role. In Peshawar, I was confined to the US consulate and the US government's guest house. I wanted to reconnect with colleagues with whom I had worked a decade earlier, before joining USAID. Between 1997 and 1999, I was based in Islamabad with a disaster preparedness organization called Focus Humanitarian Assistance (FOCUS). FOCUS is now part of the Aga Khan Development Network's Agency for Habitat. Although I could not go to a local restaurant, I could invite prescreened guests to the areas in which I was confined. I offered to buy my former colleagues dinner if they would make the trip to the guest house. Some came from Islamabad; one even flew in from Kabul to meet with me! It was great reuniting with them all and finding out how they had grown personally and professionally. We discussed the problems in Pakistan and Afghanistan, as well as the changes in disaster management and international development. Of course, we also talked about the role of the United States in the region. One former colleague told me about a village in the FATA that had a USAID-funded agriculture program. The

program supported the digging of irrigation canals to help improve agricultural productivity. He had been working in that same village under
a different program (not US-funded) when he heard about a young man
who had harbored a few Taliban visitors the previous week. That man
was a paid laborer on the USAID project. The Taliban had come to his
house and asked for food and a place to sleep. Even though he was part
of the American program, he did not hesitate to host them. He saw no
conflict between his participation in the USAID-funded activity and
his actions. His decision was driven not by his employment, but by the
Pakhtun code—a traditional ethical and cultural code of conduct that
governs social relationships.

Even in the absence of strong culture or tradition, the intellectual elite
can brainwash educated and employed individuals, building on emotions
and anger that fuels them. Many rioters who stormed the US Capitol on
January 6, 2021, were not uneducated and unemployed but "doctors, lawyers, architects and business owners."[16] Those who participated in such
violent protests that resulted in the loss of life and damaged property, for
example, those occurring in Los Angeles (Rodney King Riots), Brussels
(after Belgium lost to Morocco in the 2022 World Cup), or Washington,
DC (January 2021), were not all poor and uneducated; they paid taxes
and helped their communities develop. Across the globe, humans have
proven across that they can destroy their own communities, irrespective
of their economic, education, or employment status.

The second hypothesis about US efforts in Pakistan, Afghanistan, and
Iraq, echoed by CVE programs in Somalia or West Africa, is that if one is
employed and busy, one is less likely to turn against one's employer or
community. The mere fact that someone works, earns a decent salary,
and receives benefits does not mean they will never turn against their
employer or country. I worked for USAID for a decade and a US government contractor for another decade. Government agencies have multiple
controls in place to prevent secret or classified materials from being
stolen, sold, or removed from government buildings. This is because it
is well-known that anyone can be bought, cajoled, or blackmailed into
releasing secrets, given the right price or pressure.

Anyone, regardless of their employment or background, can choose
to steal money for personal or other kinds of gain. Our drive to improve
our own quality of life or our desire for a better education for our kids,

a simple house, or a 100-foot yacht is a fundamental carnal instinct. In 2012, the USAID Office of Inspector General reported, "over the past five years, U.S. investigations of fraud committed in development projects in Afghanistan have resulted in over 60 U.S. individuals being charged and over 40 subsequent convictions of U.S. citizens. Those U.S. citizens who were convicted received a total of approximately 600 months incarceration in the United States. These investigations resulted in recoveries and cost savings in excess of $100 million."[17]

Why would USAID assume that a Pakistani, Afghan, Somali, or Kenyan youth would hold themselves to a higher standard than a US citizen working for USAID, simply because they earn a few dollars on a public works project?

Counterintelligence experts in the US design and require training for government employees and their contractors. They rely on many acronyms to capture the motives of potential recruiters, including MICE, or "money, ideology, compromise, and ego." The training definition of "ideology" can include political, national allegiance, cultural, or political connotations. Irrespective of the trending acronym, research, or approach, religion is conspicuously sidestepped in government and corporate circles in the United States. Yet, we know that, today, "recruiters of agents abroad often pursue nonstate actors with complex mixtures of competing loyalties, including family, tribe, religion, ethnicity, and nationalism."[18] The Eastleigh assessment and design report, the KTI CVE evaluations (midterm and final), and third-party studies all found that religion plays a meaningful role in recruiting individuals to extremism.

In prisons, community centers, and rural basements, religion drives violent extremists on issues of abortion, guns, immigration, and notions of racial supremacy. Religion also plays as meaningful role in these movements, just as it played a role in the colonial powers' belief that they were superior to both Africans and Native Americans.

Only by understanding and embracing the role of religion can American officials, diplomats, and policymakers begin designing global CVE programs to help improve US peace and security. Without applying a lens that accounts for religion, we are simply programming under a false rubric of CVE and wasting public resources, time, and effort.

Programming Synergy

The Eastleigh CVE assessment validated my inherent belief that a meaningful CVE program had to address pull factors and, specifically, religion. This independent assessment increased my credibility among USAID and US embassy staff. Now I needed real case studies to validate it. I began exploring what other US government agencies were doing in Kenya. Could I apply their lessons to our programming approach? I quickly ran into the proverbial flashing, yellow warning lights and bright red "do not enter signs" when trying to apply these lessons to USAID.

As the most senior Muslim at USAID's Kenya office, I received a formal, embossed invitation from the US ambassador to attend a Ramadhan *iftar* program at the ambassador's residence. The home, located in the Muthaiga section of Nairobi, was a short drive from the embassy. Muthaiga, representing the upper social echelon of Nairobians, had fancy Victorian houses with swimming pools and servants' quarters. It hosted the famous Muthaiga Club, often depicted alongside the Norfolk Hotel in colonial movies about Kenya, including *Out of Africa,* a film based on Karen Blixen's novel of the same title. I was no stranger to the residence, having attended Fourth of July functions, closed-door meetings, and small group discussions with the ambassador and his deputy. But this was the first time attending an *iftar* program at the residence.

While the Fourth of July celebration, even in Nairobi, brings out red, white, and blue buntings, the US Marine Corps Color Guard, and the US flag, this *iftar* event was simpler and more fitting for the pious month of Ramadhan. Muslims believe that during this month, God selected the Prophet Muhammad and communicated with him through the archangel Gabriel. The month is a time of spiritual renewal in which Muslims focus on purifying their thoughts and actions, deepening their spiritual connections, and becoming better individuals and members of their communities. As part of this practice, many Muslims abstain from food and anything detrimental to themselves or others (e.g., negative thoughts and actions, overindulging, being judgmental), every day from dawn until dusk. In addition to the daily fast, practicing patience and virtue, deepening spiritual practices (e.g., saying additional prayers and reading the Quran), community service and charity, focusing on gratitude, time with family, and strengthening relationships within oneself and with others, are big parts of Ramadan. It is the most strenuous, rewarding, and transformational time of the year for many Muslims. Sunset at the end of each day is marked by breaking the fast, or the *iftar,* a communal meal taken alongside the evening prayer.

The ambassador had invited Kenya's Muslim leaders, politicians, scholars, and influencers. As an embassy representative, I was a host before I was a guest. I welcomed and guided the guests to the tables set up in the garden under a typically beautiful Nairobi evening sky. As the sun sank below the horizon, we broke our fast with a traditional course of dates and water. The hosts then led the guests into tents set up for the evening prayers. The experience moved me spiritually; for the first time in my life, I was praying alongside Kenyan Muslims of all cultures and backgrounds under a tent at the US ambassador's residence in Nairobi. For me, prayer is a three-way conversation; it is between me and my fellow sisters and brothers, who pray alongside, and between us and our creator, the one God, the same God that Jews, Christians, and Muslims reach out to for guidance, solace, strength, and forgiveness.

The Muslim prayer reminds me of the greatness of God, as we call on God using any of Their[19] many majestic names. These names are anthropomorphic descriptions that are within the capacity of humans to understand. The prayer also reminds me of our individual insignificance within the all-encompassing creator. It reminds me of our history. There are many different *tariqahs,* or paths within Islam. But each person is united in their belief that there is only one God, whom we call Allah, and the knowledge that the Holy Prophet Muhammad was God's final messenger, through whom They revealed the Qur'an. Each *tariqah* differs somewhat in its interpretations of the faith, including who has the authority to guide believers and how to interpret the Qur'an. I believe in the history, traditions, and interpretations of the Shi'a Ismaili Muslims. We believe this authority vests in a living hereditary imam, who traces his lineage directly from the Holy Prophet.

This micro-moment that evening under the tent was the real manifestation of pluralism, which is noticeably different from diversity. Diversity accepts our differences while pluralism embraces them. The word of God, as codified in the Qur'an, reverberated through my mind that night, as I took in my surroundings and the congregation: "O mankind! We created you from male and a female, and made you into nations and tribes, that ye may know each other."[20] I extend the world "knowing" to mean embracing, trusting, and working together, instead of despising and fighting one another. Violent extremism is simply the blatant opposite of this verse. It propagates violence and death among those we dislike, with whom we disagree, or those who we believe have historically been unjust to us. Recent examples include violence between Shi'a and Sunni Muslims, Palestinians and Israelis, the January 6, 2021, insurrection of the US Capitol, and America's almost daily public mass shootings. Therefore, programs that attempt to thwart violent extremism must promote pluralism and counter the narratives of hate. After the prayers, I had to set aside my spiritual and idealistic thoughts as we headed back to the tables for the *iftar* meal. I had to return from my inner thoughts to playing host and networker across the multiple conversations at my table.

The next day, I moved on to other KTI work, specifically, reviewing and recommending a grant for our Kenya Constitution programming. I discussed this example in chapter 3, explaining USAID's interpretation that we could not invite people based only on their religion to a US government funded event to discuss the content of the current and proposed constitutions. Here were two opposing approaches from one US government. On the one hand, I could not invite religious leaders to discuss a contentious clause in the Kenya's draft constitution; on the other hand, the US government was actively promoting the process by which Kenyans were seeking a new constitution. Yet the Department of State could invite only Muslim leaders to an *iftar* program at the ambassador's residence in Kenya and, in Washington, DC, the White House can host selected religious leaders on matters of national importance. For example, in 2022, the "White House Office of Public Engagement convened a meeting with a diverse group of national religious denominational leaders on reproductive rights."[21]

How can executive branches of the same US government, operating under the same constitution, have radically different interpretations of the implications of the First Amendment as described in chapter 3. In the same week, I added a third data point to this jumble. I attended a meeting between a State Department colleague, a Department of Defense colleague, and a Kenyan Muslim imam who worked at the Kenya Prisons Division. The imam was asking the US Defense Department for an *extension* of funding to continue his moderate radio programming targeting Muslim youth. Not only was the recipient selected solely based on their religion but also the programing content was promulgating a more pluralistic interpretation of Islam. The red "do not enter" sign flashed in my head; I was not even going to attempt to replicate that program by extending the reach of that imam to other radio stations and social media. All I could conclude was that USAID and the Departments of State and Defense existed in parallel and separate universes. I was constrained by the former.

The second constraint on creative and efficient programming lies in the flavors of federal funding. In the introduction to this book, I briefly described the OTI and its unique transition initiatives account, which Congress authorizes annually with special notwithstanding authority. Annual appropriations bills are thousands of pages long and include over 4,000 different accounts. USAID itself had over 70 accounts in the fiscal year (FY) of 2023.[22] Accounts may have different authorities; the transition initiatives account's authority did not extend to the many other funds we received for our CVE programming in Eastleigh and the coast. I also discussed the flow of funds among US government agencies. One of the biggest examples is AIDS programming from the Department of Health and Human Services to USAID in Kenya. The transfer of funds was difficult but not impossible. It required a significant amount of paperwork and number of approvals because it implied that the executive branch of the government was telling Congress that we have to get the money for this activity from another account because you did not give us enough here. In the US government's system of fiscal management, only Congress can appropriate funds. But there are always exceptions. Congress allows what OTI staff affectionately call "stealing authority." For example, the annual appropriation for the transition initiatives account specifically earmarked for OTI was $80 million in FY 2023. But Congress authorizes the secretary of state to take an additional amount ($15 million in FY 2023) from any other account under the same act and magically convert it to the transition initiatives fund to be used by OTI with the same authorities applicable to OTI's regular funds. This looks simple on paper in the annual appropriations bill, but the reality in the executive branch of the American government is that the regulations, bureaucracy, and processes required to do this are significantly more complex than the actual law. Suffice it to say, the ability of my colleagues and I at the Departments of State and Defense, and even those within USAID at the US embassy in Nairobi, to pool our resources to advance CVE programming was severely restricted.

Programming Opportunities

What if neither of these constraints existed? What if the US Supreme Court or Congress offered an unequivocal interpretation aligning with the State and Defense Departments? What if money could be easily pooled among agencies to advance each one's respective missions? This section offers a glimpse into what I believe the US government's peace and security programming for CVE could be if none of these constraints existed. This glimpse is anchored in my understanding as a Muslim, a development specialist, and someone who has lived in the United States, Pakistan, and Kenya, as well as the findings in the 2010 Eastleigh CVE assessment.

This 2010 assessment identified over 15 different outcomes necessary to counter the recruitment of youth into violent extremism. These outcomes included the availability of safe spaces and an increase in one's sense of identity; constructive interactions with government and community engagement; and peaceful avenues for raising, discussing, and addressing community development concerns. USAID is great at supporting programming that achieves these outcomes. However, messaging and rhetoric are extremely important. The assessment identified the need to train and equip influencers and community and religious leaders "to disseminate messages and principles of nonviolence, peace, tolerance, diversity and pluralism."[23] I believe that countering the hate messaging, the distorted interpretations of Islam's message of peace, and offering a counterfactual to a minority extremist interpretation of Islam are essential components of successful programming. The assessment team envisioned "the community at the grassroots level strongly rejects radical ideologies."[24]

Globally, Christianity flourishes today because of its pluralistic interpretations and practices. However, its history is punctuated with acts of intolerance and discrimination; Americans may not recall the massacres that the Crusades, supported by the Catholic Church, committed across

Europe on the crusaders' way to "free" Jerusalem. Muslim Americans cringed when former President George W. Bush invoked a crusade against the perpetrators of the 9/11 attacks. It sounded like a Christian leader relaunching a war against Muslims. I shudder whenever I drive through downtown Sammamish, Washington, past the street sign that reads "Crusader Way." I thought of petitioning the city for a name change but discovered that the street is private; it leads straight to a Catholic high school that is not visible from the main public street.

But Americans would recall the *Mayflower,* which brought pilgrims who did not want to belong to the Church of England. This idea of freedom of religion was enshrined in the First Amendment of the US Constitution, ratified in 1791, which "provides that Congress make no law respecting an establishment of religion or prohibiting its free exercise."[25] Yet, American rhetoric does not always match our practice. Slaves had to wait 90 years between the Declaration of Independence's claim that "all men are created equal" and attaining their freedom, while women had to wait 140 years between the Constitution's provision that our representatives be chosen by "the people" and the acknowledgment that women were "people" with the right to vote. Mormons, or members of the Church of Jesus Christ of Latter-Day Saints, were unable to practice their interpretation of Christianity and were forced to flee west in the mid-1800s, eventually settling in Utah. Native Americans were deprived of their own cultures, traditions, and religions in the late-1800s, when their youth were forced into boarding schools that promoted European traditions, language, and religions. (America did not apologize for that "blot on American history" and "a sin on our soul" until October 2024.)[26]

With significant increases in worldwide connectivity, Muslim traditions are coming into increased contact with others. Those who have the means and desire to do so can proselytize their own interpretations across countries and continents. One example is Saudi Arabia. In the wake of the 9/11 attacks on the United States, Senator Jon Kyl defined Wahhabism and the kingdom's role:

> Islam has a proud history. Many people who follow its beliefs here in the United States are hardworking citizens. But unfortunately, Mr. Chairman, there is mounting evidence that Saudi-sponsored groups are trying to hijack mainstream Islam here in the United States and in

the world and replace it with an extremist form of Islam, referred to as Wahhabism. Wahhabism is known throughout the Muslim world for its puritanical and severe approach to the teachings of the Muslim prophet Mohammed. It preaches violence against nonbelievers or infidels, and those include not just Christians, Jews, Hindus, but also Muslims who don't adhere to the strict Wahhabi faith.[27]

The 2010 Eastleigh assessment team described a local example of hijacking Islam by eroding minority beliefs in Kenya. Like Christian minority groups, Muslim minorities have always been prosecuted. Today, that prosecution is not only physical (e.g., attacks on Shia minorities in Pakistan) but also ideological and carried out through social media, YouTube, and blogs. The assessment team found, among Somali youth, a "systematic rejection of Sufi practices and approach to religion as illicit, unjustifiable innovation and deviation. Somali society was deeply steeped in Sufism, which promotes values of tolerance, nonviolence, peace, love, and compassion. Youth are led to see a Sufi approach to religion as backward."[28] As challenges and attacks on minority interpretations of Islam accelerate globally, Muslim youth are unable to find identity and meaning in the traditions of their parents. Instead, they turn to those who want to listen and explain, including those who promulgate extremist ideology.

Senator Kyl not only succinctly defined the problem but also presented his own perspective of US government peace and security CVE programming, as captured in the quotation at the beginning of this chapter. Solutions must come from Muslims themselves. My contribution to this effort is this chapter, which highlights that ideal programming must transcend the inherent systemic constraints described above. This is not theoretical; it happened informally and quietly in Kenya between 2011 and 2014.

Making it Happen

Some elements of my ideal programming took place despite these inherent systemic constraints. Some of the grantees we funded went beyond their approved scopes of work and incorporated what they thought was best for the objectives of their particular grant. They did not deviate from the grant agreements; they leveraged our assistance and did a lot more with it. This type of extension was not unusual for KTI, and we looked for and documented grantee contributions. For example, if we funded a radio station for three hourlong programs to educate listeners on the content of the proposed constitution (see chapter 3), we were thrilled when they could leverage that support to add two more sessions and design a call-in quiz show on the same topic.

How should the US government, through USAID and its implementing partners, react if the grant recipient uses other sources, including voluntary donations of time, to extend the activities and add a religious component? Lawyers can tear this apart and pontificate on the distinction between activities funded by us and a grantee's own contribution that reaches beyond the grant agreement. The line can become less blurred if the radio station were to air funded programming at a different time. But what if the call-in quiz show immediately followed our funded program? Perhaps it would be okay if the caller were to say, "This ends our USAID-funded programming." before starting the call-in show. Future legal experts should turn to three US Supreme Court cases, two involving USAID: *Agency for International Development v. Alliance for Open Society,* 591 U.S. (2020) and 570 (2013), as well as *National Institute of Family and Life Advocates v. Becerra,* 585 U.S. (2018) against the state of California. The 2013 case required that all federally funded organizations implement a policy explicitly opposing prostitution, while the 2018 and 2020 cases were about abortion. In all three cases, the Supreme Court decided against the government and for the grant recipient's free speech rights.

I recall two examples of KTI's grantees going the extra mile that legal scholars may endlessly opine about. In the first case, British author Michela Wrong published a book titled, *It's Our Turn to Eat,* documenting the story of Anglo Leasing, one of the grandest corruption schemes that cost Kenyan taxpayers more than $600 million.[29] Elite Kenyans, including senior politicians named in the book, had informally blocked its distribution in Kenya by convincing Kenya's few bookstores not to carry the book for fear of a libel suit. The British author approached USAID for assistance and, in 2013, KTI launched a multipronged distribution effort using unusual intermediaries—a newspaper, a writer's group, radio stations, and two large church groups.

One of the national church groups proposed convening facilitators from around the country, training them on the content of the book, and sending them home to disseminate the information. That is what KTI agreed to fund. However, they leveraged our support and added two components at their own cost. The facilitators were a mix of community influencers, pastors, and deacons. In addition to the USAID-funded open community sessions, the pastors voluntarily incorporated the information from the book and anticorruption messages into their sermons. Does that cross any red lines? USAID had educated the facilitators, trained them to be anticorruption advocates, and funded public nonreligious sessions. The pastors had then used that knowledge and their pulpits to amplify the message. USAID was not paying for the church services.

The second example involved developing an anticorruption study guide based on both Michela Wrong's book and the Bible. The study guide explained: "This is in line with the Council's mission of seeking to enhance the creation of a just and sustainable society. This Topical Study Guide is merely a tool to study the book by reflecting on the issues raised from a Biblical perspective, and is not intended to replace reading of the actual book."[30]

The study guide was brilliant; it appealed to its religious audience by drawing parallels between the advice in the Bible and the messages in the book. In reflecting on the strategy, author Michela Wrong stated, "Africa's clergy has a proud tradition of taking on repressive government and Kenya is no exception. The National Council of Churches of Kenya and the Catholic Justice and Peace Commission plan to debate my book alongside passages from the Bible. Church groups across the country will draw parallels between episodes of It's Our Turn to Eat and Noah's rejection of earthly corruption, Nehemiah's refusal to accept defeat and Jesus's sermons about egalitarianism and brotherhood."[31]

True development professionals know that the best way to propagate a message is to let the local civil society group own it, customize it to their audience and local context, and leverage the donor's funding to exponentially increase their impact. What more could USAID want?

In the second example, a youth group from the coast received a grant to use poetry to promote critical thinking. The Kenyan education system is focused much more on rote learning than critical thinking. As a child in a British school in Kenya, I entered many poetry competitions that judged me on my enunciation and elocution. I was forced to memorize and deliver old British poems by Yeats, Byron, and Shakespeare. Not a single poet was a contemporary figure; nor was any of them African. I was not allowed to offer my own interpretations of the poems; our teachers simply handed us the poems, told us what it meant, and told us to memorize them. Unfortunately, the same can be said of many Muslim madrassas or religious schools. Children memorize the Qur'an but do not explore or internalize its meaning.

This particular coastal youth group wanted to promote critical thinking and intellectual vitality using a multi-round, knockout poetry competition at which students would not only recite the poems but also be asked about their meaning. After the grant was awarded and the first round of competitions held, the volunteer organizers decided to introduce verses that emotionally appealed to the target audiences: the students and their parents. They selected popular verses that were historically and culturally important; they happened to be verses from the Qur'an.

When I first heard about this, I checked the grant agreement—it did not specify which poems would be used. As a Muslim, I loved it. The Qur'an is revealed in an intricate rhyming meter in which God challenges the whole of mankind to "produce the like of this Qur'an, they could not produce the like thereof, even if they backed up each other with help and support."[32] The youth organizers maintained, consistent with our assessment, that youth are often misled into believing one particular extreme interpretation of a Quranic verse rather than being encouraged to explore multiple interpretations from different sources, and allowed to develop their own personal meaning. Like their Christian pastors' sermons, these organizers were complying with the objective of the grant agreement to promote critical thinking but adding an important religious component. Once again, I thought it was a brilliant application that furthered the program objectives with a grantee contribution.

Together, these four examples (dialogue with religious leaders, targeted radio programming by moderate imams, applying religious texts to contemporary issues, and encouraging critical thinking alongside exploring multiple interpretations of religious texts) are excellent ways for local organizations to fight extremist narratives through education and pluralism. Unfortunately, USAID staff face significant restrictions because of the agency's interpretation of the First Amendment, restrictions that the Departments of State or Defense colleagues do not face. I have not been able to unearth why disparate US government agencies have such divergent interpretations of the US Constitution.

I approached the second challenge, the inherent obstacles to pooling funds from diverse accounts and agencies, and navigating the varying authorities associated with assorted flavors of money, more directly than the religion obstacle described above. We pooled money in theory but not in reality. Instead of spending months trying to transfer funds to KTI, I decided it was better to let a department that had a more liberal interpretation of the First Amendment and did not have the same constraints working with law enforcement pick up the check.

One human rights-focused civil society organization on the coast wanted to empower police and prison wardens to interact more effectively with community members when addressing extremism and radicalization, as well as better understand and use social media. A second group wanted their paralegals inside prisons to promote a better understanding of good governance and human rights, establish youth support groups in prisons, connect ex-offenders to aftercare programs, and train law enforcement officers and prison officers on risk assessments and early warnings of extremism ideology. I connected the groups with the State Department's counterterrorism fund manager in Nairobi and helped both groups advance their grant proposals.

Obstacles

I thought I had it all figured out. The two groups would get funded to work with local law enforcement and in prisons. We would remain true to the design team's vision, and we would comply with USAID's requirements. Or so I thought.

Striving for synergy and coordination among US government agencies is especially difficult given varying deployment times. Our foreign service deployment terms are short. I was the KTI deputy for six years because I was not technically with the foreign service, rather I was a personal services contractor. Many USAID foreign service officers (FSOs) in Kenya were on a four-year rotation while those of the Department of

State were on two-year rotations. In other higher risk countries such as Pakistan or South Sudan, everyone was on a one-year rotation, leaving barely enough time to get in and understand the context and culture before packing out. When designing the Eastleigh CVE program, I made an extra effort to coordinate across departments. But the USAID process took a year from the initial design to the launch of the program. Within that time, colleagues with the Departments of Defense and State had moved on. I had to restart the explanations and repeatedly secure buy-in.

For the law enforcement and prison grants, the person filling the State Department's counterterrorism advisor role switched between the time the proposal was forwarded to Washington, DC, and the approvals were secured. The new advisor had been given a host of other responsibilities and did not have the capacity to manage these two grants. However, I was a certified contracting officer's representative and could oversee the project. It fit right into our larger CVE project that had over 100 grants and the additional workload needed for two more grants would be negligible. I was too dreamy. The bureaucratic dragon slayed that idea. USAID management told me that while it was a noble idea, it was impossible for a USAID employee to manage a Department of State program in that it would violate the US Antideficiency Act, which "prohibits federal agencies from obligations or expending federal funds in advance or in excess of an appropriation, and from accepting voluntary services."[33] In USAID's interpretation, if Congress had given the Department of State funds for a grant program targeting law enforcement overseas, it had to manage that program itself. USAID could not volunteer to do it for them. Sound complex and bureaucratic? It is. That is the nature of working for a large government machine and the downside is that finding synergies is extremely difficult.

The second problem is the role of headquarters and field offices. While we were all based at the US embassy in Nairobi, all OTI's big decisions, funding, and contracts were managed out of Washington, DC. The State Department had its own center of gravity a mile away on the other side of the White House. The Pentagon was technically in another state, three miles away from USAID's Washington, DC, office, and the US Africa command headquarters (and funding) came from Stuttgart, Germany. After securing buy-in and funding for the Eastleigh and Coast CVE program, ensuring no overlap, maximizing synergy for the program, and kicking it off, I received a text message from one of our program officers. She was attending a project activity in Eastleigh and saw a billboard that she wanted me to investigate. It was advertising a crowdsourcing website for the same youth that we were targeting and for the same purpose— countering extremism. I opened my browser and went to the website. After a few clicks, I found the byline. I froze. It said the site was sponsored by the US embassy in Nairobi. I could not believe it; I was disappointed and frustrated. It took more than one phone call to solve the mystery; the effort was funded and managed in Washington, DC, and the Defense Department personnel who had initiated it while stationed in Nairobi were no longer posted to Kenya. They had left before I had conceived the Eastleigh program but the slow and faithful US government bureaucracy had designed, initiated, and funded the Defense Department program. My efforts to engage across the other side, to pull in all agencies and individuals, and to leverage each other's strengths had been in vain.

USAID's CVE Mandate

The US Congress, through the Foreign Assistance Act, has mandated the president to align assistance with American foreign policy and to priori- tize assistance where there is the "greatest opportunity to . . . reduce child- hood and adolescent exposure to or engagement in violent extremism or extremist ideologies."[34] This clause, added in the 2017 amendments to the act, is found in a section titled, "Assistance to Promote Sustainable, Qual- ity Basic Education."[35] Had this clause existed when I was with USAID, the development specialists I worked with would have maintained that it means teaching secular school students about kindness, dialogue, and good governance, as well as providing them with a basic education that allows them to secure employment, raise a family, and be good people. I believe it means teaching about pluralism and tolerance, especially in Islam, in all education facilities including *madrassas.*

The USAID staff I interacted with are guided by the ludicrous belief that USAID's role is not to change perceptions or attitudes toward religion. I found this nonsensical because changing someone's percep- tions or attitude toward handwashing or education is no different from changing their perception about extremism. In all three examples, the development professional is attempting to change behavior by first changing a perception.

The confusion about the flow of CVE funding and the concern and pushback from development practitioners must have percolated up to Washington, DC, because, in the introductory letter attached to the 2011 USAID CVE policy, the USAID administrator stated: "Clarifying USAID's role in the context of violent extremism and insurgency does not come without controversy. Some hold strong views on whether development agencies generally—and USAID in particular—should engage on these issues. . . . By not confronting where we can those development related factors that drive conflict and, specific to this policy, violent extremism and insurgency, we will ignore the plight of many around the world in great need."[36]

USAID in Kenya has not shied away from CVE efforts. The October 2020–October 2025 CDCS boldly identifies programming under the second development objective (resilience) and the fourth (region). However, such objectives cannot be realized given the self-imposed constraint, the inability to embrace the importance of religion, and the externally imposed constraint, USAID's interpretation of the First Amendment.

A Brookings Institution 2015 paper, "Integrating Religious Engagement into Diplomacy: Challenges and Opportunities," focused on constraints within the State Department that echoes my analysis of USAID. The authors noted that "most Western diplomats engage these issues from a distinct disadvantage . . . in which issues of identity, culture, and faith are largely irrelevant" and that "any effort to better appreciate the role of religion in foreign affairs must involve at least some modicum of willingness to examine the assumptions we hold about the place of religion in society."[37]

Second, the significant differences in USAID's interpretation of the influence of the First Amendment in our program design will squash our local partners' creativity and our ability to support those best able to counter extremism. These are Muslims, as noted by Senator Kyl in 2004 (see the quotation at the beginning of this chapter). The Brookings Institute recognized that "legal concerns tend to be raised most frequently in connection with programs organized and run by the State Department and other foreign policy agencies such as USAID. Most of these involve US foreign assistance funds being used to support activities by faith-based organizations or the participation in US government programs by religious leaders."[38]

If USAID staff cannot design a program that invites religious leaders to discuss a proposed constitution from a religious angle and head off any extremist rhetoric, we cannot succeed. As a born Muslim, Western educated man who has lived in Kenya, Pakistan, and the United States, I am extremely comfortable with religious engagement. However, the Brookings Institute states, "the fact of the matter is, however, that very few Foreign Service officers and other diplomats possess either sufficient understanding of religion or the necessary skillsets to effectively undertake religious engagement."[39] The report also echoed the discrepancies among agency interpretations that I found: "Further complicating matters is the fact that the legal guidance provided to US agencies asking about this kind of work tend to varies widely from agency to agency and, within the same agency, from case-to-case. Fear of falling on the wrong side of the law has sometimes had a chilling effect on State Department officers contemplating new programs with a large focus on religious engagement."[40]

USAID's CVE programs cannot succeed with this chilling effect and USAID's legal interpretations. Few USAID development specialists have the spirit of OTI breathed into them when they start working for the agency. Nor are they able to challenge the bureaucracy or take risks. Few have an interest to learn about Islam. Even fewer have the time, inclination, or patience to work across agencies to pool ideas and funding. The same holds true regarding slowly developing trust with local organizations.

If one looks hard enough, one will find breadcrumbs left by others that lead to my conclusion. For example, The State Department's Office of Inspector General (OIG) does not appear to see a role for USAID in CVE programming. For example, in the "Audit of the Department of State Implementation of Policies Intended To Counter Violent Extremism" (2019), the OIG recommended that the State Department's "Bureau of Counterterrorism and Countering Violent Extremism seek designation from the Secretary of State to be the controlling authority on countering violent extremism issues and policy."[41] The same report recommended that the bureau, with other offices at the State Department (and not USAID), "develop and implement a single definition for what constitutes a countering violent extremism program or project."[42] This approach casts aside the joint USAID–State Department efforts to define foreign assistance and develop a common framework for reporting on foreign assistance programming, as discussed in chapter 2. I believe it is because of the inherent, unarticulated belief among the Departments of States and Defense staff that USAID should not be in this programming space. This belief does not represent any official or unofficial policy, it is simply a collective belief that I picked up on during informal discussions across three continents.

The US government's GAO offers its own breadcrumb. In a July 2008 report titled, "Combatting Terrorism. Actions Needed to Enhance Implementation of Trans-Sahara Counterterrorism Partnership," the office concluded that "although the agencies measure activities' outputs, such as the number of foreign military personnel trained, they do not measure their activities' outcomes in combating terrorism—for instance, any decrease in extremism in the targeted countries."[43] In other words, USAID must address CVE programming head-on and, in my opinion, this means acknowledging the role that faith plays. Absent this acknowledgment, for whatever reason, including the desire to remain politically correct, USAID should exit this space.

Conclusion

Some readers may be offended by my conclusion about the inherent weaknesses in USAID's attitude and ability to address violent extremism given that its practitioners are not equipped with the right mindset and tools. Other readers may vehemently oppose my accusation that religion is used as an instigator of violence. However, I would like to suggest that someone's individual beliefs may actually be further informed by more recent studies conducted since we completed the Kenyan experiment; these studies were actually informed by the Eastleigh pilot.[44] One example was a 2016 CVE study administered in Jordan that debunked the prevailing simplistic USAID perception that extremism can be addressed through jobs and community participation. The 2016 report published the following:

However, worldviews and personal motivations examined against a given environment are a much more useful approach and facilitate the identification of three clusters of motivations: opportunistic (remuneration, boredom, or purposelessness), retributive (a desire to redress an injustice and/or take revenge, effect political change, or achieve personal redemption) and ideological (yearnings of salvation and/or a desire to restore the 'true nature' of Islam).[45]

The report, based on 120 depth interviews, 4,800 guided questionnaires, and 20 expert interviews across 12 governorates, elaborates on this third cluster: "It is also a pathway that provides more ideological and sociopolitical certainty to individuals suffering from an identity crisis and with a deep need for belonging. It also offers an honorable exit from life for desperate individuals resigned to escape their daily lives as well as an avenue for individuals who seek to make amends for past misdeeds."[46] A 2017 European study found that "interviews conducted in Egypt indicated that supporters of the government view the basis of extremism as the political Islam groups and their religious discourse, which exploits social, economic and political problems to broaden the extremism."[47] The Combatting Terrorism Center at West Point's journal, the *CTC Sentinel,* found that "economics, education, and religious ideology have all played roles in pushing young Jordanians toward the Islamic State."[48]

CVE programming is important to secure long-term peace in Kenya. The PARADISE mnemonic's components of *P*eace; *A*cceptance of diversity, equality, and pluralism; *R*ule of law and human rights; and *S*tewardship of neighbors and communities should be reflected in the US government's CVE programming. Kenya's history of terrorist attacks and the struggles that Kenya's neighbors face testify to the significant violent extremism afflicting Kenya.

If US development assistance wants to remain relevant in US foreign policy and national security, it has two choices: Either it must address violent extremism head-on by acknowledging and addressing the role of religion, or it needs to explicitly stop programming and reject all CVE-related funding. Neither choice is easy. The first requires USAID to make a conscious, top-down effort, one that requires legislative and judiciary support, to be more explicit in addressing pull factors inclusive of religion. One of my OTI colleagues introduced me to my favorite metaphor—"nibbling at the edges." Given this set of choices, USAID must stop nibbling at the edges of CVE programming and dive into it headfirst. This would require Congress to define its CVE objectives within the context of America's national security and explicitly task USAID with CVE programming. The courts would have to drive the agency's interpretation of the non-establishment clause in the First Amendment by finding harmony across departments. Countering extremism requires engaging with Muslims and their religious leaders, not to "establish" a particular religion but to promote tolerance and pluralism with the goal of making America safer. USAID would have to align its interpretation with other departments and agencies and work much more closely with the Departments of State and Defense to leverage each other's strengths and synergize overseas programming. USAID would have to define CVE programs and train its staff and implementing partners on the role of religion and supporting local, creative ideas.

CONCLUSION

Either you have journeyed with me through this entire book or are jumping ahead to the conclusion. If you are in the former cohort, you will understand what I mean when I say this book is both a personal memoir and a textbook on peace and security, using the example of Kenya in the aftermath of its flawed 2007 general election. If you are in the latter cohort, having jumped ahead, perhaps this conclusion will prove this claim.

I spent a decade working for USAID, the American government's primary foreign assistance arm. I spent three years at USAID's head-quarters in Washington, DC, and seven at the US embassy in Nairobi. I also ran into many USAID and Department of State personnel scattered around the nine countries I visited in my official roles. Some of those visits were extremely short—three days in N'djamena, Chad; five in Bogota, Colombia; and 10 in Amman, Jordan. Others were much longer—four weeks in Peshawar, Pakistan, and six in Juba, South Sudan. The latter two were not on anyone's top tourism destinations and I was largely confined to the office and US government housing. I became quite comfortable traveling in an armored vehicle or forced to stick to my assigned protective service personnel.

My mind is always working; my friends and family complain that it never stops. Therefore, each of these environments provided an opportunity to think and engage with professional colleagues. What else is there to do on a restricted compound for a three-day weekend or in a six-hour car ride? I tried talking about USAID and foreign assistance, Congress and appropriations, peace and security programming, religion, and international politics. For a variety of reasons, many colleagues never wanted to talk about these bigger issues.

Some were working a day job to secure a government pension in retirement. Once, I tried congratulating a long-serving foreign service officer, whom I had met at USAID in Nairobi because he had been recognized for completing 25 years of service. He dismissed me, shook his head, frowned, and mumbled, "I hate it here, I just need to finish my term for my pension."[1] Other USAID staff dropped the "US" from USAID; they wanted no association with the US government and instead pretended that USAID was a charity or foundation whose goal was alleviating poverty or facilitating development. They would cut me off when I pointed out that our raison d'être was national security and foreign policy, or when I reminded them that Congress appropriated US taxpayer money for us to manage.

A few conversations were mindboggling to me, as a logical guy with a systems engineering degree. I had to force myself to stop talking. On a long car ride to Peshawar with an American economist brandishing a PhD, I mentioned I wanted to buy carpets when I returned to Islamabad. He maintained that the price of carpets should be cheaper in Peshawar because it was closer to Afghanistan, which was one source of the carpets. Having lived in Islamabad for two years and frequented Peshawar before joining USAID, I knew the best carpet shops were in Islamabad because the capital had more expatriates and tourists. With more demand and more shops, prices were more competitive. He would not budge, relying solely on economic theory and ignoring local contexts.

Failed Linkages

Unable to engage in intellectually honest conversations about USAID's purpose, mission, and, specifically, USAID's role in promoting peace and security for the United States, I turned to published documents. While USAID's presentation of peace, security, and foreign policy terms continues to evolve, as described in chapter 2, one should never ignore the original rationale for establishing the organization. In 1962, former President Kennedy was unambiguous in his remarks when signing the first amendments to the year-old Foreign Assistance Act: "It is our national obligation and in our national interest and **security** to work for a world in which there is a chance for national sovereignty and national independence."[2] The former president also countered those who did not believe in the relationship between America's national security and international, nonmilitary assistance, emphasizing that "the amount of money that is involved in the nonmilitary areas are a fraction of what we spend on our national defense every year, and yet this is very much related to our **national security** and is as important dollar for dollar as any expenditure for national defense itself.[3]

In 2012, CRS noted that "U.S. foreign aid is intended to be a tool for fighting poverty, enhancing bilateral relationships, and/or protecting U.S. security and commercial interests."[4] CRS blamed Congress, stating, "over the years [Congress] added dozens of new, though often overlapping, aid objectives."[5] The service then concluded its report by criticizing the direction USAID has taken in protecting America's national security. The report explains that the cause for the failure is "that aid provided for development objectives is often conflated with aid provided for political and security purposes."[6] This is a stark and poignant accusation. It emphasizes a central confusion: Is aid supposed to be for development objectives only, used only to assist other nations improve their citizens' quality of life? Or is development assistance supposed to be more intentionally aimed at providing security? If the latter, then whose security is at stake, America's, our allies', or both?

With the rollout of the February 2015 National Security Strategy under former President Obama, Diane Ohlbaum explained her theory as to why development has not been able to play its intended role in national security: "Development advocates and practitioners have often resisted justifying their work on national security grounds, fearing that development objectives would be sacrificed on the altar of security imperatives."[7] Ohlbaum claims that development practitioners, between 2005 and 2015, resisted playing the national security card. Her claim implies that USAID staff knew about the nexus between development and national security but chose not to rely on it. Many USAID Foreign Service Officers, especially all the ones I interacted with, fundamentally oppose this belief and struggle to articulate its intended nexus, even behind closed doors or off the record. If her claim were true, if the officers understood the nexus, the effect would have trickled overseas and permeated overarching country strategies or discussions. It did not.

While CRS blames overlapping aid objectives and Diane Ohlbaum faults an active intellectual resistance, the Bookings Institution blames the absence of an explicit linkage. In a 2017 study, "Development as a featured theme in US National Security Strategies since 2002,"[8] George Ingram explored development in national security strategies, expecting to find a direct, articulated, intentional, and proven nexus between foreign assistance and national security. Instead, he laments: "The Bush and Obama strategies positioned the U.S. role in development as part of a global effort that tied our country's national interest with progress elsewhere in the world, *even where there is no overt linkage.*"[9]

Perhaps USAID does not get an A+ for an overt linkage because, first, the vast majority of its foreign assistance programs do not intentionally consider peace and security. Second, peace and security programming does not use all the tools in the USAID toolbox. As long as USAID staff ignore national security, or treat it as a tertiary objective, they cannot be intentional about it. Recall USAID's 2014 mission statement's use of the word "while:" "We partner to end extreme poverty and to promote resilient, democratic societies *while* advancing our security and prosperity."[10] USAID's primary purpose was not America's security and prosperity; its primary purpose was the other country's poverty alleviation and democracy building. By 2018 (and as of 2024), the "while" had evolved into an "and," making the two goals equal: "On behalf of the American people, we promote and demonstrate democratic values abroad, and advance a free, peaceful, and prosperous world."[11] However, in making these two goals equal, the mission statement dropped its focus on America's security and prosperity. Now, USAID has morphed into assuming the role of the United Nations, not that of a US government agency. How can long-term USAID staff unravel this constantly swinging pendulum and not resist justifying their work on national security grounds?

Chapter Summary

Chapter 2 addressed the meaning of the phrase "peace and security." I described how I interpret its constituent words, how they are used in international and domestic governing documents, and why the concept is explicitly important for America's national security. Chapter 2 is the academic analysis of a phrase, a chapter sandwiched between four others that describe how the US government tried to promote America's peace and security while trying to assist Kenya to recover from its postelection violence. Each of these four chapters focused on a different type of support, some successful, others not.

The journey began in chapter 1 on a positive note, presenting a successful effort to assist Kenya initiate reforms to its judiciary. Chapter 3 discussed USAID's role in the development, promotion, and adoption of Kenya's new constitution in 2010, a process made possible only because of the devastating postelection violence. Those who were unfortunate enough to be killed or displaced because of the postelection violence were seen as martyrs for the nation: Their blood and tears gave rise to a new governing document. The United States played a pivotal role in helping Kenya through its journey of establishing a new constitution despite the roadblocks and potholes along the road. The debate about Kenya's Constitution is eternal; Kenya will continue to struggle to fully implement it, much as the United States struggled to give everyone the right to vote and continues to struggle to balance the Second Amendment with safety and security. Kenya's Constitution also took a place on the world's peace and security stage, playing a role in the 2024 Haiti crisis. Chapter 4 showed that USAID unsuccessfully dabbled in Kenya's eternal and undefined land reform movement, a problem with both historical and contemporary parallels in the United States.

These three chapters (on Kenya's judiciary, Kenya's Constitution, and land reform in the nation) offer lessons on governance programming. They also showcase what I believe US peace and security programming should and should not be. The last chapter tackles arguably the most critical topic in peace and security studies, one that researchers and practitioners are only starting to understand. Congress and the executive allocate a lot of money for CVE, even in the United States. Yet, on more than one occasion, USAID colleagues admitted that they labeled their development programming as "CVE" simply to use CVE money. The fifth chapter explores the role of religion as frontstage in justifying acts of violence across all faiths but offstage at USAID. Religion is the foundation that is blatantly missing between USAID programming and the CVE objectives it purports to achieve. I also contrast the religion-based approaches of USAID with those of the Departments of State and Defense.

Peacebuilding and Reconciliation

My readers are perhaps asking about two topics I chose not to cover—peacebuilding and reconciliation. I acknowledge these conflicts are extremely critical for local peace and can become flashpoints for larger eruptions of violence. Yet, I have noticeably omitted these topics because I believe that local conflict mitigation, listening, trauma recovery, and other forms of peace and reconciliation—dialogues over cattle rustling, ethnic tolerance, or local resources—are matters that should not percolate up to a US government's program on peace and security as it impacts the United States.

I also recognize and appreciate the role that the peace and reconciliation industry had on USAID's Kenya program. When we launched KTI in mid-2008, we started searching for astute Kenyan program officers. In the end, the KTI final evaluation team noted that "KTI [had] hired and given considerable autonomy to a cadre of young highly trained and sophisticated professionals. . . . The [Program Development Officers], grant managers and procurement officers were all highly skilled professionals, highly motivated, analytical in approach and highly sensitive to the political nature of their working environment."[12] Many of our program officers had accumulated regional experience and were motivated to return to Kenya after the postelection violence.

KTI did engage in some local peace and reconciliation activities, representing as much as 16 percent of all grants. We funded groups as disparate as religious groups, local government, and women's and youth groups to dialogue; resolve local conflict over cattle, water, or land; and engage in nonviolent interactions among diverse groups living in the same geographical area. A few of these grants were tied to other, broader objectives and themes discussed in this book—countering violent extremism, educating people about the new constitution, and land reform. Others were not linked to other aims; instead, they focused on local-level intertribal conflict over resources and power.

Author's Message

This book has helped me unravel the mystery of USAID's attempts to play a role in America's peace and security. I now understand that the term itself is widely used, yet ill-defined. A lack of an established definition prevents development practitioners from accurately accounting for US peace and security initiatives overseas, resulting in underreporting initiatives that the United States should be showcasing. As USAID staff cannot consistently design intentional, efficient, and effective programs that promote America's peace and security, USAID programs sometimes use the wrong tool from the programming toolbox.

Hopefully, this book provides a broader perspective to students pursuing peace and security degrees and those who teach them. It provides students, professors, development practitioners, policymakers, and diplomats with a broader perspective of the peace and security sector, deemphasizing arms deals, intelligence gathering, drones, military training, and bilateral negotiations, while emphasizing the powerful role of other types of traditional programming. Third, it offers the American taxpayer, those funding USAID initiatives overseas, an appreciation of why overseas programming is important for our own national security, as reflected in the February 2024 White House press statement at the beginning of the book. It also offers the American taxpayer detailed examples of how USAID designs and implements programs under the peace and security umbrella.

As Kenya began recovering from its tumultuous 2007 election and the subsequent violence, which ended with the signing of the February 2008 peace agreement, USAID's primary mechanism for helping Kenya with short-term, strategic interventions in support of the agreement was the Kenya Transition Initiative (KTI). It was intentional, using USAID's complete toolbox to help advance peace and security, or PARADISE, in Kenya to advance our US peace and security. None of KTI's support was military focused. The essential ingredients of peace and security, or what I call "secure peace," are depicted by the mnemonic, PARADISE:

- **P**eace, or the absence of war, conflict, crime, and turmoil
- **A**cceptance of our diversity, equality, and pluralism
- **R**ule of law and human rights

- **A**dministration of government services and responsibilities
- **D**emocracy or a government with people's representation and voice
- **I**nnovation allowing each new generation to be better placed than the previous one
- **S**tewardship of neighbors, communities, humanity, and the earth
- **E**conomic growth

Foreign policy and international development professionals, especially those working on Africa, hopefully, can now better appreciate the intricacies of nonmilitary peace and security programming. Instead of shying away from it, they can recognize that development interventions commonly used for other objectives such as judicial and constitutional reform can play a tremendous and powerful role in advancing America's peace and security objectives. They may also be able to use all the tools from the development assistance toolbox, when appropriate, to advance US peace and security, while simultaneously enabling other countries to improve their governance and quality of life. Former President Biden certainly believed in this broader application of peace and security programming. In an address to University of Nairobi students in 2010, spoken while he served as vice president, noted, that "the truth is, better governance is not just an end in itself, it is your path to a lasting democratic stability and your ultimate stability. And, I might add—presumptuous of me, as an outsider, to say—it's the best route to economic prosperity, sparking job creation, opening up opportunity, and improving the way of life for Kenyans everywhere."[13]

NOTES

Introduction

1. "Ballots to Bullets: Organized Political Violence and Kenya's Crisis of Governance," Human Rights Watch, Mar. 16, 2008, https://www.hrw.org/report/2008/03/16/ballots-bullets/organized-political-violence-and-kenyas-crisis-governance.

2. "Dashboard," ForeignAssistance.gov, www.foreignassistance.gov, accessed Jan. 11, 2022.

3. Mission, Vision and Values," USAID, https://www.usaid.gov/who-we-are/mission-vision-values, captured Jan. 26, 2019 (site discontinued).

4. Office of Transitions Initiative (OTI), *Kenya Last Quarterly Report*, Chemonics, Mar. 31, 2014, https://pdf.usaid.gov/pdf_docs/PA00K6HV.pdf (site discontinued).

5. I was not hired as a foreign services officer (FSO) but as a personal services contractor, with almost all the rights, privileges, and benefits of an FSO for the duration of the specific job posting.

6. Bush v. Gore, 531 U.S. 98 (2000).

7. Michael Ranneberger, "Reform, Partnership, and the Future of Kenya," speech given to the American Chamber of Commerce, State Department, Nairobi, Kenya, Jan. 26, 2010, https://reliefweb.int/report/kenya/reform-partnership-and-future-kenya-speech-us-ambassador-michael-ranneberger-american.

8. Ranneberger, "Reform."

9. Ranneberger, "Reform."

10. Ranneberger, "Reform."

11. Joel D. Barkan, "Kenya After Moi," *Foreign Affairs* 83, no. 1 (2004): 87–100.

12. Barkan, "Kenya After Moi."

13. Joel D. Barkan et al., *Kenya Transition Initiative, Final Evaluation*, report commissioned by and presented to USAID, Oct. 2013. Prepared by Barkan et al. on behalf of The QED Group, LLC, under Task Order #62 of the Prog. Dev. Quickly II (PDQII) IQC, no. DOTI-00-08-00017-00.

14. The term "NGO," for "nongovernmental organization," is often misinterpreted to refer narrowly to nonprofit entities. I use the term to denote anything that is not associated directly with a government or the United Nations. Within the context of international development, the term encompasses all of civil society—businesses, nonprofit development entities, academia, and for-profit development contractors.

15. Exec. Order No. 10,973, 3 C. F. R. 26 FR 10496 (1961).

16. Foreign Affairs Reform and Restructuring Act of 1998, 5 U.S.C. §104 (1998).

17. Foreign Affairs Reform and Restructuring Act.

18. Foreign Affairs Reform and Restructuring Act.

19. *Alumni Association Forum* (blog), USAID Alumni Association, Feb. 7, 2015, http://www.usaidalumni.org/uaa-forum/general-discussion/raj-shah-the-second-worst-usaid-administrator-in-30-years/, captured Oct. 2018 (site discontinued).

20. USAID, Congressional Budget Justification, 2023, https://www.usaid.gov/sites/default/files/documents/FY2023-Congressional-Budget-Justification.pdf (site discontinued).

21. NASA, *FY 2023 President's Budget Request,* 2023, https://www.nasa.gov/sites/default/files/atoms/files/fy23_nasa_budget_request_summary.pdf; US Department of Transportation, *Budget Estimates, Fiscal Year 2023,* Federal Aviation Administration, https://www.transportation.gov/sites/dot.gov/files/2022–03/FAA_Buget_Estimates_FY23.pdf; National Oceanic and Atmospheric Administration, *Budget Summary FY 2023,* https://www.noaa.gov/sites/default/files/2022–05/508_Compliant_Final_FY23_NOAA_Blue_Book_Budget_Summary.pdf.

22. Office of Inspector General (OIG), "Inspection of Embassy Nairobi," ISPI-12–38A, Aug. 2012, https://www.stateoig.gov/report/isp-i-12-38a.

23. Physical display at the former USAID library and public information center on the mezzanine level of the Ronald Reagan Building in Washington, DC; captured July 2008.

24. These contractors were USAID's top vendors. See, for example, "Archived Content," USAID, https://2012-2017.usaid.gov/results-and-data/budget-spending/top-40-vendors (site discontinued).

25. OTI, "Where We Work," USAID, https://www.usaid.gov/stabilization-and-transitions/where-we-work, captured Dec. 24, 2022 (site discontinued).

26. OTI, "Where We Work."

27. "Mission," USAID.

28. OTI, *A Decade of Transition, 1994–2004,* USAID, http://www.globalcorps.com/sitedocs/oti10yearreport.pdf.

29. State, Foreign Operations, and Related Programs Appropriations Bill, 2023, H.R. 117–401, 117th Cong. (2022).

30. USAID, "Appendix: Police Reform," *KTI Final Report, 2014–2019,* Kenya Transition Initiative, www.kenyati.com (site discontinued).

31. Michela Wrong, "Adventures of a Book in Africa," *Standpoint,* June 24, 2009, http://www.standpointmag.co.uk/node/1703/full, accessed Dec. 20, 2020.

1. Judicial Reform

1. Peter Kagwanja and Roger Southall, "Introduction: Kenya: A Democracy in Retreat?," *Journal of Contemporary African Studies* 27, no. 3 (2009): 259–77.
2. Raila Odinga (@RailaOdinga), "Re: Statement on Court Ruling," X, Sept. 5, 2022, https://x.com/RailaOdinga/status/1566751566178263041.
3. Willy Mutunga, "Circular on Dress Code and Address," *Chief Justice Issues Circular C. J.* 90, Aug. 23, 2011, http://kenyalaw.org/kl/index.php?id=835.
4. See, for example, Elisabeth Lindenmayer and Josie Lianna Kaye, *A Choice for Peace? The Story of Forty-One Days of Mediation in Kenya,* International Peace Institute, Aug. 2009, https://www.ipinst.org/wp-content/uploads/pub lications/kenyamediation_epub.pdf; "Statement of Principles on Long-Term Issues and Solutions," Kenya National Dialogue and Reconciliation, May 23, 2008, https://www.peaceagreements.org/viewmasterdocument/688.
5. See, for example, "Why Martha Karua is Kenya's 'Iron Lady,'" *Daily Nation,* July 14, 2022, https://nation.africa/kenya/blogs-opinion/letters/why -martha-karua-is-kenya-s-iron-lady--3878760.
6. *Encyclopedia Britannica Online,* s.v. "Bush v. Gore," accessed Oct. 21, 2022, https://www.britannica.com/event/Bush-v-Gore/Majority-opinion.
7. William Cummings et al., "By the Numbers: President Donald Trump's Failed Efforts to Overturn the Election," *USA Today,* Jan. 6, 2021, https://www .usatoday.com/in-depth/news/politics/elections/2021/01/06/trumps-failed -efforts-overturn-election-numbers/4130307001/ (site discontinued).
8. Jude Sheerin, "January 6 Hearing: Trump Accused of Attempted Coup," BBC, June 10, 2022, https://www.bbc.co.uk/news/world-us-canada-61753870.
9. Joe Biden, "Remarks by Vice President Joe Biden to University Students in Nairobi, Kenya," speech given at the Kenyatta International Conference Center, Nairobi, Kenya, June 9, 2010, the White House, Office of the Vice President, https://obamawhitehouse.archives.gov/the-press-office/remarks -vice-president-joe-biden-university-students-nairobi-kenya.
10. See, for example, Maya Gainer, "How Kenya Cleaned Up Its Courts," *Foreign Policy,* July 9, 2016, https://foreignpolicy.com/2016/07/09/how-kenya -cleaned-up-its-courts/; Republic of Kenya, *Final Report of the Task Force on Judicial Reforms,* July 2010, http://kenyalaw.org/kl/fileadmin/pdfdownloads /Final_Report_of_the_Task_Force_on_Judicial_Reforms.pdf.
11. USAID, "Appendix: Judiciary Reform," *KTI Final Report, 2014–2019.*
12. Cary Anderson, email to the author from a Connected Justice Solutions Architect at Cisco Systems Inc., June 15, 2011.

13. Mbogo, personal conversation with the author, Eldoret Magistrate's Court, 2009.

14. Maya Gainer, "Transforming the Courts: Judicial Sector Reforms in Kenya, 2011–2015," Innovations for Successful Societies, Princeton Univ., Nov. 2015, https://successfulsocieties.princeton.edu/sites/g/files/toruqf5601/files/MG_OGP_Kenya_FORMATTED_02Dec2015_0.pdf.

15. USAID, "Gifts and Donations and Dollar Trust Fund Management," chap. 628, USAID Automated Directive System, 2011, https://2017-d2020.usaid.gov/sites/default/files/documents/1868/628.pdf.

16. "Judicial Performance Improvement," World Bank Group, Proj. ID: P105269, last updated May 30, 2022, https://projects.worldbank.org/en/projects-operations/project-detail/P105269.

17. The World Bank, *Implementation Completeness and Results Report,* IDA 51810, presented to the Republic of Kenya for the Judicial Performance Improvement, May 30, 2022, https://documents1.worldbank.org/curated/en/174721654782927709/pdf/Kenya-Judicial-PerformanceImprovement-Project.pdf.

18. Mugambe Kiai, "Kenya: Why Hire a Lawyer When You Can Pay the Judge?," *Standard,* Jan. 26, 2003, https://allafrica.com/stories/200301271086.html; personal communication between the author and a Nairobi-based lawyer, c. 2013.

19. Caroline Elkins, *Imperial Reckoning: The Untold Story of Britain's Gulag in Kenya* (Henry Holt, 2005).

20. Elkins, *Imperial Reckoning.*

21. John Bingham, "Asif Ali Zardari: Life and Style of Pakistan's Mr 10 Per Cent," *Telegraph,* Aug. 3, 2010, https://www.telegraph.co.uk/news/worldnews/asia/pakistan/7923479/Asif-Ali-Zardari-life-and-style-of-Pakistans-Mr-10-Per-Cent.html.

22. "Corruption Index," Trading Economics, https://tradingeconomics.com/country-list/corruption-index.

23. David Anderson, *Histories of the Hanged: Britain's Dirty War in Kenya and the End of Empire* (Norton, 2005).

24. Anderson, *Histories of the Hanged.*

25. Anderson, *Histories of the Hanged.*

26. Munir Ahmed, "Report: Killing of Pakistani Journalist in Kenya 'Planned,'" *AP,* Dec. 7, 2022, https://apnews.com/article/africa-pakistan-journalists-islamabad-67fc48f4c2f42fea603df6f4eac425bf.

27. Thomas Escrit, "ICC Judges Agree to Withdrawal of Kenyatta Charges," *Reuters,* Mar.13, 2015, https://www.reuters.com/article/uk-kenya-icc-idUKKBN0M91SD20150313/.

28. US Sen., Roll Call Vote, 117th Congress—1st Session, "Guilty or Not Guilty (Article of Impeachment Against Former President Donald John Trump)," H.Res. 24, Feb. 13, 2021, https://www.senate.gov/legislative/LIS/roll_call_votes/vote1171/vote_117_1_00059.htm.

29. USAID, *Guidance for Promoting Independence and Impartiality,* Office of Democracy and Governance, Technical Publication Series, Jan. 2002, https://peacemaker.un.org/sites/default/files/document/files/2022/07/usaidguidanceforpromotingjudicialindependenceandimpartiality2002.pdf.

30. Patricia Kameri Mbote and Migai Akech, *Kenya: Justice Sector and the Rule of Law* (Open Society Initiative for Eastern Africa, International Environmental Law Research Centre, 2011), https://www.ielrc.org/content/a1104.pdf.

31. International Commission of Jurists, Kenya Section, "Summary of Issues to be Highlighted in ICJ Mission Report for Release to the Press," Apr. 6, 2005, https://web.archive.org/web/20160304083836/http://www.icj-kenya.org/index.php/media-centre/press-releases/221-summary-of-issues-to-be-highlighted-in-icj-mission-report-for-release-to-the-press.

32. The chief justice was given six months to vacate their office and could apply for a lower court position if desired and vetted; the other two were given 12 months to vacate their offices.

33. USAID Kenya, *Country Development Cooperation Strategy 2014–2020.*

34. USAID, *Country Development Cooperation Strategy (CDCS) October 2020–October 2025,* executive summary, https://www.msiworldwide.com/wp-content/uploads/2023/10/Kenya_CDCS_External_Sept_2021.pdf.

35. USAID, *Country Development Cooperation Strategy (CDCS) October 2020–October 2025.*

36. Kenya Const. of 2010, cl. 138(4)(a).

37. Kenya Const. of 2010, cl. 138(4)(a).

38. Nanjala Nyabola, "Why Did Kenya's Supreme Court Annul the Elections?" *Al Jazeera,* Sept. 2, 2017, https://www.aljazeera.com/opinions/2017/9/2/why-did-kenyas-supreme-court-annul-the-elections.

39. Nyabola, "Annul."

40. Alex Marquadt, "US Determines Saudi Crown Prince is Immune in Case Brought by Jamal Khashoggi's Fiancée," CNN, Nov. 18, 2022, https://edition.cnn.com/2022/11/17/politics/saudi-crown-prince-immunity-state-department-jamal-khashoggi/index.html.

41. Julian E. Barnes and David E. Sanger, "Saudi Crown Prince Is Held Responsible for Khashoggi Killing in U.S. Report," *New York Times,* Feb. 16, 2021, https://www.nytimes.com/2021/02/26/us/politics/jamal-khashoggi-killing-cia-report.html; see also, Office of the Director of National Intelligence, "Assessing the Saudi Government's Role in the Killing of Jamal Khashoggi," Feb. 11, 2021, https://www.dni.gov/files/ODNI/documents/assessments/Assessment-Saudi-Gov-Role-in-JK-Death-20210226v2.pdf.

42. Andrew Glass, "This Day in Politics. United States Invades Panama, Dec. 20, 1989," *Politico,* Dec. 12, 2018, https://www.politico.com/story/2018/12/20/united-states-invades-panama-1989-1067072.

43. Ted Dagne, "Kenya: The December 2007 Elections and the Challenges Ahead," Congressional Research Service, Sept. 17, 2008, https://www.everycrs

report.com/files/20080917_RL34378_a1924cc669bf807094f5772f5f5252e48aad 383d.pdf.

44. "Ringera-List Judges Eye Millions in Damages," *Nation,* Nov. 13, 2010, updated July 3, 2020, https://nation.africa/kenya/news/ringera-list-judges-eye -millions-in-damages--745506.

45. Barkan et al., *Kenya Transition Initiative, Final Evaluation.*

2. Defining Peace and Security

1. United Nations, "United Nations Charter: Preamble," https://www.un .org/en/about-us/un-charter/preamble, captured Feb. 15, 2025.

2. All figures in this chapter are from "Dashboard," ForeignAssistance. gov, Jan. 11, 2022.

3. Aga Khan IV, "Address to Both Houses of the Parliament of Canada in the House of Commons Chamber," Feb. 27, 2014, https://the.akdn/en/resources -media/resources/speeches/address-both-houses-parliament-canada-house -commons-chamber-his-highness-the-aga-khan.

4. "About the Agency," Peace Corps, https://www.peacecorps.gov/about/; "The Origins of USIP," United States Institute of Peace, https://www.usip.org/ about/origins-usip, captured Feb. 15, 2025.

5. "TSA by the Numbers," Transportation Security Administration, https:// www.tsa.gov/news/press/factsheets/tsa-numbers, captured Feb. 15, 2025.

6. United Nations, "Preamble."

7. "Peace and Security," UNWomen, https://www.unwomen.org/en/what -we-do/peace-and-security, accessed Oct. 1, 2021.

8. "Global Issues: Peace and Security," United Nations, https://www.un .org/en/global-issues/peace-and-security, accessed Feb. 2025.

9. Constitute, https://constituteproject.org./constitutions, accessed Dec. 2022.

10. Const. of Angola of 2010, art. 202.

11. Kenya Const. of 2010, art. 238.1.

12. International Peace and Security Act of 1961, Pub. L. No. 87–195.

13. International Peace and Security Act of 1961, Sec. 501. (22 U.S.C. 2301).

14. Women, Peace, and Security Act of 2017, Pub. L. No. 115–68.

15. Women, Peace, and Security Act, Sec. 4.

16. Mandated by $603 of the Goldwater-Nichols Department of Defense Reorganization Act of 1986, Pub. L. No. 99–433, 100 Stat. 992 (1986).

17. The White House, "National Security Strategy of the United States," 2010, https://obamawhitehouse.archives.gov/sites/default/files/rss_viewer/ national_security_strategy.pdf.

18. Ryan J. Reilly and Ken Dilanian, "Intel Community Escapes Major Criticism by Jan. 6 Committee for Missing 'Foreseeable' Capitol Violence," *NBC,* Dec. 22, 2022, https://www.nbcnews.com/politics/justice-department/

intel-community-escapes-major-criticism-jan-6-committee-missing-forese
-rcna62628.

19. The White House, "National Security Strategy of the United States," 2015, https://obamawhitehouse.archives.gov/sites/default/files/docs/2015_national_security_strategy_2.pdf.

20. The White House, "National Security Strategy of the United States," 2017, p. 38, https://trumpwhitehouse.archives.gov/wp-content/uploads/2017/12/NSS-Final-12-18-2017-0905.pdf.

21. The White House, "National Security Strategy," 2017, p. 38.

22. The White House, "Interim National Security Strategic Guidance," 2021, https://bidenwhitehouse.archives.gov/wp-content/uploads/2021/03/NSC-1v2.pdf.

23. Foreign Assistance Act of 1961, Pub. L. 87–195, 22 U.S.C. 2151. As amended.

24. "Research," Institute for Peace and Security Studies, Addis Ababa Univ., https://ipss-addis.org/what-we-do/academic-and-applied-research/, captured Dec. 5, 2022.

25. "Youth, Peace, and Society," Columbia Climate School Advanced Consortium on Cooperation, Conflict, and Complexity, Columbia Univ., https://ac4.climate.columbia.edu/yps, captured Dec. 30, 2022.

26. "Women Are Critical to Achieving Sustainable Peace," Georgetown Institute for Women, Peace and Security, https://giwps.georgetown.edu/, captured Dec. 30, 2022.

27. "About," Center of Peace and Security Studies, Univ. of CA San Diego, https://cpass.ucsd.edu/about/index.html#About, captured Dec. 30, 2022.

28. "Branding," USAID, https://www.usaid.gov/branding, accessed Sept. 2018 and Dec. 2022.

29. "Mission," USAID, captured Mar. 17, 2024.

30. "Mission," USAID, captured Dec. 24, 2024. Emphasis added.

31. "On behalf of the American people, we promote and demonstrate democratic values abroad, and advance a free, peaceful, and prosperous world. In support of America's **foreign policy**, the U.S. Agency for International Development leads the U.S. Government's international development and disaster assistance through partnerships and investments that save lives, reduce poverty, strengthen democratic governance, and help people emerge from humanitarian crises and progress beyond assistance," USAID, www.usaid.gov/who-we-are/mission-vision-values, Mar. 23, 2019 (site discontinued). Emphasis added.

32. US Department of State and USAID, *Joint Strategic Plan, FY 2018–2022*, Feb. 2018, https://www.state.gov/wp-content/uploads/2018/12/Joint-Strategic-Plan-FY-2018-2022.pdf.

33. "Mission," USAID, captured Jan. 29, 2014. Emphasis added.

34. US Department of State, "Secretary Marco Rubio Appointed as Acting Administrator for the United States Agency for International Development (USAID)," press release, Feb. 3, 2025, https://www.state.gov/secretary-marco

-rubio-appointed-as-acting-administrator-for-the-united-states-agency-for
-international-development-usaid/.

35. Departments of Agriculture, Defense, Energy, Health and Human
Services, Homeland Security, Justice, Labor, State, Interior, and Treasury; the
Air Force (listed separately from Defense), Environmental Protection Agency,
Peace Corps, USAID, Trade and Development Agency, African Development
Foundation, and the US International Development Finance Corporation;
Departments of Commerce and Transportation, Federal Trade Commission,
and Millennium Challenge Corporation.

36. USAID and the Departments of Health and Human Services, Defense,
and State, as well as the Peace Corps; USAID and the Departments of Justice,
State, and Interior.

37. Refer to ForeignAssistance.gov.

38. An obligation is a binding agreement that the US government enters
into with a vendor or grantee to provide funding. This term applies to both
acquisition (the purchase of specific goods or services) and assistance
(financial or in-kind support to an organization that helps it accomplish a
public purpose); "Glossary of Terms," Operational Policy, USAID, https://
2012-2017.usaid.gov/sites/default/files/documents/1868/glossary.pdf (site
discontinued).

39. US Department of State, "Updated Foreign Assistance Standardized
Program Structure and Definitions," Apr. 19, 2016, https://2009-2017.state.
gov/f/releases/other/255986.htm#PS42.

40. US Department of State, "Updated Foreign Assistance."

41. US Department of State, "Updated Foreign Assistance."

42. US Department of State, "Updated Foreign Assistance."

43. The primary program areas noted on the ForeignAssistance.gov
dashboard are: Peace and Security ($293b); Health ($152b); Humanitarian
Assistance ($107b); Economic Growth ($86b); Democracy, Human Rights and
Governance ($66b); and Education and Social Services ($31b). There are two
others: Multi-Sector ($45b) and Program Support ($43b).

44. The rest of the Defense Department's obligations concerning Kenya
are for health.

45. Dustin Jones, "Why a Submarine Deal Has France at Odds with the U.S.,
U.K. and Australia," National Public Radio, Sept. 19, 2021, https://www.npr.org
/2021/09/19/1038746061/submarine-deal-us-uk-australia-france, captured Jan.
12, 2022.

46. "The U.S. Gives Egypt $1.5 Billion a Year in Aid. Here's What It Does,"
Washington Post, July 9, 2013, https://www.washingtonpost.com/news/wonk/
wp/2013/07/09/the-u-s-gives-egypt-1-5-billion-a-year-in-aid-heres-what-it-
does/, captured Jan. 17, 2022.

47. US Department of State, "Updated Foreign Assistance."

48. US Department of State, "Updated Foreign Assistance."

49. US Department of State, "Updated Foreign Assistance."

50. Abraham Lincoln, "The Gettysburg Address," speech given in Gettysburg, PA, Nov. 19, 1863, Library of Congress, https://www.loc.gov/resource/rbpe.24404500.

51. Foreign Assistance Act of 1961. As amended; emphasis added.

52. Xan Rice, "Background: The Lord's Resistance Army," *Guardian,* Oct. 20, 2007, https://www.theguardian.com/katine/2007/oct/20/about.uganda, retrieved Jan. 12, 2022.

53. The White House, "National Security Strategy," 2017.

54. International Peace and Security Act of 1961.

55. Tariq Ali, *Winston Churchill: His Times His Crimes* (Verso, 2022).

56. Macharia Kamau, "US Intervention in Kenya? No Thanks.," *African Arguments,* Mar. 6, 2018, https://africanarguments.org/2018/03/us-intervention-in-kenya-no-thanks/.

57. Mark Bellamy and Johnnie Carson, "How and Why the US Should Intervene in Kenya," *African Arguments,* Feb. 27, 2018, https://africanarguments.org/2018/02/how-and-why-the-us-should-intervene-in-kenya/.

58. Kamau, "US Intervention in Kenya?"

59. Bellamy and Carson, "Why the US Should Intervene."

60. Bellamy and Carson, "Why the US Should Intervene." Emphassis added.

61. US Africa Command Public Affairs, "Langley Makes First Visit to Africa as Commander," US Africa Command, Sept. 1, 2022, https://www.africom.mil/pressrelease/34687/langley-makes-first-visit-to-africa-as-commander.

62. Biden, "Remarks by Vice President."

63. The White House, "Interim National Security Strategic Guidance."

64. US Africa Command Public Affairs, "AFRICOM Commander Conducts Visit to Manda Bay," US Africa Command, Jan. 17, 2021, https://www.africom.mil/pressrelease/33416/africom-commander-conducts-visit-to-manda-bay, captured Oct. 9, 2021; "Welcome to Camp Lemonnier, Djibouti," US Navy, https://cnreurafcent.cnic.navy.mil/Installations/Camp-Lemonnier-Djibouti/, captured Feb. 17, 2025.

65. Select Comm. to Study Governmental Operations with Respect to Intelligence Activities, Sen. Rep. 94–465 (1975), https://www.intelligence.senate.gov/sites/default/files/94465.pdf.

66. John F. Kennedy, "Remarks Upon Signing the Foreign Assistance Act," speech given at the White House, Aug. 1, 1962, American Presidency Project, Univ. of CA Santa Barbara, https://www.presidency.ucsb.edu/documents/remarks-upon-signing-the-foreign-assistance-act.

67. Galeeb Kachra, *How I Changed the World in My Own Unique Ways,* selfpub., 2021.

68. The White House, "Interim National Security Strategic Guidance."

69. The White House, "Interim National Security Strategic Guidance."

70. The White House, "National Security Strategy," 2010.

71. *Collins Dictionary,* s.v. "help (*v.*)," captured Dec. 30, 2022, https://www.collinsdictionary.com/us/dictionary/english/help.

72. *Collins Dictionary,* s.v. "Assist (*v.*)," captured Dec. 30, 2022, https://www.collinsdictionary.com/us/dictionary/english/assist.

73. Margareta Cederfelt, "International Observers Increase Trust in US Elections," OSCEPA, Oct. 28, 2022, https://www.oscepa.org/en/news-a-media/op-eds/international-observers-increase-trust-in-us-elections.

74. *Reuters,* "USA: World Lines Up to Help After Katrina," news release, Sept. 5, 2005, Reliefweb, https://reliefweb.int/report/united-states-america/usa-world-lines-help-after-katrina.

75. Biden, "Remarks by Vice President."

3. A New Dawn

1. The media, policy analysts, and the public have heralded the process that led up to enacting Kenya's 2010 Constitution as a "New Dawn." A Google search on Jan. 1, 2022, of "New Dawn" +"Kenya" +"Constitution" yielded about 683,000 results. However, the term "New Dawn" predated Kenya's constitutional process and has been applied to other major Kenyan political events such as the nation's 2002 election.

2. See Michael Lecher, *The Constitution of Medina: Muhammad's First Legal Document* (Darwin, 2004), for a compilation of research; see also Yetkin Yildirim, "The Medina Charter: A Historical Case of Conflict Resolution," *Islam and Christian-Muslim Relations* 20, no. 4 (2009): 439–50.

3. U.S. Const. Preamble.

4. Kenya Const. of 2010, chap. 14, art. 283(1).

5. Kenya Const. of 2010, chap. 14, art. 283(1).

6. Willy Mutunga, "2010 Constitution of Kenya."

7. Aga Khan III, "O Ocidente devia aceitar que o islão não separa o mundo e a fé" ["The West Should Accept That Islam Does Not Separate the World and Faith"], interview with António Marujo and Faranaz Keshavjee, *Paroquias de Portugal* (July 23, 2008), https://www.paroquias.org/noticias.php?n=7548.

8. Cornelia Glinz, "Kenya's New Constitution: A Transforming Document or Less Than Meets the Eye?," *Verfassung Und Recht in Übersee / Law and Politics in Africa, Asia and Latin America* 44, no. 1 (2011): 60–80, http://www.jstor.org/stable/43239778.

9. Glinz, "Kenya's New Constitution."

10. Mary L. Dudziak, "Working Towards Democracy: Thurgood Marshall and the Constitution of Kenya," *Duke Law Journal* 56, no. 3, Dec. 2006.

11. Dudziak, "Working Towards Democracy."

12. Mary L. Dudizak, "Thurgood Marshall's Bill of Rights for Kenya," *Green Bag 2d* 11 (2008): 207, https://ssrn.com/abstract=1134026.

13. Naomi Gichuki, "Kenya's Constitutional Journey: Taking Stock of Achievements and Challenges," *Law in Africa* 18 (2015): 130–38, https://doi.org/10.5771/2363-6270-2015-1-130.

14. Smith Hempstone, *Rogue Ambassador: An African Memoir* (Univ. of the South Press, 1997).

15. Hempstone, *Rogue Ambassador.*

16. Hempstone, *Rogue Ambassador.*

17. Hempstone, *Rogue Ambassador.*

18. Kenya Human Rights Commission, "Wanjiku's Journey: Tracing Kenya's Quest for a New Constitution and Reporting on the 2010 National Referendum," Nov. 2010, https://khrc.or.ke/wp-content/uploads/2023/12/WANJIKUS-JOURNEY-Tracing-Kenyas-Quest-for-a-New-Constitution-Reporting-on-the-2010-Referendum.pdf.

19. Janne Holemén, "Nation-Building in Kenyan Secondary School Textbooks," *Education Inquiry* 2, no. 1 (2011): 79–91, DOI: 10.3402/edui.v2i1.21964.

20. *Final Report of the Committee of Experts on Constitutional Review,* Committee of Experts, Oct. 11, 2020, https://katibaculturalrights.wordpress.com/wp-content/uploads/2016/04/coe_final_report-2.pdf.

21. *Final Report,* Committee of Experts.

22. *Final Report,* Committee of Experts.

23. "Kenya: From Moi to Kibaki," Wilson Center, Sept. 11, 2003, https://www.wilsoncenter.org/event/kenya-moi-to-kibaki.

24. "Kenya: From Moi to Kibaki."

25. "Top Diplomat: U.S. Should Push Africa Reform," Tell Me More, National Public Radio, Dec. 10, 2009, https://www.npr.org/templates/story/story.php?storyId=121279843.

26. "Kenya: From Moi to Kibaki."

27. Implemented by National Democratic Institute, International Republican Institute, and International Foundation for Electoral Systems; US Government Accountability Office (GAO), Rep. GAO-12–35, Oct. 2011.

28. This text and some of the subsequent paragraphs are adapted from an annex to a USAID final report that I helped author. The annex is titled "USAID/KENYA Support to the Constitution Reform Process Through the Kenya Transition Initiative (KTI)." It was published in 2014 with the USAID/KTI multimedia final report that was hosted for five years on www.kenyati.com (site discontinued).

29. *Final Report,* Committee of Experts.

30. *Final Report,* Committee of Experts.

31. Whereas the grant programs of many public and private donors are accessible only to organizations sophisticated enough to understand the application process, submit appropriate proposals, and meet rigid qualification criteria, USAID's OTI seeks to award its grants to new and untested local partners. Rather than conducting competitions that can take months to judge,

OTI helps groups with good ideas put together quick and effective action plans. OTI then offers them in-kind support, often in the form of office equipment, building supplies, or professional services. By procuring these items directly, OTI avoids the problem of transferring cash to organizations lacking the administrative and bookkeeping capacities to manage it properly. See OTI, *A Decade of Transition, 1994–2004.*

32. Constitution of Kenya Review Act, No. 9 of 2008, Government of Kenya, cl. 26.

33. For example, the UK Department for International Development released $550,000.

34. *Final Report,* sec. 6.4.8, Committee of Experts.

35. GAO, GAO-12–35.

36. Xan Rice, "Kenya Investigates Attempt to Sabotage New Constitution," *Guardian,* May 21, 2010, https://www.theguardian.com/world/2010/may/21/kenya-investigates-constitution-sabotage.

37. Aga Khan III, "The Aga Khan's World View," interview with John Stackhouse, *Globe and Mail,* May 28, 2010, https://www.theglobeandmail.com/news/world/the-aga-khans-world-view/article4321039/.

38. Kenya Const. of 2010, art. 262, cl. 31(7) (2010) and cl. 12(3) (2010).

39. Aga Khan III, "The Aga Khan's World View."

40. Statista, https://www.statista.com/, captured Feb. 12, 2022.

41. "Elections," Washington Secretary of State, https://www.sos.wa.gov/elections/, captured Feb. 12, 2022.

42. Concerning a recent referendum proposed in Washington state for a property tax increase for schools, lawn signs read "No to unfair taxes" and "Vote yes for our children."

43. Statista, https://www.statista.com/, captured Dec. 30, 2022. Data for Washington state (23.8 percent) is dated 2021; data for Kenya (3.5 percent) is based on Kenya's 2019 census.

44. James Ratemo, *Standard,* May 12, 2010.

45. Emmanuel Igunza, "Kenya's BBI Blocked in Blow to President Uhuru Kenyatta," BBC, Mar. 31, 2022, https://www.bbc.com/news/world-africa-60941860.

46. OIG, US Department of State, "Inspection of Embassy Nairobi, Kenya," Rep. ISPI-12–38A, Aug. 2012, https://www.stateoig.gov/report/isp-i-12-38a.

47. Scott Gration, "Fmr. Amb. Scott Gration Speaks Out on Clinton E-Mails," interview with Michael Smerconish, CNN Press Room, Mar. 8, 2015, https://cnnpressroom.blogs.cnn.com/2015/03/08/cnn-exclusive-fmr-amb-scott-gration-speaks-out-on-clinton-emails/.

48. David Martosko,"Hillary Clinton's State Department Ousted Ambassador to Kenya After He Set Up Private Email System in Embassy Bathroom," *Daily Mail,* Mar. 5, 2015.

49. Hempstone, *Rogue Ambassador,* 115.

50. Hempstone, *Rogue Ambassador*, 113.

51. Hempstone, *Rogue Ambassador*, 130.

52. Hempstone, *Rogue Ambassador*, 134.

53. Stephen Makabila, "Two Grand Farewell Parties for Outgoing US Ambassador," *Standard*, Apr. 24, 2011, https://www.standardmedia.co.ke/article/2000033867/two-grand-farewell-parties-for-outgoing-us-ambassador.

54. Makabila, "Farewell Parties."

55. Makabila, "Farewell Parties."

56. Ranneberger, "Reform."

57. Ranneberger, "Reform."

58. Ranneberger, "Reform."

59. Ranneberger, "Reform."

60. Ranneberger, "Reform."

61. Ranneberger, "Reform."

62. Biden, "Remarks by Vice President Joe Biden to University Students in Nairobi, Kenya."

63. Ranneberger, "Reform."

64. Ranneberger, "Reform."

65. Although I was a personal services contractor and not a civil or foreign service member, I am still bound by the same disclosure policies.

66. *Collins Dictionary*, s.v. "Mission (*n.*)," captured Feb. 19, 2025, https://www.collinsdictionary.com/us/dictionary/english/mission.

67. Hempstone, *Rogue Ambassador*, 8.

68. Personal communication between a USAID Foreign Service Officer and the author at the US Embassy, Nairobi, c. 2010.

69. FOIA.gov, https://www.foia.gov, captured Feb. 6, 2022.

70. GAO, Rep. GAO-12–35.

71. GAO, Rep. GAO-12–35.

72. GAO, Rep. GAO-12–35.

73. GAO, Rep. GAO-12–35.

74. Jeff Sagnip, "GAO Finds USAID-Funded Organization Pushed Pro-Abortion Language in Kenya Constitution," US Congressman Chris Smith, press release, Nov. 16, 2011, https://chrissmith.house.gov/news/documentsingle.aspx?DocumentID=269304.

75. U.S. Const. amend. I.

76. Muhsin Hassan, "The Lost Boys of Eastleigh: Ideology, Identity, and the Appeal of al-Shabaab" (master's thesis, Princeton Univ., 2012). See, for example, chap. 5, "Establishment Conundrum," which explores the US government's inconsistent application of the First Amendment's Establishment Clause in various peace and security and USAID development programs across the globe.

77. Mutunga, "The 2010 Constitution of Kenya." Mutunga's work was derived from an inaugural lecture delivered at the Univ. of Fort Hare's Distinguished

Lecture Series on Oct. 16, 2014, and from a speech given at the launching of the Judiciary Transformation Framework on May 31, 2012.

78. Mutunga, "The 2010 Constitution of Kenya."

79. *Final Report,* Committee of Experts.

80. Dudziak, "Working Towards Democracy."

81. Kenya Const. of 2010, chap. 17, art. 259.

82. Kenya Const. of 2010, chap. 4, art. 27(8).

83. Ken Opala, "Kenya's High Court Blocks Proposal to Send Police Support to Haiti," Global Initiative Against Transnational Crime, Feb. 5, 2024, https://globalinitiative.net/analysis/kenyas-high-court-blocks-proposal -police-support-haiti/.

84. Mwangi S. Kimenyi, "Kenya: A Country Redeemed after a Peaceful Election," Brookings Institution, Apr. 2, 2013, https://www.brookings.edu/blog/ upfront/2013/04/02/kenya-a-country-redeemed-after-a-peaceful-election/.

85. Bellamy and Carson, "Why the US Should Intervene."

86. "Kenya Presidential Election Cancelled by Supreme Court," BBC, Sept. 1, 2017, https://www.bbc.co.uk/news/world-africa-41123329.

87. Ranneberger, "Reform."

88. Kimenyi, "Kenya."

89. Barkan, "Kenya After Moi."

90. Barkan et al., *Kenya Transition Initiative.*

4. Mother Earth

1. Ambreena Manji, *The Struggle for Land and Justice in Kenya* (James Currey, 2020).

2. Ranneberg, "Reform."

3. "Statement of Principles," Kenya National Dialogue and Reconciliation.

4. National Foreign Assessment Center, *Africa Review,* CIA, rep. RP AR 78–005, Sept. 1, 1978, https://www.cia.gov/readingroom/docs/CIA-RDP79T00 912A002700010012-7.pdf.

5. "Program Cycle," USAID, https://2017–2020.usaid.gov/project-starter/ program-cycle, captured Sept. 9, 2022 (site discontinued).

6. USAID, *Country Development Cooperation Strategy (CDCS) October 2020–October 2025.* The USAID mission "held 16 separate consultation events, engaging with more than 900 Kenyans across all 47 counties, listening to the voices of the private sector, civil society, and public sector at both the national and county levels."

7. Natasha Turak, "Iran Is Calling for the U.S. to Be Thrown Out of the World Cup After Flag Change," CNBC, Nov. 28, 2022, https://www.cnbc.com /2022/11/28/iran-is-calling-for-the-us-to-be-thrown-out-of-the-world-cup -after-flag-change.html.

8. Ed Pilkington, "Black Pastor Arrested While Watering Neighbor's Flowers in Alabama," *Guardian,* Aug. 22, 2022, https://www.theguardian.com/us-news/2022/aug/31/alabama-black-pastor-arrested-watering-flowers-michael-jennings; Amir Vera and Laura Ly, "White Woman Who Called Police on a Black Man Bird-Watching in Central Park has been Fired," CNN, May 26, 2020, https://edition.cnn.com/2020/05/26/us/central-park-video-dog-video-african-american-trnd/index.html.

9. Rebecca Samervelle, "Mumbai: Accused in Rape Case Acquitted as Teen Turns Hostile," *Times of India,* June 26, 2022, https://timesofindia.indiatimes.com/city/mumbai/mumbai-accused-in-rape-case-acquitted-as-teen-turns-hostile/articleshow/92465948.cms.

10. David Fahrenthold, "Trump Recorded Having Extremely Lewd Conversation About Women in 2005," *Washington Post,* Oct. 8, 2016, https://www.washingtonpost.com/politics/trump-recorded-having-extremely-lewd-conversation-about-women-in-2005/2016/10/07/3b9ce776-8cb4-11e6-bf8a-3d26847eeed4_story.html.

11. DFID collaborated with KTI and provided funds to the latter for a decentralization program in 2014. In 2020, DFID was dissolved and absorbed into the UK Foreign Commonwealth and Development Office, the British equivalent of the US Department of State; Ivica Petrikova and Melita Lazell, "'Securitized' UK Aid Projects in Africa: Evidence from Kenya, Nigeria and South Sudan," *Development Policy Review* 40, no. 1 (2021), https://doi.org/10.1111/dpr.12551.

12. Emmanuel Macron et al., "The Climate Is Already Collapsing in Africa—But Its Nations Have a Plan," *Guardian,* Nov. 4, 2022, https://www.theguardian.com/commentisfree/2022/nov/04/climate-breakdown-africa-plan.

13. John Bruce, "Kenya Land Policy: Analysis and Recommendations," Prepared for USAID by ARD Inc., May 2009, https://landportal.org/library/resources/kla2649/kenya-land-policy-analysis-and-recommendations.

14. Barkan et al., *Kenya Transition Initiave.*

15. Examples include the Njonjo Commission of Inquiry into Land Law systems (Kenya Government Commission, 1999), the *Report of the Commission of Inquiry into the Illegal/Irregular Allocation of Public Land* (Ndung'u, 2004), and the Truth, Justice, and Reconciliation Commission of Kenya Report (2012).

16. Regarding the term "development partner": I grew up in Kenya using the term "donor." USAID and its counterparts across the globe (Japan's JICA, Canada's CIDA, Britain's DFID, and Sweden's SIDA) were donors. Now they are referred to as "development partners" because they are supposed to represent a partnership, not a charity. This semantic distinction and my opinion on it are not the focus of this book; perhaps I will unravel it in a future book.

17. The total sold was $127.7 million between 2008 and 2014, when KTI was active, that is, obligated by the Department of Defense for Kenya. For example, $19 million worth was sold in 2014 under Sec. 1206 of the Train and Equip Program, which "builds partnership capacity for time-sensitive, new

and emerging counterterrorist operations and supports military and stability operations in which the US armed forces are a participant." Data query performed via ForeginAssistance.gov, Nov. 2, 2022.

18. Richard Cox, *Kenyatta's Country* (Federick A. Praeger, 1966).

19. Human Rights Watch, "Ballots to Bullets."

20. Robert Wanjala, "Land Reform Centre-Stage in Kenyan Election: Delays in Enacting Legislation to Address Longstanding Grievances Make Land as Potent an Election Issue as Ever," Institute for War and Peace Reporting, Mar. 1, 2013, https://iwpr.net/global-voices/land-reform-centre-stage-kenyan-election.

21. Wanjala, "Land Reform."

22. Uhuru Kenyatta was constitutionally time-barred from running again Kenya's 2022 election but he threw his weight behind Raila Odinga's campaign instead of his own vice president's, William Ruto, who would go on to win the election.

23. Presidential Communication Services, "President Kenyatta Kicks Off Issuance Of 1 Million Title Deeds," *Capital News,* June 22, 2022, https://www.capitalfm.co.ke/news/2022/06/president-kenyatta-kicks-off-issuance-of-1-million-title-deeds/.

24. Darunee Sukaran, "Kenyan Farmers Turn to Avocados in the Face of a Changing Climate," *Sustainability Times,* Oct. 20, 2020, https://www.sustainability-times.com/environmental-protection/kenyan-farmers-turn-to-avocados-in-the-face-of-a-changing-climate/; Daniel Workman, "Avocados Exports By Country," World's Top Exports, https://www.worldstopexports.com/avocados-exports-by-country/, captured Oct. 16, 2022.

25. Emmanul Igunza, "Kenyan Vigilantes Taking on Avocado Gangs," BBC, Jan. 16, 2022, https://www.bbc.co.uk/news/world-africa-59989656.

26. Penn Central Transportation Co. v. New York City, 438 U.S. 104 (1978).

27. Elkins, *Imperial Reckoning.*

28. Cox, *Kenyatta's Country.*

29. Erin O'Brien, *Irregular and Illegal Land Acquisition by Kenya's Elites: Trends, Processes, and Impacts of Kenya's Land-Grabbing Phenomenon,* International Land Coalition, 2011, https://land.igad.int/index.php/documents-1/countries/kenya/investment-3/642-irregular-and-illegal-land-acquisition-by-kenya-s-elites-trends-processes-and-impacts-of-kenya-s-land-grabbing-phenomenon/file. Prepared in collaboration with The Kenya Land Alliance.

30. O'Brien, "Irregular and Illegal Land Acquisition."

31. Manji, *The Struggle for Land.*

32. See, for example, Thomas Pakenham, *The Scramble for Africa: White Man's Conquest of the Dark Continent from 1876 to 1912* (Avon, 1992).

33. Manji, *The Struggle for Land.*

34. Saul David, "Slavery and the 'Scramble for Africa,'" BBC, https://www.bbc.co.uk/history/british/abolition/scramble_for_africa_article_01.shtml, last updated Feb. 17, 2011.

35. See, for example, Cox, *Kenyatta's Country.* Cox maintains that this legend is true.

36. See, for example, "How Kilimanjaro Ended Up in Tanzania," *Nation,* July 14, 2013; "In Depth in Kilimanjaro," *Frommer's,* https://www.frommers.com/destinations/kilimanjaro/in-depth-in-kilimanjaro, captured Feb. 22, 2025.

37. Cox, *Kenyatta's Country.*

38. Mary Serumaga, "The New Lunatic Express: Lessons not Learned from the East African Railway," *The Elephant,* June 16, 2018, https://www.theelephant .info/features/2018/06/16/the-new-lunatic-express-lessons-not-learned-from -the-east-african-railway.

39. Kaushik Patowary, "Lunatic Express: The Railway That Gave Birth to Kenya," *Amusing Planet,* Mar. 15, 2019, https://www.amusingplanet.com/2019/03/lunatic-express-train-that-gave-birth.html.

40. Elkins, *Imperial Reckoning.*

41. Amos Kareithi, "The Lunatic Express: Was it Doomed from the Beginning?" *Standard,* 2019, https://www.standardmedia.co.ke/counties/article/2001323010/doomed-from-the-cradle-the-lunatic-express.

42. Panos Mourdoukoutas, "Why is China Building in Africa," *Forbes,* Sept. 21, 2019, https://www.forbes.com/sites/panosmourdoukoutas/2019/09/21/why-is-china-building-africa.

43. Africa Defense Forum, "Chinese Debts Push Some African Countries to Edge of Default," *Africa Defense Forum Magazine,* US Africa Command, Aug. 30, 2022, https://adf-magazine.com/2022/08/chinese-debts-push-some-african -countries-to-edge-of-default/.

44. Joyska Nunez-Medina, "The Story of Chinese Laborers and the Reconstruction South," May 5, 2022, Tennesse State Museum, https://tnmuseum.org /Stories/posts/the-story-of-chinese-laborers-and-the-reconstruction-south.

45. Samuel Kanzugu, "Kenya: Cargo Train Spells Doom for Truck Drivers," *Nation,* July 24, 2018, https://nation.africa/kenya/news/cargo-train-spells-doom for-over-500-truckdrivers-70270.

46. Anderson, *Histories of the Hanged.*

47. Elkins, *Imperial Reckoning.*

48. Manji, *The Struggle for Land.*

49. Robert J. Miller, "The Doctrine of Discovery, Manifest Destiny, and Oregon," (working paper, Christian Aboriginal Infrastructure Developments), https://caid.ca/DocDisManDesOre2008.pdf.

50. Eric Cain, "Broken Treaties, an Oregon Experience," Oregon Public Broadcasting, Mar. 3, 2017, https://www.opb.org/television/programs/oregon-experience/article/broken-treaties-oregon-native-americans/.

51. Native Registration Ordinance of 1920; see *The Official Gazette of the Colony of Kenya and the East Africa Protectorate* 22, no. 727, Aug. 18, 1920, https://archive.gazettes.africa/archive/ke/1920/ke-government-gazette-dated-1920 -08-18-no-727.pdf.

52. Jena Hughes et al., *Historical Context of Racist Planning: A History of How Planning Segregated Portland,* Bureau of Planning and Sustainability, Portland. gov, Sept. 2019, https://www.portland.gov/sites/default/files/2019–12/portland racistplanninghistoryreport.pdf.

53. Truth, Justice, and Reconciliation Commission of Kenya, *Commissions of Inquiry—CIVE Report (Waki Report) (2008),* IX (Government [of Kenya] Documents and Regulations), 23, https://digitalcommons.law.seattleu.edu/cgi/viewcontent.cgi?article=1004&context=tjrc-gov.

54. Truth, Justice, and Reconciliation Commission of Kenya, *Commissions of Inquiry.*

55. Elkins, *Imperial Reckoning.*

56. Manji, *The Struggle for Land;* Elkins, *Imperial Reckoning.*

57. Elkins, *Imperial Reckoning.*

58. Michael Burleigh, *Small Wars, Faraway Places: Global Insurrection and the Making of the Modern World, 1945–1965* (Penguin, 2014).

59. I discuss the Mau Mau effort in chap. 5.

60. Elkins, *Imperial Reckoning.*

61. Elkins, *Imperial Reckoning.*

62. Manji, *The Struggle for Land.*

63. Bruce, "Kenya Land Policy."

64. Francesca Di Matteo, "The Politicisation of Land Policy Reform in Contemporary Kenya," in *Kenya in Motion 2000–2020,* ed. Marie-Aude Fouéré et al., trans. Sara Stavchansky (Africae, 2021), 199–222, https://doi.org/10.4000/books.africae.2510.

65. Rasna Warah, "The Sins of the Father: Why Lifestyle Audits Cannot Resolve Land-Related Historical Injustices," *Elephant,* June 28, 2018, https://www.theelephant.info/features/2018/06/28/the-sins-of-the-father-why-lifestyle-audits-cannot-resolve-land-related-historical-injustices.

66. Manji, *The Struggle for Land.*

67. Manji, *The Struggle for Land.*

68. Manji, *The Struggle for Land.*

69. Manji, *The Struggle for Land.*

70. Manji, *The Struggle for Land.*

71. Manji, *The Struggle for Land.*

72. Manji, *The Struggle for Land.*

73. USAID, *Country Development Cooperation Strategy (CDCS) October 2020–October 2025.*

74. Aga Khan IV, "Address."

75. "Statement of Principles," Kenya National Dialogue and Reconciliation.

76. USAID, *Country Development Cooperation Strategy (CDCS) October 2020–October 2025.*

77. Manji, *The Struggle for Land.*

78. Paul Ndiritu Ndung'u, *Report of the Commission of Inquiry into the Illegal/Irregular Allocation of Public Land* (Nairobi, Government Printer, 2004), https:

//kenyalaw.org/kl/fileadmin/CommissionReports/A_Report_of_the_Land
_Commission_of_Inquiry_into_the_Illegal_or_Irregular_Allocation_of_Land
_2004.pdf.

79. Consider the examples I provide in the next section on land grabbing. One example focuses on the people who went to court—the former MP and the ministry of lands staff. The middleman was a businessman who initially and illegally bought the public land parcel from the Kenya Railways Corporation (also known as Kenya Railways). The media paint him, briefly, as a victim; see Sharon Mwende, "Court Postpones MP Arama's Sentencing," *Star,* June 9, 2022; Alpgonce Mung'aha, "Former Nakuru Land Registrar Charged with Fraud, Freed on Sh2m bond," *Star,* July 3, 2018.

80. Mfonobong Nsehe, "Kenyan Millionaire Uhuru Kenyatta Officially Wins Presidential Election," *Forbes,* Mar. 9, 2013, https://www.forbes.com/sites/mfonobongnsehe/2013/03/09/kenyan-millionaire-uhuru-kenyatta-officially-wins-presidential-election.

81. Prior to Matiangi joining the Kenyatta government in 2013, he was the chief of party for for the USAID-funded Parliament Strengthening Program, run by the State University of New York (SUNY). KTI collaborated with and co-funded the program. Matiangi selected me to be his deputy chief of party for a subsequent USAID-funded decentralization program, also with SUNY; Vincent Achuka, "How Much is William Ruto Worth? Matiangi Unmasks 'Hustler,'" *Nation,* Sept. 2, 2021, https://nation.africa/kenya/news/how-much-is-william-ruto-worth-matiang-i-unmasks-hustler--3534658.

82. Japhet Ruto, "Raila Odinga: List of Expensive Properties and Companies Owned by ODM Leader," TUKO, Aug. 2, 2022, https://www.tuko.co.ke/business-economy/434064-raila-odinga-list-properties-companies-owned-by-odm-leader/.

83. The Supreme Court of Kenya, National Land Commmission v. Attorney-General and 5 Others, adv. op. no. 2 of 2014, http://kenyalaw.org/caselaw/cases/view/116512/.

84. Ministry of Lands, Republic of Kenya, "Sessional Paper No. 3 of 2009 on National Land Policy," 2009, https://lands.go.ke/wp-content/uploads/2023/11/Sessional-paper-on-Kenya-National-Land-Policy.pdf.

85. National Foreign Assessment, *Africa Review.*

86. See land investigations such as the Njonjo Commission of Inquiry into Land Law systems (1999) and *Report of the Commission of Inquiry into the Illegal/Irregular Allocation of Public Land* (Ndung'u, 2004), or broader international findings such as the Panama Papers (2016).

87. "Court Removes Restrictions on Beach Plot Ownership," *Business Daily Africa,* Mar.14, 2014, https://www.businessdailyafrica.com/bd/economy/court-removes-restrictions-on-beach-plot-ownership-2053974.

88. James Mbaka, "Why Raila is Walking a Tightrope Over Land Issue," *Star,* Feb. 28, 2020, https://www.the-star.co.ke/siasa/2020-02-28-why-raila-is-walking-a-tightrope-overland-issue.

89. Mbaka, "Why Raila is Walking a Tightrope Over Land Issue."

90. Christine Mungai, "Kenya: Why Raila & Ruto Remain Quiet on Land Justice Issues," *Africa Report,* June 20, 2022, https://www.theafricareport.com/215008/kenya-why-raila-ruto-remain-quiet-on-land-justice-issues/.

91. Warah, "The Sins of the Father."

92. Sam Omwenga, "The Ruto Dilemma," *Star,* Jan. 31, 2020, https://www.the-star.co.ke/siasa/2020–01–31-the-ruto-dilemma/.

93. USAID, *Country Development Cooperation Strategy (CDCS) October 2020–October 2025.*

94. USAID, *Country Development Cooperation Strategy (CDCS) October 2020–October 2025.*

95. Barkan et al., *Kenya Transition Initiative.*

96. *Report on Private Investigations on Allocation of Taifa Park: A Case Study on Theft of Public Utility Land in Kenya,* Pelican Investigations Services, for Nyanza Youth Coalition, Mar. 17, 2010, KTI grant no. DAIKTI0042.

97. Roger Southall, "The Ndungu Report: Land and Graft in Kenya," *Review of African Political Economy* 32, no. 103 (2005): 142–51, quoted in Manji, *The Struggle for Land.*

98. Mung'aha, "Nakuru Land Registrar."

99. Mwende, "Postpones."

100. Manji, *The Struggle for Land.*

101. See, for example, Kenya Land Alliance and Kenya National Commission for Human Rights, *Unjust Enrichment, the Making of Land Grabbing Millionaires,* 2011, https://kenyalandalliance.or.ke/; see also O'Brien, "Irregular and Illegal Land Acquisition by Kenya's Elites."

102. Omwenga, "The Ruto Dilemma."

103. Rajiv Shah, "Remarks by USAID Administrator Dr. Rajiv Shah: Transforming Development Through Science, Technology, and Innovation," speech, July 13, 2010, https://2012-2017.usaid.gov/news-information/speeches/remarks-usaid-administrator-dr-rajiv-shah-transforming-development-through (site discontinued).

104. Manji, *The Struggle for Land.*

105. Dennis Ndiritu, "The National Land Commission: What Have We Gained?," *Nairobi Law Monthly,* Oct. 8, 2019, https://nairobilawmonthly.com/the-national-land-commission-what-have-we-gained/.

106. Daniel Wesangula, "Swazuri: Forever in Summer Amid Murmurs over Lifestyle," *Saturday Standard,* Dec. 20, 2016, https://www.standardmedia.co.ke/nairobi/article/2001284379/swazuri-forever-in-summer-amid-murmurs-over-lifestyle.

107. Wesangula, "Swazuri."

108. Christine Perkins, "A History of Corruption in the United States," Harvard Law Today, Sept. 23, 2020, https://hls.harvard.edu/today/a-history-of-corruption-in-the-united-states/.

109. Anderson, *Histories of the Hanged.*

110. Anderson, *Histories of the Hanged.*

111. Anderson, *Histories of the Hanged.*

112. Endangered Species Conservation Act of 1973, Pub. L. 93–205, 87 Stat. 884.

113. US Fish and Wildlife Service and National Marine Fisheries Service, *Endangered Species Consultation Handbook, Procedures for Conducting Consultation and Conference Activities Under Section 7 of the Endangered Species Act,* Mar. 1998, https://www.fws.gov/sites/default/files/documents/ endangered-species-consultation-handbook.pdf.

114. Aaron Gordon, "Why Doesn't America Build Things?," *Vice,* Aug. 22, 2022, https://www.vice.com/en/article/93a39e/why-doesnt-america-build-things.

115. John Ndiso and Maggie Fick, "Demolitions to Protect River Sparks Rows in Kenyan Capital," *Reuters,* Aug. 17, 2018, https://www.reuters.com/ article/world/demolitions-to-protect-river-spark-rows-in-kenyan-capital -idUSKBN1L21EK/; "Kenya Tears Down 'Illegal' Upmarket Mall," BBC, Aug. 10, 2018, https://www.bbc.co.uk/news/world-africa-45144151.

116. Mwangi Mwaura, "Demolitions in Nairobi: Settler Colonialism and the Elimination of the Native," Opinion, *Elephant,* Nov. 11, 2022, https://www .theelephant.info/opinion/2022/11/11/demolitions-in-nairobi-settler-colonial ism-and-the-elimination-of-the-native/.

117. Gabe Joselaw, "Kenyan Construction Problems Blamed on Corruption," *Voice of America,* Jan. 15, 2015, https://www.voanews.com/a/corruption-lies -behind-construction-problems-kenya/2600197.html.

118. Environment and Land Court at Malindi, Rep. of Kenya, Malindi Law Society & 12 Others v. Attorney General & 2 Others, pet. 19 and 291 of 2016 (Consolidated) [2021] KEELC [4748] (KLR) (Oct. 29, 2021), http://kenyalaw.org/case law/cases/view/221739/.

119. Centre for Rights Education and Awareness, "Tracing the Journey: Towards Implementation of the Two Thirds Gender Principle," 2019, https:// home.creaw.org/wp-content/uploads/2019/11/Tracing-the-Journey-Two- Thirds.pdf.

120. Joe Biden, "Remarks by President Biden on the Infrastructure Investments Made at Portland International Airport," speech given at Portland Air National Guard Base, Portland, OR, Apr. 21, 2022, the White House, https:// bidenwhitehouse.archives.gov/briefing-room/speeches-remarks/2022/04/21/ remarks-by-president-biden-on-the-infrastructure-investments-made-at -portland-international-airport/.

121. Christine Cube, "Resilience 2021: For Every $1 Spent on a Resilient Runway at PDX, Oregon Will Save $50," National Institute of Building Sciences (blog), Apr. 21, 2021, https://www.nibs.org/blog/resilience-2021-every-1-spent -resilient-runway-pdx-oregon-will-save-50.

122. Petrikova and Lazell, "'Securitized.'"

123. Petrikova and Lazell, "'Securitized.'"

124. Clarissa Augustinas and GLTN Team, "UN-Habitat and Chair of the Development Partners Group on Lands," as reported in USAID, "Appendix: Land Reform," *KTI Final Report, 2014–2019,* www.kenyati.com (site discontinued).

125. Law Society of Kenya, "Audit Report on the Nairobi, Mombasa, Thika, and Nakuru Land Registries," Feb. 2012.

126. Barkan et al., *Kenya Transition Initiative.*

127. USAID, "Appendix: Land Reform," *KTI Final Report, 2014–2019.*

128. USAID, "Appendix: Land Reform," *KTI Final Report, 2014–2019.*

129. USAID, "Appendix: Land Reform," *KTI Final Report, 2014–2019.*

130. "ArdhiSasa" was launched in 2021. The word literally translates into English as "Land Now," but I think of it as "Land Records Now."

131. Mung'aha, "Nakuru Land Registrar"; Mwende, "Postpones."

132. Uhuru Kenyatta, "Presidential Proclamation," *Kenya Gazette* 119, no. 102, Nairobi, July 21, 2017, https://new.kenyalaw.org/akn/ke/officialGazette/2017-07-21/102/eng@2017-07-21.

133. Environment and Land Court at Malindi, Rep. of Kenya, Malindi Law Society & 12 Others v. Attorney General & 2 Others, pet. 19 and 291 of 2016 (Consolidated) [2021] KEELC [4748] (KLR) (Oct. 29, 2021), http://kenyalaw.org/caselaw/caselawreport/?id=221739.

134. Grace Ashford, "Why a Native American Nation Is Challenging the U.S. Over a 1794 Treaty," *New York Times,* Mar. 15, 2024, https://www.nytimes.com/2024/03/15/nyregion/onondaga-reparations-lawsuit.html.

135. Brian Patrick Green, "Regarding Reparations, the US Should Adhere to the Highest Standards of Justice," Markkula Center for Applied Ethics, Santa Clara Univ., July 15, 2020, https://www.scu.edu/ethics-spotlight/ethics-and-systemic-racism/regarding-reparations-the-us-should-adhere-to-the-highest-standards-of-justice/.

136. Ministry of Lands, Republic of Kenya, "Sessional Paper No. 3."

137. Bruce, "Kenya Land Policy."

138. The Taifa Park story is narrated in Kachra, *How I Changed the World.*

139. SIDA, *Development Cooperation Sweden and Kenya Thematic Priorities Guide Swedish Development Cooperation,* 2010, https://www.sida.se/content assets/f52ec8bd5afa4b6eafff61e795e45680/14938.pdf.

140. Odenda Richard Lumumba, "Kenya Land Policy Making, Implementation and Outcomes: This Far," *African Journal on Land Policy and Geospatial Sciences* 3, no. 1, (2020): 143–56, https://ageconsearch.umn.edu/record/334263/files/17826–50334-1-PB.pdf.

141. Sel. Comm. on International Development, "Annex 2: DFID Property Rights Programmes and Projects: Notes on DFID Regional and Global Programmes," UK Parliament, May 2006, https://publications.parliament.uk/pa/cm200506/cmselect/cmintdev/921/921we05.htm.

142. Sel. Comm. on International Development, "Annex 2: DFID Property Rights Programmes and Projects."

143. Lumumba, "Kenya Land Policy Making."

144. Chris Mullins, *Decline and Fall* (Profile, 2011), quoted in Lumumba, "Kenya Land Policy Making," 148.

145. Lumumba, "Kenya Land Policy Making."

146. Truth, Justice, and Reconciliation Commission of Kenya, *Commissions of Inquiry—CIVE Report (Waki Report) (2009)*; Government of Kenya, *Kenya: Commission of Inquiry into the Post Election Violence (CIPEV) Final Report*, Oct. 16, 2008, https://reliefweb.int/report/kenya/kenya-commission-inquiry-post-election-violence-cipev-final-report.

147. USAID, *Country Development Cooperation Strategy (CDCS) October 2020–October 2025*.

148. Petrikova and Lazell "'Securitized.'"

149. Bruce, "Kenya Land Policy."

150. Petrikova and Lazell, "'Securitized.'"

5. Countering Violent Extremism

1. The White House, "National Security Strategy," 2006, https://history.defense.gov/Portals/70/Documents/nss/nss2006.pdf.

2. The White House, "National Security Strategy," 2006.

3. US Departement of State, "The 2010 Quadrennial Diplomacy and Development Review (QDDR): Leading Through Civilian Power," https://2009-2017.state.gov/s/dmr/qddr/2010/index.htm.

4. USAID, "The Development Response to Violent Extremism and Insurgency," https://2017-2020.usaid.gov/news-information/factsheets/development-response-violent-extremism (site discontinued).

5. Gallup Organization, "How Religious Are Americans?," 2021, https://news.gallup.com/poll/358364/religious-americans.aspx.

6. Paul Marshall, "Misunderstanding bin Laden's 2002 Letter to America," *Providence Magazine,* Hudson Institute, Nov. 24, 2023, https://www.hudson.org/religious-freedom/misunderstanding-bin-laden-2002-letter-americans-paul-marshall.

7. Biden, "Remarks by Vice President."

8. "20 Killed in Bomb Attack on Norfolk," *Nation,* Sept. 15, 2013, https://nation.africa/lifestyle/1950774-1993444-format-xhtml-tt6skxz/index.html.

9. Aaslin Laing, "Nairobi Assault: Kenyan Terrorist Attacks Since 1980," *Telegraph,* Sept. 21, 2013, https://www.telegraph.co.uk/news/worldnews/africaandindianocean/kenya/10325230/Nairobi-assault-Kenyan-terrorist-attacks-since-1980.html.

10. US Department of Defense, "Department of Defense Press Briefing on U.S. Africa Command Investigation of Jan. 5, 2020, Al-Shabaab Attack at the Cooperative Security Location in Manda Bay, Kenya," press release, Mar. 10,

2022, https://www.defense.gov/News/Transcripts/Transcript/Article/296324/department-of-defense-press-briefing-on-us-africa-command-investigation-of-jan/, captured Aug. 12, 2022.

11. USAID, "Eastleigh Youth Engagement Project Assessment and Design," contract DOTI-00-03-00004-00/03, Development Alternatives Incorproated, 2010.

12. Examples include QED Group, "Mid-Term Evaluation of Three Countering Violent Extremism Projects" (for USAID, Feb.13, 2013), https://pdf.usaid.gov/pdf_docs/pdacx479.pdf (site discontinued); Khalil James and Martine Zeuthen, "Qualitative Study on Countering Violent Extremism (CVE) Programming Under the KTI," 2013, https://www.integrityglobal.com/wp-content/uploads/KTI-End-of-Programme-Qualitative-Study-R.pdf; James Khalil and Martine Zeuthen, "A Case Study of Counter Violent Extremism (CVE) Programming: Lessons from OTI's Kenya Transition Initiative," *Stability: International Journal of Security and Development* 3, no. 1 (2014): 31, http://doi.org/10.5334/sta.ee; Sara Savage et al., "Preventing Violent Extremism in Kenya through Value Complexity: Assessment of Being Kenyan Being Muslim," *Journal of Strategic Security* 7, no. 3 (2014): 1–26, http://dx.doi.org/10.5038/1944-0472.7.3.1; and Mushin Hassan, "Understanding Drivers of Violent Extremism: The Case of al-Shabab and Somali Youth, CTC," *Sentinal, Combatting Terrorism Center at West Point* 5, no. 8 (2012): 18–20, https://ctc.westpoint.edu/wp-content/uploads/2012/08/CTCSentinel-Vol5Iss84.pdf.

13. OTI, "Pakistan Political Transition Initiative," fact sheet, USAID, https://2017-2020.usaid.gov/stabilization-and-transitions/closed-programs/pakistan (site discontinued).

14. OTI, "Pakistan."

15. OTI, "Pakistan."

16. Masood Farivar, "Who Were the US Capitol Rioters?," *Voice of America*, Feb. 12, 2021, https://www.voanews.com/a/usa_who-were-us-capitol-rioters/6201956.html.

17. Office of Inspector General, "Former Development Contractor Sentenced to 3 Years in Prison and $10,000 Fine," press release, May 3, 2012, https://oig.usaid.gov/node/75, captured Oct. 3, 2018.

18. Randy Burkett, "Rethinking an Old Approach. An Alternative Framework for Agent Recruitment: From MICE to RASCLS," *Studies in Intelligence* 57, no. 1 (2013): 7–17.

19. God is neither male nor female. The Arabic word "Allah" is a gender neutral term.

20. Qur'an 49:13.

21. The White House, "Readout of Meeting with Religious Denominational Leaders on Reproductive Rights," press release, June 22, 2022, https://bidenwhitehouse.archives.gov/briefing-room/statements-releases/2022

/06/06/readout-of-vice-president-harriss-meeting-with-faith-leaders-on
-reproductive-rights/.

22. Bureau of the Fiscal Service, *Federal Account Symbols and Titles: The FAST Book*, Treasury Financial Manual Supplement, US Department of the Treasury, https://fiscal.treasury.gov/reference-guidance/fast-book/.

23. USAID, "Eastleigh."

24. USAID, "Eastleigh."

25. U.S. Const. amend. I.

26. Rachel Looker, "Biden Apologises for Indian Boarding Schools 'Blot on History,'" BBC, Oct. 25, 2024, https://www.bbc.com/news/articles/c704z4qxzeno.

27. *Terrorism: Two Years After 9/11, Connected the Dots, First Session, Before the Subcommittee on Terrorism, Technology, and Homeland Security of the Committee on the Judiciary, US Sen.*, 108th Cong. J-108–30 (Sept. 10, 2003) (statement of Jon Kyl, Senator), https://www.govinfo.gov/content/pkg/CHRG-108shrg93083/html/CHRG-108shrg93083.htm.

28. USAID, "Eastleigh."

29. Brian Ngugi, "Sh200m Anglo Leasing Cash in Swiss Banks Frozen," *Business Daily*, July 24, 2018, https://www.businessdailyafrica.com/bd/news/sh200m-anglo-leasing-cash-in-swiss-banks-frozen-2212172.

30. National Council of Churches of Kenya, *It's Our Turn to Eat: The Story of a Kenyan Whistleblower* (NCCK, 2013), https://chriskinyanjuikamau.files.wordpress.com/2013/07/its-our-turn-to-eat-ncck-study-guide.pdf.

31. Wrong, "Adventures of a Book in Africa."

32. Qur'an, 17:88, interpreted by Yusuf Ali, 1946.

33. GAO, "Antideficiency Act Resources," https://www.gao.gov/legal/appropriations-law-decisions/resources, captured Aug. 19, 2018.

34. Foreign Assistance Act of 1961, 22 U.S.C. 2151c, §105(c), sub. 4.

35. Foregin Assistance Act of 1961 2017 Appropriations, Pub. L. No. 115–56, H.R. 601, 115th Cong. (2017).

36. USAID, "Development Response."

37. Sara Silvestri, "Integrating Religious Engagement into Diplomacy: Challenges and Opportunities," Brookings Institution, Jan. 29, 2015, https://www.brookings.edu/articles/integrating-religious-engagement-into-diplomacy-challenges-opportunities/.

38. Silvestri, "Integrating."

39. Silvestri, "Integrating."

40. Silvestri, "Integrating."

41. OIG, *Audit of the Department of State Implementation of Policies Intended To Counter Violent Extremism*, AUDMERO-19–27 (US Dep. of St., June 2019), US Department of State, https://www.oversight.gov/sites/default/files/documents/reports/2019–07/AUDMERO-19–27.pdf.

42. OIG, *Audit*.

43. GAO, *Combatting Terrorism: Actions Needed to Enhance Implementation of Trans-Sahara Counterterrorism Partnership* (rep. to Comm. on Foreign Affairs, H.R. GAO-08-806, 2008), https://www.gao.gov/assets/gao-08-860.pdf.

44. Also see QED Group, "Mid-Term Evaluation"; Khalil and Zeuthen, "Qualitative Study"; Khalil and Zeuthen, "A Case Study"; Savage et al., "Preventing Violent Extremism"; Hassan, "Understanding Drivers."

45. Madison Springfield, *Factors Impacting Propensity and Influence Pathways Toward Violent Extremism in Jordan. Nationwide Study—Executive Summary,* Nov. 2016.

46. Madison Springfield, *Factors.*

47. European Union, *The Role of the Sub-National Authorities from the Mediterranean Region in Addressing Radicalisation and Violent Extremism of Young People,* EU Comm. of the Regions, rep. cat. no. QG-01-17–803-ENN (2017), 10.2863/241902.

48. Sean Yom and Katrina Sammour, "Counterterrorism and Youth Radicalization in Jordan: Social and Political Dimensions," *CTC Sentinel* 10, no. 4 (2017): 25–30, https://ctc.westpoint.edu/wp-content/uploads/2017/05/CTC-Sentinel_Vol10Iss44.pdf.

Conclusion

1. Anonymous, personal conversation, USAID Kenya Office, 2009.

2. Kennedy, "Remarks." Emphasis added.

3. Kennedy, "Remarks." Emphasis added.

4. Marian Leonardo Lawson, "Does Foreign Aid Work? Efforts to Evaluate U.S. Foreign Assistance" (Congressional Research Service, 7–5700, R42827, Nov. 19, 2012), https://fas.org/sgp/crs/row/R42827.pdf.

5. Lawson, "Does Foreign Aid Work?" For example, the clause "the suppression of the illicit manufacturing of and trafficking in narcotic and psychotropic drugs" was added in 1971; "to alleviate human suffering caused by natural and manmade disasters" was added in 1975; and "to enhance the antiterrorism skills of friendly countries by providing training and equipment" and "to strengthen the bilateral ties of the United States with friendly governments by offering concrete [antiterrorism] assistance" were added in 1983.

6. Lawson, "Does Foreign Aid Work?"

7. "Strength Through Development," May 29, 2014, MFAN, https://oldsite.modernizeaid.net/2014/05/strength-through-development/, retrieved Aug. 19, 2018.

8. George Ingram, "Development as a Featured Theme in US National Security Strategies Since 2002," Brookings Institution, Dec. 22, 2017, https://www.brookings.edu/blog/upfront/2017/12/22/development-as-a-featured-theme-in-us-national-security-strategies-since-2002/.

9. Ingram, "Development." Emphasis added.
10. "Mission," USAID. Emphasis added.
11. "Mission," USAID, retrieved Aug. 25, 2018.
12. Barkan et al., *Kenya Transition Initiative.*
13. Biden, "Remarks by Vice President."

BIBLIOGRAPHY

Achuka, Vincent. "How Much Is William Ruto Worth? Matiangi Unmasks 'Hustler.'" *Nation,* Sept. 2, 2021. https://nation.africa/kenya/news/how -much-is-william-ruto-worth-matiang-i-unmasks-hustler--3534658.

Africa Defense Forum. "Chinese Debts Push Some African Countries to Edge of Default." *Africa Defense Forum Magazine,* Aug. 30, 2022. https://adf-mag azine.com/2022/08/chinese-debts-push-some-african-countries-to-edge -of-default/.

Aga Khan IV. "Address to Both Houses of the Parliament of Canada in the House of Commons Chamber." Feb. 27, 2014. https://the.akdn/en/re-sources-media/resources/speeches/address-both-houses-parliament-canada-house-commons-chamber-his-highness-the-aga-khan.

Aga Khan IV. "The Aga Khan's World View." Interview with John Stackhouse. *Globe and Mail,* May 28, 2010. https://www.theglobeandmail.com/news/ world/the-aga-khans-world-view/article4321039/.

Aga Khan IV. "O Ocidente devia aceitar que o islão não separa o mundo e a fé" ["The West Should Accept that Islam Does Not Separate the World and Faith"]. Interview with António Marujo and Faranaz Keshavjee. *Paroquias de Portugal,* July 23, 2008. https://www.paroquias.org/noticias. php?n=7548.

Ahmed, Munir. "Report: Killing of Pakistani Journalist in Kenya 'Planned.'" *AP,* Dec. 7, 2022. https://apnews.com/article/africa-pakistan-journalists-islamabad-67fc48f4c2f42fea603df6f4eac425bf.

Ali, Tariq. *Winston Churchill: His Times His Crimes.* Verso, 2022.

Alumni Association Forum (blog). USAID Alumni Association. Feb. 7, 2015. http://www.usaidalumni.org/uaa-forum/general-discussion/raj-shah-the -second-worst-usaid-administrator-in-30-years/. Captured Oct. 2018. Site discontinued.

Anderson, David. *Histories of the Hanged: The Dirty War in Kenya and the End of Empire.* W. W. Norton, 2005.

Ashford, Grace. "Why a Native American Nation Is Challenging the U.S. Over a 1794 Treaty." *New York Times,* Mar. 15, 2024. https://www.nytimes. com/2024/03/15/nyregion/onondaga-reparations-lawsuit.html.

Augustinas, Clarissa, and GLTN Team. "UN-Habitat and Chair of the Development Partners Group on Lands." As reported in "Appendix: Land Reform,"
KTI Final Report, 2014–2019, www.kenyati.com. Site discontinued.

Barkan, Joel D. "Kenya after Moi." *Foreign Affairs* 83, no. 1 (2004): 87–100.
https://doi.org/10.2307/20033831.

Barkan, Joel D., Njuguna Ng'ethe, and Jacqueline Klopp. *Kenya Transition
Initiative, Final Evaluation.* Oct. 2013. Report commissioned by and
presented to USAID. Unpublished manuscript.

Barnes, Julian E., and David E. Sanger. "Saudi Crown Prince Is Held Responsible for Khashoggi Killing in U.S. Report." *New York Times,* Feb. 16, 2021.
https://www.nytimes.com/2021/02/26/us/politics/jamal-khashoggi-killing
-cia-report.html.

BBC. "Kenya Presidential Election Cancelled by Supreme Court." Sept. 1, 2017.
https://www.bbc.co.uk/news/world-africa-41123329.

BBC. "Kenya Tears Down 'Illegal' Upmarket Mall." Aug. 10, 2018. https://www
.bbc.co.uk/news/world-africa-45144151.

Bellamy, Mark, and Johnnie Carson. "How and Why the US Should Intervene
in Kenya." *African Arguments,* Mar. 6, 2018. https://africanarguments.org/
2018/02/how-and-why-the-us-should-intervene-in-kenya/.

Biden, Joe. "Remarks by President Biden on the Infrastructure Investments
Made at Portland International Airport." Speech given at Portland Air
National Guard Base, Portland, OR. Apr. 21, 2022. The White House.
https://bidenwhitehouse.archives.gov/briefing-room/speeches-re-
marks/2022/04/21/remarks-by-president-biden-on-the-infrastructure-
investments-made-at-portland-international-airport/.

Biden, Joe. "Remarks by Vice President Joe Biden to University Students in
Nairobi, Kenya." Speech given at the Kenyatta International Conference
Center. Nairobi, Kenya. June 9, 2010. The White House. Office of the Vice
President. https://obamawhitehouse.archives.gov/the-press-office/
remarks-vice-president-joe-biden-university-students-nairobi-kenya.

Bingham, John. "Asif Ali Zardari: Life and Style of Pakistan's Mr 10 Per Cent."
Telegraph, Aug. 3, 2010. https://www.telegraph.co.uk/news/worldnews/
asia/pakistan/7923479/Asif-Ali-Zardari-life-and-style-of-Pakistans-Mr-10
-Per-Cent.html.

Bruce, John. "Kenya Land Policy: Analysis and Recommendations." May 2009.
https://landportal.org/library/resources/kla2649/kenya-land-policy-anal
ysis-and-recommendations.

Bureau of the Fiscal Service. *Federal Account Symbols and Titles: The FAST
Book.* US Department of the Treasury. https://fiscal.treasury.gov/reference
-guidance/fast-book/.

Burkett, Randy. "Rethinking an Old Approach. An Alternative Framework for
Agent Recruitment: From MICE to RASCLS," *Studies in Intelligence* 57, no.
1 (2013): 7–17.

Burleigh, Michael. *Small Wars, Faraway Places: Global Insurrection and the Making of the Modern World, 1945–1965*. Penguin, 2014.

Business Daily Africa. "Court Removes Restrictions on Beach Plot Ownership." Mar. 14, 2014. https://www.businessdailyafrica.com/bd/economy/court-removes-restrictions-on-beach-plot-ownership-2053974.

Cain, Eric. "Broken Treaties, an Oregon Experience." Oregon Public Broadcasting. Mar. 3, 2017. https://www.opb.org/television/programs/oregon-experience/article/broken-treaties-oregon-native-americans/.

Cederfelt, Margareta. "International Observers Increase Trust in US Elections." OSCEPA. Oct. 28, 2022. https://www.oscepa.org/en/news-a-media/op-eds/international-observers-increase-trust-in-us-elections.

Center of Peace and Security Studies. "About." Univ. of CA San Diego. https://cpass.ucsd.edu/about/index.html#About. Captured Dec. 30, 2022.

Centre for Rights Education and Awareness. "Tracing the Journey: Towards Implementation of the Two Thirds Gender Principle." 2019. https://home.creaw.org/wp-content/uploads/2019/11/Tracing-the-Journey-Two-Thirds.pdf.

Columbia Climate School Advanced Consortium on Cooperation, Conflict, and Complexity. "Youth, Peace, and Society." Columbia Univ. https://ac4.climate.columbia.edu/yps. Captured Dec. 30, 2022.

Committee of Experts. *Final Report of the Committee of Experts on Constitutional Review*. Oct. 11, 2020. https://katibaculturalrights.wordpress.com/wp-content/uploads/2016/04/coe_final_report-2.pdf.

Cox, Richard. *Kenyatta's Country*. Federick A. Praeger, 1966.

Cube, Christine. "Resilience 2021: For Every $1 Spent on a Resilient Runway at PDX, Oregon Will Save $50." *National Institute of Building Sciences* (blog). Apr. 21, 2021. https://www.nibs.org/blog/resilience-2021-every-1-spent-resilient-runway-pdx-oregon-will-save-50.

Cummings, William et al. "By the Numbers: President Donald Trump's Failed Efforts to Overturn the Election." *USA Today*. Jan. 6, 2021. https://www.usatoday.com/in-depth/news/politics/elections/2021/01/06/trumps-failed-efforts-overturn-election-numbers/4130307001/.

Dagne, Ted. "Kenya: The December 2007 Elections and the Challenges Ahead." Congressional Research Service. Sept. 17, 2008. https://www.everycrsreport.com/files/20080917_RL34378_a1924cc669bf807094f5772f5f5252e48aad383d.pdf.

Daily Nation. "Why Martha Karua is Kenya's 'Iron Lady.'" July 14, 2022. https://nation.africa/kenya/blogs-opinion/letters/why-martha-karua-is-kenya-s-iron-lady—3878760.

David, Saul. "Slavery and the 'Scramble for Africa.'" BBC. Last updated Feb. 17, 2011. https://www.bbc.co.uk/history/british/abolition/scramble_for_africa_article_01.shtml.

Di Matteo, Francesca. "The Politicisation of Land Policy Reform in Contemporary Kenya." In *Kenya in Motion 2000–2020*, edited by Marie-Aude

Fouéré et al. Translated by Sara Stavchansky. Africae, 2021. Generated Oct. 2022. http://books.openedition.org/africae/2510.

Dudziak, Mary L. "Thurgood Marshall's Bill of Rights for Kenya." *Green Bag 2d* 11 (2008): 207. https://ssrn.com/abstract=1134026.

Dudziak, Mary L. "Working Towards Democracy: Thurgood Marshall and the Constitution of Kenya," *Duke Law Journal* 56, no. 3 (2006): 721–80.

Elkins, Caroline. *Imperial Reckoning, the Untold Story of Britain's Gulag in Kenya.* Henry Holt, 2005.

Escrit, Thomas. "ICC Judges Agree to Withdrawal of Kenyatta Charges." *Reuters,* Mar.13, 2015. https://www.reuters.com/article/uk-kenya-icc-idUK KBN0M91SD20150313/.

European Committee of the Regions. *The Role of the Sub-National Authorities from the Mediterranean Region in Addressing Radicalisation and Violent Extremism of Young People.* European Union, 2017. doi:10.2863/241902.

Fahrenthold, David. "Trump Recorded Having Extremely Lewd Conversation About Women in 2005." *Washington Post,* Oct. 8, 2016. https://www.wash ingtonpost.com/politics/trump-recorded-having-extremely-lewd-conve rsation-about-women-in-2005/2016/10/07/3b9ce776–8cb4–11e6-bf8a-3d2 6847eeed4_story.html.

Farivar, Masood. "Who Were the US Capitol Rioters?" *Voice of America,* Feb. 12, 2021. https://www.voanews.com/a/usa_who-were-us-capitol-rioters /6201956.html.

ForeignAssistance.gov. Dashboard. Accessed Jan. 11, 2022. www.foreignassis tance.gov.

Frommers. "In Depth in Kilimanjaro." https://www.frommers.com/destina tions/kilimanjaro/in-depth-in-kilimanjaro, captured Feb. 22, 2025.

Gainer, Maya. "How Kenya Cleaned up Its Courts." *Foreign Policy.* July 9, 2016. https://foreignpolicy.com/2016/07/09/how-kenya-cleaned-up-its-courts/, and the July 2010.

Gainer, Maya. "Transforming the Courts: Judicial Sector Reforms in Kenya, 2011–2015." Innovations for Successful Societies. Princeton Univ. Nov. 2015. https://successfulsocieties.princeton.edu/sites/g/files/toruqf5601/files/ MG_OGP_Kenya_FORMATTED_02Dec2015_0.pdf.

Gallop Organization. "How Religious Are Americans?" 2021. https://news.gal lup.com/poll/358364/religious-americans.aspx.

Georgetown Institute for Women, Peace and Security. "Women are Critical to Achieving Sustainable Peace." https://giwps.georgetown.edu/. Captured Dec. 30, 2022.

Gichuki, Naomi. "Kenya's Constitutional Journey: Taking Stock of Achieve-ments and Challenges." *Law in Africa* 18 (2015): 130–38. https://doi.org/10. 5771/2363–6270–2015–1–130.

Glass, Andrew. "This Day in Politics. United States Invades Panama, Dec. 20, 1989." *Politico,* Dec. 12, 2018. https://www.politico.com/story/2018/12/20/ united-states-invades-panama-1989-1067072.

Glinz, Cornelia." Kenya's New Constitution: A Transforming Document or Less than Meets the Eye?" *Verfassung Und Recht in Übersee / Law and Politics in Africa, Asia and Latin America* 44, no. 1 (2011): 60–80. http://www .jstor.org/stable/43239778.

Gordon, Aaron. "Why Doesn't America Build Things?" *Vice*, Aug. 22, 2022. https://www.vice.com/en/article/93a39e/why-doesnt-america-build-things.

Government Accountability Office. "Antideficiency Act Resources." https:// www.gao.gov/legal/appropriations-law-decisions/resources. Captured Aug. 19, 2018.

Government Accountability Office. *Combatting Terrorism: Actions Needed to Enhance Implementation of Trans-Sahara Counterterrorism Partnership.* Report to Commission on Foreign Affairs. https://www.gao.gov/assets/ gao-08–860.pdf.

Government Accountability Office. "Foreign Assistance: Clearer Guidance Needed on Compliance Overseas with Legislation Prohibiting Abortion -Related Lobbying." GAO-12–35. Oct. 2011. https://www.gao.gov/assets/ a585759.html.

Gratian, Scott. "Fmr. Amb. Scott Gration Speaks Out on Clinton E-Mails." Interview with Michael Smerconish. CNN. Mar. 8, 2015. https://cnnpress room.blogs.cnn.com/2015/03/08/cnn-exclusive-fmr-amb-scott-gration -speaks-out-on-clinton-emails/.

Green, Brian Patrick. "Regarding Reparations, the US Should Adhere to the Highest Standards of Justice." Markkula Center for Applied Ethics. Santa Clara Univ. July 15, 2020. https://www.scu.edu/ethics-spotlight/ethics-and -systemic-racism/regarding-reparations-the-us-should-adhere-to-the -highest-standards-of-justice/.

Hassan, Muhsin. "The Lost Boys of Eastleigh: Ideology, Identity, and the Appeal of al-Shabaab." Master's thesis. Princeton Univ., 2012.

Hassan, Muhsin. "Understanding Drivers of Violent Extremism: The Case of al-Shabab and Somali Youth, CTC." *Sentinal, Combatting Terrorism Center at West Point* 5, no. 8 (2012): 18–20. https://ctc.westpoint.edu/wp-content/ uploads/2012/08/CTCSentinel-Vo15Iss84.pdf.

Hempstone, Smith. *Rogue Ambassador: An African Memoir.* Univ. of the South, 1997.

Holemén, Janne. "Nation-Building in Kenyan Secondary School Textbooks." *Education Inquiry* 2, no. 1 (2011): 79–91. DOI: 10.3402/edui.v2i1.21964.

Hughes, Jena et al. *Historical Context of Racist Planning: A History of How Planning Segregated Portland.* Bureau of Planning and Sustainability. Portland.gov. Sept. 2019. https://www.portland.gov/sites/default/files/2019 -12/portlandracistplanninghistoryreport.pdf.

Human Rights Watch. "Ballots to Bullets: Organized Political Violence and Kenya's Crisis of Governance." Mar. 16, 2008. https://www.hrw.org/re- port/2008/03/16/ballots-bullets/organized-political-violence-and-kenyas -crisis-governance.

Igunza, Emmanuel. "Kenyan Vigilantes Taking on Avocado Gangs." BBC. Jan. 16, 2022, https://www.bbc.co.uk/news/world-africa-59989656.

Igunza, Emmanuel. "Kenya's BBI Blocked in Blow to President Uhuru Kenyatta." BBC. Mar. 31, 2022. https://www.bbc.com/news/world-africa-60941860.

Ingram, George. "Development as a Featured Theme in US National Security Strategies since 2002." Brookings Institute. Dec. 22, 2017. https://www.brookings.edu/blog/upfront/2017/12/22/development-as-a-featured-theme-in-us-national-security-strategies-since-2002/.

Institute for Peace and Security Studies. "Research." Addis Ababa Univ. https://ipss-addis.org/what-we-do/academic-and-applied-research/. Captured Dec. 05, 2022.

International Commission of Jurists. "Summary of Issues to be Highlighted in ICJ Mission Report for Release to the Press." Apr. 6, 2005. https://web.archive.org/web/20160304083836/http://www.icj-kenya.org/index.php/media-centre/press-releases/221-summary-of-issues-to-be-highlighted-in-icj-mission-report-for-release-to-the-press.

James, Khalil, and Martine Zeuthen. "A Case Study of Counter Violent Extremism (CVE) Programming: Lessons from OTI's Kenya Transition Initiative." *Stability: International Journal of Security and Development* 3, no. 1 (2014). http://doi.org/10.5334/sta.ee.

James, Khalil, and Martine Zeuthen. "Qualitative Study on Countering Violent Extremism (CVE) Programming Under the KTI." 2013. https://www.integrityglobal.com/wp-content/uploads/KTI-End-of-Programme-Qualitative-Study-R.pdf.

Jones, Dustin. "Why a Submarine Deal Has France at Odds with the U.S., U.K. and Australia." National Public Radio. Sept. 19, 2021. https://www.npr.org/2021/09/19/1038746061/submarine-deal-us-uk-australia-france. Captured Jan. 12, 2022.

Joselaw, Gabe. "Kenyan Construction Problems Blamed on Corruption." *Voice of America,* Jan. 15, 2015. https://www.voanews.com/a/corruption-lies-behind-construction-problems-kenya/2600197.html.

Kachra, Galeeb. *How I Changed the World in My Own Unique Ways.* Self-published, 2021.

Kagwanja, Peter, and Roger Southall. "Introduction: Kenya: A Democracy in Retreat?" *Journal of Contemporary African Studies* 27, no. 3 (2009): 259–77.

Kamau, Macharia. "US Intervention in Kenya? No Thanks." *African Arguments,* Mar. 6, 2018. https://africanarguments.org/2018/03/us-intervention-in-kenya-no-thanks/.

Kanzugu, Samuel. "Kenya: Cargo Train Spells Doom for Truck Drivers." *Nation,* July 24, 2018. https://nation.africa/kenya/news/cargo-train-spells-doom-for-over-500-truckdrivers-70270.

Kareithi, Amos. "The Lunatic Express: Was it Doomed from the Beginning?" *Standard,* 2019. https://www.standardmedia.co.ke/counties/article/200132301/doomed-from-the-cradle-the-lunatic-express.

Kiai, Mugambe. "Kenya: Why Hire a Lawyer When You Can Pay the Judge?" *Standard,* Jan. 26, 2003. https://allafrica.com/stories/200301271086.html.

Kennedy, John F. "Remarks Upon Signing the Foreign Assistance Act." Speech given at the White House, Aug. 1, 1962. American Presidency Project. Univ. of CA Santa Barbara. https://www.presidency.ucsb.edu/documents/remarks -upon-signing-the-foreign-assistance-act.

Kenya Human Rights Commission. "Wanjiku's Journey: Tracing Kenya's Quest for a New Constitution and Reporting on the 2010 National Referendum." Nov. 2010. https://khrc.or.ke/storage/2023/12/WANJIKUSJOURNEY -Tracing-Kenyas-Quest-fora-New-Constitution-Reporting-on-the-2010 -Referendum.pdf.

Kenya Land Alliance and Kenya National Commission for Human Rights. *Unjust Enrichment: The Making of Land Grabbing Millionaires.* 2011. https:// kenyalandalliance.or.ke/.

Kenya National Dialogue and Reconciliation. "Public Statement Kenya National Dialoge and Reconciliation Mediated by H. E. Kofi Annan and the Panel of Eminent African Personalities." Feb. 11, 2008. http://196.202.208 .106:8080/xmlui/handle/123456789/3658.

Kenya National Dialogue and Reconciliation. "Statement of Principles on Long-Term Issues and Solutions." May 23, 2008. https://www.peaceagree- ments.org/viewmasterdocument/688.

Kenyatta, Uhuru. "Presidential Proclamation." *Kenya Gazette* 119, no. 102. July 21, 2017. https://new.kenyalaw.org/akn/ke/officialGazette/2017-07-21/102/ eng@2017-07-21.

Kimenyi, Mwangi S. "Kenya: A Country Redeemed after a Peaceful Election." Brookings Institution. Apr. 2, 2013. https://www.brookings.edu/blog/ upfront/2013/04/02/kenya-a-country-redeemed-after-a-peaceful-election/.

Laing, Aaslin. "Nairobi Assault: Kenyan Terrorist Attacks Since 1980." *Telegraph,* Sept. 21, 2013. https://www.telegraph.co.uk/news/worldnews/ africaandindianocean/kenya/10325230/Nairobi-assault-Kenyan-terrorist -attacks-since-1980.html.

Law Society of Kenya. "Audit Report on the Nairobi, Mombasa, Thika, and Nakuru Land Registries." Feb. 2012.

Lawson, Marian Leonardo. "Does Foreign Aid Work? Efforts to Evaluate U.S. Foreign Assistance." Congressional Research Service. Nov. 19. 2012. https:// fas.org/sgp/crs/row/R42827.pdf.

Lecher, Michael. *The Constitution of Medina: Muhammad's First Legal Document.* Darwin, 2004.

Lincoln, Abraham. "The Gettysburg Address." Speech given in Gettysburg, PA. Nov. 19, 1863. Library of Congress, https://www.loc.gov/resource/rbpe .24404500.

Lindenmeyer, Elisabeth, and Josie Lianna Kaye. "A Choice for Peace? The Story of Forty-One Days of Mediation in Kenya." International Peace

Institute. Aug. 2009. https://www.ipinst.org/wp-content/uploads/publi cations/kenyamediation_epub.pdf.

Looker, Rachel. "Biden Apologises for Indian Boarding Schools 'Blot on History.'" BBC. Oct. 25, 2024. https://www.bbc.com/news/articles/c704z4qxzeno.

Lumumba, Odenda. "Kenya Land Policy Making, Implementation and Outcomes This Far." *African Journal on Land Policy and Geospatial Sciences* 3, no. 1 (2020): 143–56. https://revues.imist.ma/index.php/AJLPGS/article/view/17826.

Macron, Emmanuel, Macky Sall, and Mark Rutte. "The Climate Is Already Collapsing in Africa—But Its Nations Have a Plan." *Guardian,* Nov. 4, 2022. https://www.theguardian.com/commentisfree/2022/nov/04/climate-break down-africa-plan.

Madison Springfield. *Factors Impacting Propensity and Influence Pathways Toward Violent Extremism in Jordan. Nationwide Study—Executive Summary.* Nov. 2016. https://jordankmportal.com/resources/factors-impacting-pro pensity-and-influence-pathways-toward-violent-extremism-in-jordan.

Makabila, Stephen. "Two Grand Farewell Parties for Outgoing US Ambassa- dor." *Standard,* Apr. 24, 2011. https://www.standardmedia.co.ke/article/ 2000033867/two-grand-farewell-parties-for-outgoing-us-ambassador.

Manji, Ambreena. *The Struggle for Land and Justice in Kenya.* James Currey, 2020.

Marquadt, Alex. "US Determines Saudi Crown Prince is Immune in Case Brought by Jamal Khashoggi's Fiancée." CNN. Nov. 18, 2022, https://edition .cnn.com/2022/11/17/politics/saudi-crown-prince-immunity-state-depart ment-jamal-khashoggi/index.html.

Marshall, Paul. "Misunderstanding bin Laden's 2002 Letter to America." *Providence Magazine.* Hudson Institute. Nov. 24, 2023. https://www.hudson .org/religious-freedom/misunderstanding-bin-laden-2002-letter-ameri cans-paul-marshall.

Martosko, David. "Hillary Clinton's State Department Ousted Ambassador to Kenya After He Set Up Private Email System in Embassy Bathroom." *Daily Mail,* Mar. 5, 2015.

Mbaka, James. "Why Raila is Walking a Tightrope Over Land Issue." *Star,* Feb. 28, 2020. https://www.the-star.co.ke/siasa/2020–02–28-why-raila-is-walk ing-a-tightrope-overland-issue.

Mbote, Patricia Kameri, and Migai Akech. *Kenya: Justice Sector and the Rule of Law.* Jan. 2011. Open Society Initiative for Eastern Africa, International Law Research Center, 2011. https://www.ielrc.org/content/a1104.pdf.

MFAN. "Strength Through Development." May 29, 2014. https://oldsite.mod ernizeaid.net/2014/05/strength-through-development/. Retrieved Aug. 19, 2018.

Miller, Robert J. "The Doctrine of Discovery, Manifest Destiny, and Oregon." Working paper. Christian Aboriginal Infrastructure Developments. https:// caid.ca/DocDisManDesOre2008.pdf.

Mourdoukoutas, Panos. "Why is China Building in Africa." *Forbes,* Sept. 21, 2019. https://www.forbes.com/sites/panosmourdoukoutas/2019/09/21/why-is-china-building-africa.

Muiruri, Mwangi. "We concede Defeat but We Made a Wise Choice in Raila, Say Kikuyu Elders." *Nation,* Aug. 15, 2022. https://nation.africa/kenya/counties/muranga/our-choice-of-raila-remains-wisest-stand-say-kikuyu-elders-3914574.

Mullins, Chris. *Decline and Fall* (Profile, 2011).

Mung'aha, Alpgonce. "Former Nakuru Land Registrar Charged with Fraud, Freed on Sh2m Bond." *Star,* July 4, 2018. https://theinformer.co.ke/former-nakuru-land-registrar-charged-with-fraud/.

Mungai, Christine. "Kenya: Why Raila & Ruto Remain Quiet on Land Justice Issues." *Africa Report,* June 20, 2022. https://www.theafricareport.com/215008/kenya-why-raila-ruto-remain-quiet-on-land-justice-issues/.

Mutunga, Willy. "The 2010 Constitution of Kenya and its Interpretation: Reflections from the Supreme Court's Decisions." *Speculum Juris* 1 (2015). https://www.saflii.org/za/journals/SPECJU/2015/6.html.

Mutunga, Willy. "Circular on Dress Code and Address," *Chief Justice Issues Circular C. J.* 90, Aug. 23, 2011. http://kenyalaw.org/kl/index.php?id=835.

Mutunga, Willy. "Progress Report on the Transformation of the Judiciary: The First 120 Days." Speech given in Nairobi, Kenya. Oct. 19, 2011. http://www.judiciary.go.ke/portal/assets/downloads/speeches/.

Mwaura, Mwangi. "Demolitions in Nairobi: Settler Colonialism and the Elimination of the Native." Opinion. *Elephant,* Nov. 11, 2022. https://www.theelephant.info/op-eds/2022/11/11.

Mwende, Sharon. "Court Postpones MP Arama's Sentencing." *Star,* June 9, 2022. https://www.the-star.co.ke/news/2022–06–09-court-postpones-mp-aramas-sentencing.

Nation. "20 Killed in Bomb Attack on Norfolk." Sept. 15, 2013. https://nation.africa/lifestyle/1950774-1993444-format-xhtml-tt6skxz/index.html.

Nation. "How Kilimanjaro Ended Up in Tanzania." July 14, 2013. https://nation.africa/kenya/life-and-style/dn2/how-kilimanjaro-ended-up-in-tanzania-875650.

Nation. "Ringera-List Judges Eye Millions in Damages." *Nation,* Nov. 13, 2010, updated July 03, 2020. https://nation.africa/kenya/news/ringera-list-judges-eye-millions-in-damages—745506.

National Council of Churches. *It's Our Turn to Eat: The Story of a Kenyan Whistleblower* (NCCK, 2013). https://chriskinyanjuikamau.files.wordpress.com/2013/07/its-our-turn-to-eat-ncck-study-guide.pdf.

National Foreign Assessment Center. *Africa Review.* CIA, rep. RP AR 78–005. Sept. 1, 1978. https://www.cia.gov/readingroom/docs/CIA-RDP79T00912A002700010012-7.pdf.

National Public Radio. "Top Diplomat: U.S. Should Push Africa Reform." Tell Me More. Dec. 10, 2009. https://www.npr.org/templates/story/story.php ?storyId=121279843.

Ndiritu, Dennis. "The National Land Commission: What Have We Gained?" *Nairobi Law Monthly,* Oct. 8, 2019. https://nairobilawmonthly.com/index .php/2019/10/08/the-national-land-commission-what-have-we-gained/.

Ndiso, John, and Maggie Fick. "Demolitions to Protect River Sparks Rows in Kenyan Capital." *Reuters,* Aug. 17, 2018. https://www.reuters.com/article/ world/demolitions-to-protect-river-spark-rows-in-kenyan-capital-idUSK BN1L21EK/.

Ndung'u, Paul Ndiritu. *Report of the Commission of Inquiry into the Illegal/ Irregular Allocation of Public Land.* Nairobi, Government Printer, 2004. https://kenyalaw.org/kl/fileadmin/CommissionReports/A_Report_of_the _Land_Commission_of_Inquiry_into_the_Illegal_or_Irregular_Allocation _of_Land_2004.pdf.

Ngugi, Brian. "Sh200m Anglo Leasing Cash in Swiss Banks Frozen. *Business Daily Africa,* July 24, 2018. https://www.businessdailyafrica.com/bd/news/ sh200m-anglo-leasing-cash-in-swiss-banks-frozen-2212172.

Nsehe, Mfonobong. "Kenyan Millionaire Uhuru Kenyatta Officially Wins Presidential Election." *Forbes,* Mar. 9, 2013. https://www.forbes.com/sites/ mfonobongnsehe/2013/03/09/kenyan-millionaire-uhuru-kenyatta-offi cially-wins-presidential-election.

Nunez-Medina, Joyska. "The Story of Chinese Laborers and the Reconstruction South." May 5, 2022. Tennesse State Museum. https://tnmuseum.org/Stories/ posts/the-story-of-chinese-laborers-and-the-reconstruction-south.

Nyabola, Nanjala. "Why did Kenya's Supreme Court Annul the Elections?" *Al Jazeera,* Sept. 2, 2017. https://www.aljazeera.com/opinions/2017/9/2/why -did-kenyas-supreme-court-annul-the-elections.

O'Brien, Erin. *Irregular and Illegal Land Acquisition by Kenya's Elites: Trends, Processes, and Impacts of Kenya's Land-Grabbing Phenomenon.* International Land Alliance. Jan. 2011. https://land.igad.int/index.php/documents -1/countries/kenya/investment-3/642-irregular-and-illegal-land-acquisi tion-by-kenya-s-elites-trends-processes-and-impacts-of-kenya-s-land -grabbing-phenomenon/file.

Office of the Director of National Intelligence. "Assessing the Saudi Government's Role in the Killing of Jamal Khashoggi." Feb. 11, 2021, https://www .dni.gov/files/ODNI/documents/assessments/Assessment-Saudi-Gov-Role -in-JK-Death-20210226v2.pdf.

Office of Inspector General. *Audit of the Department of State Implementation of Policies Intended to Counter Violent Extremism.* US Department of State. June 2019. https://www.oversight.gov/sites/default/files/documents/re ports/2019-07/AUDMERO-19-27.pdf.

Office of Inspector General. "Former Development Contractor Sentenced to 3 Years in Prison and $10,000 Fine." Press release. May 3, 2012. https://oig. usaid.gov/node/75. Captured Oct. 3, 2018.

Office of Inspector General. "Inspection of Embassy Nairobi, Kenya." Rep. ISPI-12–38A. Aug. 2012. https://www.stateoig.gov/report/isp-i-12–38a.

Office of Transitions Initiative. *A Decade of Transition, 1994–2004*. USAID. http://www.globalcorps.com/sitedocs/oti10yearreport.pdf.

Office of Transitions Initiative. *Kenya Last Quarterly Report*. Chemonics. Mar. 31, 2014. https://pdf.usaid.gov/pdf_docs/PA00K6HV.pdf.

Office of Transitions Initiative. "Pakistan Political Transition Initiative." Fact sheet. USAID. https://2017–2020.usaid.gov/stabilization-and-transitions/closed-programs/pakistan. Site discontinued.

Office of ITransitions Initiative. "Where We Work." https://www.usaid.gov/stabilization-and-transitions/where-we-work. Captured Dec. 24, 2022.

Ohlbaum, Diana. "Strength Through Development." May 29th, 2014. http://modernizeaid.net/2014/05/strength-through-development/. Retrieved Aug. 19, 2018. Site discontinued.

Omwenga, Sam. "The Ruto Dilemma." *Star,* Jan. 31, 2020. https://www.the-star.co.ke/siasa/2020–01–31-the-ruto-dilemma/.

Opala, Ken. "Kenya's High Court Blocks Proposal to Send Police Support to Haiti." Global Initiative Against Transnational Crime, Feb. 5, 2024. https://globalinitiative.net/analysis/kenyas-high-court-blocks-proposal-police-support-haiti/.

Pakenham, Thomas. *The Scramble for Africa: White Man's Conquest of the Dark Continent from 1876 to 1912*. Avon, 1992.

Patowary, Kaushik. "Lunatic Express: The Railway That Gave Birth to Kenya." *Amusing Planet,* Mar. 15, 2019. https://www.amusingplanet.com/2019/03/lunatic-express-train-that-gave-birth.html.

Pelican Investigations Services. *Report on Private Investigations on Allocation of Taifa Park: A Case Study on Theft of Public Utility Land in Kenya*. Nyanza Youth Coalition. Mar. 17, 2010. KTI grant no. DAIKTI0042.

Pelosi, Nancy. Annual Session of the NATO Parliamentary Assembly. Award acceptance speech. Oct. 11, 2021. https://www.dvidshub.net/video/817179/annual-session-nato-parliamentary-assembly-nancy-pelosi-award-acceptance.

Perkins, Christine. "A History of Corruption in the United States." Harvard Law Today, Sept. 23, 2020. https://hls.harvard.edu/today/a-history-of-corruption-in-the-united-states/.

Petrikova, Ivica, and Melita Lazell. "'Securitized' UK Aid Projects in Africa: Evidence from Kenya, Nigeria, and South Sudan." *Development Policy Review* 40, no. 1 (2021). https://doi.org/10.1111/dpr.12551.

Pilkington, Ed. "Black Pastor Arrested While Watering Neighbor's Flowers in Alabama." *Guardian,* Aug. 22, 2022. https://www.theguardian.com/us

-news/2022/aug/31/alabama-black-pastor-arrested-watering-flowers-mi-chael-jennings.

Presidential Communication Services. "President Kenyatta Kicks Off Issuance Of 1 Million Title Deeds." *Capital News,* June 22, 2022. https://www.capital fm.co.ke/news/2022/06/president-kenyatta-kicks-off-issuance-of-1-million -title-deeds/.

QED Group. "Mid-Term Evaluation of Three Countering Violent Extremism Projects." Feb.13, 2013. https://pdf.usaid.gov/pdf_docs/pdacx479.pdf. Site discontinued.

Ranneberger, Michael. "Reform, Partnership, and the Future of Kenya." Speech to the American Chamber of Commerce in Nairobi, Kenya. Jan. 26, 2010. https://reliefweb.int/report/kenya/reform-partnership-and-future-kenya -speech-us-ambassador-michael-ranneberger-american.

Ratemo, James. *Standard,* May 12, 2010.

Reilly, Ryan J., and Ken Dilanian. "Intel Community Escapes Major Criticism by Jan. 6 Committee for Missing 'Roreseeable' Capitol Violence." *NBC,* Dec. 22, 2022. https://www.nbcnews.com/politics/justice-department/intel-commu nity-escapes-major-criticism-jan-6-committee-missing-forese-rcna62628.

Republic of Kenya. "Advisory Opinion Reference 2 of 2014: National Land Commission v Attorney-Genearl & 5 Others." Dec. 2, 2015. Kenya Law. https: //kenyalaw.org/caselaw/cases/view/116512.

Republic of Kenya. *Final Report of the Task Force on Judicial Reforms.* July 2010. http://kenyalaw.org/kl/fileadmin/pdfdownloads/Final_Report_of_ the_Task_Force_on_Judicial_Reforms.pdf.

Republic of Kenya. "Petition 19 & 291 of 2016 (Consolidated): Malindi Law Society & 12 Others v. Attorney General & 2 Others." Kenya Law. Oct. 29, 2021. https://kenyalaw.org/caselaw/cases/view/221739/.

Republic of Kenya. "Sessional Paper No. 3 of 2009 on National Land Policy." 2009. https://lands.go.ke/wp-content/uploads/2023/11/Sessional-paper-on-Kenya-National-Land-Policy.pdf.

Reuters. "USA: World Lines Up to Help After Katrina." News release. Sept. 5, 2005. https://reliefweb.int/report/united-states-america/usa-world-lines -help-after-katrina.

Rice, Xan. "Background: The Lord's Resistance Army." *Guardian,* Oct. 20, 2007. https://www.theguardian.com/katine/2007/oct/20/about.uganda. Retrieved Jan. 12, 2022.

Rice, Xan. "Kenya Investigates Attempt to Sabotage New Constitution." *Guardian,* May 21, 2010. https://www.theguardian.com/world/2010/may/21 /kenya-investigates-constitution-sabotage.

Ruto, Japhet. "Raila Odinga: List of Expensive Properties and Companies Owned by ODM Leader." TUKO. Aug. 2, 2022. https://www.tuko.co.ke/bus iness-economy/434064-raila-odinga-list-properties-companies-owned -by-odm-leader/.

Sagnip, Jeff. "GAO Finds USAID-Funded Organization Pushed Pro-Abortion Language in Kenya Constitution." US Congressman Chris Smith. Press release. Nov. 16, 2011. https://chrissmith.house.gov/news/documentsingle .aspx?DocumentID=269304.

Samervelle, Rebecca. "Mumbai: Accused in Rape Case Acquitted as Teen Turns Hostile." *Times of India,* June 26, 2022. https://timesofindia.indiatimes.com/ city/mumbai/mumbai-accused-in-rape-case-acquitted-as-teen-turns-hos tile/articleshow/92465948.cms.

Savage, Sara, Anjum Khan, and Jose Liht. "Preventing Violent Extremism in Kenya through Value Complexity: Assessment of Being Kenyan Being Muslim." *Journal of Strategic Security* 7, no. 3 (2014): 1–26. http://dx.doi.org /10.5038/1944–0472.7.3.1.

Select Committee on International Development. "Annex 2: DFID Property Rights Programmes and Projects: Notes on DFID Regional and Global Programmes." UK Parliament. May 2006. https://publications.parliament .uk/pa/cm200506/cmselect/cmintdev/921/921we05.htm.

Select Committee to Study Governmental Operations with Respect to Intelligence Activities. S. 94–496. 94th Cong. Nov. 20, 1975. https://www .intelligence.senate.gov/sites/default/files/94465.pdf.

Serumaga, Mary. "The New Lunatic Express: Lessons not Learned from the East African Railway." Opinion. *The Elephant,* June 16, 2018. https://www .theelephant.info/features/2018/06/16/the-new-lunatic-express-lessons -not-learned-from-the-east-african-railway.

Shah, Rajiv. "Remarks by USAID Administrator Dr. Rajiv Shah: Transforming Development Through Science, Technology, and Innovation." Speech, July 13, 2010. https://2012-2017.usaid.gov/news-information/speeches/remarks -usaid-administrator-dr-rajiv-shah-transforming-development-through. Site discontinued.

Sheerin, Jude. "January 6 Hearing: Trump Accused of Attempted Coup." BBC. June 10, 2022. https://www.bbc.co.uk/news/world-us-canada-61753870.

SIDA. *Development Cooperation Sweden and Kenya Thematic Priorities Guide Swedish Development Cooperation.* 2010. https://www.sida.se/contentassets /f52ec8bd5afa4b6eafff61e795e45680/14938.pdf.

Silvestri, Sara. "Integrating Religious Engagement into Diplomacy: Challenges and Opportunities." Brookings Institution. Jan. 29, 2015. https://www.brook ings.edu/articles/integrating-religious-engagement-into-diplomacy-chal lenges-opportunities/.

Southall, Roger. "The Ndungu Report: Land and Graft in Kenya," *Review of African Political Economy* 32, no. 103 (2005): 142–51.

Sukaran, Darunee. "Kenyan Farmers Turn to Avocados in the Face of a Chang-ing Climate." *Sustainability Times,* Oct. 20, 2020. https://www.sustainability -times.com/environmental-protection/kenyan-farmers-turn-to-avocados -in-the-face-of-a-changing-climate/.

Transportation Security Administration. "TSA by the Numbers." https:// www.tsa.gov/news/press/factsheets/tsa-numbers. Captured Feb. 15, 2025.

Truth, Justice, and Reconciliation Commission of Kenya. *Commissions of Inquiry—CIVE Report (Waki Report) (2008)*. Government [of Kenya] Documents and Regulations. https://digitalcommons.law.seattleu.edu/cgi /viewcontent.cgi?article=1004&context=tjrc-gov.

Truth, Justice, and Reconciliation Commission of Kenya. *Commissions of Inquiry—CIVE Report (Waki Report) (2009)*.

Turak, Natasha. "Iran Is Calling for the U.S. to Be Thrown Out of the World Cup After Flag Change." CNBC, Nov. 28, 2022. https://www.cnbc.com/2022/11/28/ iran-is-calling-for-the-us-to-be-thrown-out-of-the-world-cup-after-flag -change.html.

United Nations. "Global Issues: Peace and Security." https://www.un.org/en/ global-issues/peace-and-security, accessed Feb. 2025.

United Nations. "United Nations Charter: Preamble." https://www.un.org/en/ about-us/un-charter/preamble#:~:text=Accordingly%2C%20our%20 respective%20Governments%2C%20through,known%20as%20the%20 United%20Nations, captured Feb. 15, 2025.

UNWomen. "Peace and Security." https://www.unwomen.org/en/what-we-do /peace-and-security. Accessed Oct. 1, 2021.

US Africa Command Public Affairs. "AFRICOM Commander Conducts Visit to Manda Bay." US Africa Command, Jan. 17, 2021. https://www.africom. mil/pressrelease/33416/africom-commander-conducts-visit-to-manda- bay. Captured Oct. 9, 2021.

USAID. Congressional Budget Justification, 2023. https://www.usaid.gov/sites /default/files/documents/FY2023-Congressional-Budget-Justification.pdf. Site discontinued.

USAID. *Country Development Cooperation Strategy (CDCS) October 2020–October 2025*. https://www.msiworldwide.com/wp-content/uploads/2023/10/ Kenya_CDCS_External_Sept_2021.pdf.

USAID. *Country Development Cooperation Strategy (CDCS) 2014–2020*.

USAID. "The Development Response to Violent Extremism and Insurgency." https://www.usaid.gov/sites/default/files/documents/1870/VEI_Policy_ Final.pdf (site discontinued).

USAID. "Eastleigh Youth Engagement Project Assessment and Design." December 2010. Contract DOTI-00–03–00004–00/03. Development Alter- natives Incorporated, 2010.

USAID. "Gifts and Donations and Dollar Trust Fund Management." 2011. https://2017–2020.usaid.gov/sites/default/files/documents/1868/628.pdf. Site discontinued.

USAID. *Guidance for Promoting Independence and Impartiality*. Jan. 2002. https: //peacemaker.un.org/sites/default/files/document/files/2022/07/usaidguid anceforpromotingjudicialindependenceandimpartiality2002.pdf.

USAID. *KTI Final Report, 2014–2019.* Kenya Transition Initiative. www.kenyati
.com. Site discontinued.

USAID. Office of Transition Initiatives. website at https://www.usaid.gov/sta
bilization-and-transitions. Site discontinued.

US Department of Defense. "Department of Defense Press Briefing on U.S.
Africa Command Investigation of Jan. 5, 2020, Al-Shabaab Attack at the
Cooperative Security Location in Manda Bay, Kenya." Press release. Mar.
10, 2022. https://www.defense.gov/News/Transcripts/Transcript/Article
/2963240/department-of-defense-press-briefing-on-us-africa-command
-investigation-of-jan/. Captured Aug. 12, 2022.

US Department of Defense. "Department of Defense Press Briefing on U.S.
Africa Command Investigation of Jan. 5, 2020, Al-Shabaab Attack at the
Cooperative Security Location in Manda Bay, Kenya." Mar. 10, 2022.
https://www.defense.gov/News/Transcripts/Transcript/Article/2963240/
department-of-defense-press-briefing-on-us-africa-command-investiga-
tion-of-jan/. Retrieved Aug. 12, 2022.

US Department of Defense. "Langley Makes First Visit to Africa as Commander." Africa Command Public Affairs. Sept. 1, 2022. https://www.afri
com.mil/pressrelease/34687/langley-makes-first-visit-to-africa-as-com
mander.

US Department of State. "The 2010 Quadrennial Diplomacy and Development Review (QDDR): Leading Through Civilian Power." https://2009-2017
.state.gov/s/dmr/qddr/2010/index.htm.

US Department of State. *Joint Strategic Plan, FY 2018–2022.* US Department of
State. USAID. 2018. https://www.state.gov/wp-content/uploads/2018/12/
Joint-Strategic-Plan-FY-2018-2022.pdf.

US Department of State. "Secretary Marco Rubio Appointed as Acting Administrator for the United States Agency for International Development (USAID)."
Press Release. Feb. 3, 2025. https://www.state.gov/secretary-marco
-rubio-appointed-as-acting-administrator-for-the-united-states-agency
-for-international-development-usaid/.

US Department of State. "Updated Foreign Assistance Standardized Program
Structure and Definitions." Apr. 19, 2016. https://2009-2017.state.gov/f/
releases/other/255986.htm#PS42.

US Fish and Wildlife Service and National Marine Fisheries Service. *Endangered Species Consultation Handbook, Procedures for Conducting Consultation and Conference Activities Under Section 7 of the Endangered Species Act.*
Mar. 1998. https://www.fws.gov/sites/default/files/documents/endangered
-species-consultation-handbook.pdf.

US Navy. "Welcome to Camp Lemonnier, Djibouti." https://cnreurafcent.cnic.
navy.mil/Installations/Camp-Lemonnier-Djibouti/. Captured Feb. 17, 2025.

Vera, Amir, and Laura Ly. "White Woman Who Called Police on a Black Man
Bird-Watching in Central Park has been Fired." CNN. May 26, 2020.

https://edition.cnn.com/2020/05/26/us/central-park-video-dog-video-african-american-trnd/index.html.

Wanjala, Robert. "Land Reform Centre-Stage in Kenyan Election: Delays in Enacting Legislation to Address Longstanding Grievances Make Land as Potent an Election Issue as Ever." Institute for War and Peace Reporting. Mar. 1, 2013. https://iwpr.net/global-voices/land-reform-centre-stage-kenyan-election.

Warah, Rasna. "The Sins of the Father: Why Lifestyle Audits Cannot Resolve Land-Related Historical Injustices." *Elephant,* June 28, 2018. https://www.theelephant.info/features/2018/06/28/the-sins-of-the-father-why-lifestyle-audits-cannot-resolve-land-related-historical-injustices.

Washington Post. "The U.S. Gives Egypt $1.5 Billion a Year in Aid. Here's What it Does." July 9, 2013. https://www.washingtonpost.com/news/wonk/wp/2013/07/09/the-u-s-gives-egypt-1-5-billion-a-year-in-aid-heres-what-it-does/. Captured Jan. 17, 2022.

Washington Secretary of State. "Elections." https://www.sos.wa.gov/elections/. Captured Feb. 12, 2022.

Wesangula, Daniel. "Swazuri: Forever in Summer Amid Murmurs over Lifestyle." *Saturday Standard,* Dec. 20, 2016. https://www.standardmedia.co.ke/nairobi/article/2001284379/swazuri-forever-in-summer-amid-murmurs-over-lifestyle.

White House, The. "Interim National Security Strategic Guidance." 2021. https://bidenwhitehouse.archives.gov/wp-content/uploads/2021/03/NSC-1v2.pdf.

White House, The. "Readout of Meeting with Religious Denominational Leaders on Reproductive Rights." Press release. June 22, 2022. https://bidenwhitehouse.archives.gov/briefing-room/statements-releases/2022/06/06/readout-of-vice-president-harriss-meeting-with-faith-leaders-on-reproductive-rights/.

White House, The. "Statement from White House Press Secretary Karine Jean-Pierre on the State Visit of President William Ruto and First Lady Rachel Ruto of Kenya." Press release. Feb. 16, 2024. https://bidenwhitehouse.archives.gov/briefing-room/statements-releases/2024/02/16/statement-from-press-secretary-karine-jean-pierre-on-the-state-visit-of-president-william-ruto-and-first-lady-rachel-ruto-of-kenya/.

Wilson Center. "Kenya: From Moi to Kibaki." Sept. 11, 2003. https://www.wilsoncenter.org/event/kenya-moi-to-kibaki.

World Bank. *Implementation Completeness and Results Report.* Presented to the Republic of Kenya for the Judicial Performance Improvement. May 30, 2022. https://documents1.worldbank.org/curated/en/174721654782927709/pdf/Kenya-Judicial-PerformanceImprovement-Project.pdf.

World Bank. "Judicial Performance Improvement." Last updated May 30, 2022. https://projects.worldbank.org/en/projects-operations/project-detail/P105269.

Workman, Daniel. "Avocados Exports by Country." World's Top Exports. https://
www.worldstopexports.com/avocados-exports-by-country/. Captured Oct.
16, 2022.

Wrong, Michela. "Adventures of a Book in Africa." *Standpoint,* June 24, 2009.
http://www.standpointmag.co.uk/node/1703/full. Accessed Dec. 20, 2009.

Yildirim, Yetkin. "The Medina Charter: A Historical Case of Conflict Resolution." *Islam and Christian–Muslim Relations* 20, no. 4 (2009): 439–50. DOI:
10.1080/09596410903194894.

Yom, Sean, and Katrina Sammour. "Counterterrorism and Youth Radicalization in Jordan: Social and Political Dimensions." *CTC Sentinel* 10, no. 4
(2017): 25–30. https://ctc.westpoint.edu/wp-content/uploads/2017/05/
CTC-Sentinel_V0110Iss44.pdf.

INDEX

abortion, 6, 12–14, 17, 112, 122, 151, 192, 200

administrator: provincial, 151; regional, 166; USAID, 10–12, 52, 160, 206

Afghanistan, 17, 48, 57–58, 109, 185, 187, 190–92, 212

Aga Khan, 93, 94, 149, 190

al-Qaeda, 58, 186

al-Shabaab, 59, 188–89

Amendments: Kenyan Constitution, 92, 100, 107, 152; US First, 114, 116, 133, 181, 195, 203, 206, 210; US Second, 215

Annan, Kofi, 22, 88, 126, 149. *See also* United Nations

assassination, 31, 36, 48, 69, 70, 84

ballot, 34, 35, 39, 95, 118–20

Bellamy, William, 62–64, 87, 121

Biden, Joseph: election of, 22; hosting visitors, 1, 8; policy, 36, 49; speech, 23, 64, 76, 107, 167, 185, 218

British: colonial rule, 29, 30, 62, 82, 85, 101, 133–35, 138–47, 162, 174, 177, 185; constitution, 6, 82, 85–86; media and literature, 30, 93, 103, 121, 186, 202; policy, 6, 176, 188

Bush, George W., 119, 198, 214

Capitol, US, 23, 32, 37, 65, 191, 195

Carson, Johnnie, 62–63, 87–88, 121

CDCS, 25, 34, 125, 127, 129, 148, 153, 155–56, 173–74, 178–79, 206

China, 64, 141–42, 144

Christian, 19, 58, 62, 83, 102, 109, 143, 183, 198–99, 202

CIA, 69, 127, 150–51

Clinton, Hillary Rodham, 62, 77, 103, 106

commission: CIPEV, 178; CoE, 88, 89–93, 112, 117–18; Constitution of Kenya

Review, 85–86; IEBC, 36, 98; IIEC, 89, 97–98; legislative committee, 33, 69, 92, 150, 164, 165, 177, 181; national land, 161, 171, 175; rose, 30, 162–63

communism, 47, 58, 69,

Congo: Belgian, 109, 138; Democratic Republic of, 14, 19, 58, 69, 182

Congress, 9–13, 15, 17, 19–20, 27, 47, 50, 53, 57–58, 60, 68, 84, 112, 114, 163–65, 167, 196–98, 204–5, 210–13, 215, 217

constitution, US, 20, 79–80, 95, 114–15, 198, 203

corruption, 22, 24, 26, 29–32, 34, 38, 40, 78, 86, 129, 133–34, 159, 161–64, 166–68, 171, 183, 200–201

COVID-19, 59, 78, 136

Department of Defense, 52, 56, 115, 182, 195

Department of Interior, 13, 81, 150

Department of State, 8–11, 14, 19, 28, 51–52, 56, 102, 104, 110, 114–15, 127, 182, 185, 195, 204, 206–8, 211

development partner, 23, 25, 32, 40, 96, 132, 148–49, 153, 155–56, 162, 167–69, 171, 176–77, 179–80, 189

devolution, 64, 107, 188

DFID, 129, 168, 176, 177, 179

Eastleigh, 188, 189, 192, 196–97, 199, 204, 205, 208

Eldoret, 5, 24–27, 32, 40, 94, 105, 106

Elite, 150–55; British, 138, 140, 148, 151, 153; Kenyan, 31–32, 34, 78, 83, 85, 87, 130, 137, 160–61, 165–66, 168, 175, 179–80, 191, 200

ethnicity, 87, 125, 127–30, 148, 174, 192

extremism, 4, 7, 48, 108; violent, 50, 55, 58, 114, 125, 181–210, 216

Printed in the United States
by Baker & Taylor Publisher Services